Arranging Stories

Arranging Stories

Framing Social Commentary in Short Story Collections by Southern Women Writers

Heather A. Fox

University Press of Mississippi / Jackson

The University Press of Mississippi is the scholarly publishing agency of the Mississippi Institutions of Higher Learning: Alcorn State University, Delta State University, Jackson State University, Mississippi State University, Mississippi University for Women, Mississippi Valley State University, University of Mississippi, and University of Southern Mississippi.

www.upress.state.ms.us

The University Press of Mississippi is a member of the Association of University Presses.

First printing 2022
∞

Library of Congress Cataloging-in-Publication Data

Names: Fox, Heather A., author.
Title: Arranging stories : framing social commentary in short story collections by southern women writers / Heather A. Fox.
Description: Jackson : University Press of Mississippi, 2022. | Includes bibliographical references and index.
Identifiers: LCCN 2022017931 (print) | LCCN 2022017932 (ebook) | ISBN 9781496840516 (hardback) | ISBN 9781496840509 (trade paperback) | ISBN 9781496840493 (epub) | ISBN 9781496840486 (epub) | ISBN 9781496840479 (pdf) | ISBN 9781496840462 (pdf)
Subjects: LCSH: American literature—Southern States—History and criticism. | American literature—Women authors—History and criticism. | Social justice in literature. | Short story. | LCGFT: Literary criticism.
Classification: LCC PS374.S5 F69 2022 (print) | LCC PS374.S5 (ebook) | DDC 813/.010992870975—dc23/eng/20220611
LC record available at https://lccn.loc.gov/2022017931
LC ebook record available at https://lccn.loc.gov/2022017932

British Library Cataloging-in-Publication Data available

For Jamie, Marshall, Brendan, and Violet

Books are to be call'd for, and supplied, on the assumption that the process of reading is not a half sleep, but, in the highest sense, an exercise, a gymnast's struggle; that the reader is to do something for himself, must be on the alert, must himself or herself construct indeed the poem, argument, history, metaphysical essay—the text furnishing the hints, the clue, the start or frame-work. Not the book needs so much to be the complete thing, but the reader of the book does.

—Walt Whitman, *Democratic Vistas* (1871)

Contents

Acknowledgments

This book began with an interest in stories and a visit to an archive that included a gracious tour of the Katherine Anne Porter Room at the University of Maryland's Hornbake Library. Almost a decade later, the project evolved to include materials from special collections and archives libraries at the University of Alabama, the University of Virginia, the University of Florida, the University of South Florida, the University of Maryland, Princeton University, the Missouri Historical Society, the University of Michigan, the State Library and Archives of Florida, and the St. Louis Public Library.

Whether in person or through correspondence, I am indebted to the insights from the archivists at these institutions, who contributed to the development of this project. In particular, Beth Alvarez and Flo Turcotte shared their time and knowledge about Porter's and Marjorie Kinnan Rawlings's archives during my visits. Alvarez also introduced me to the Katherine Anne Porter Society, and I learned from its members as well as from the members and resources of the Kate Chopin International Society. Nancy Dupree and Jennifer Cabanero made my visit to the A. S. Williams III Americana Collection and W. S. Hoole Special Collections Library at the University of Alabama productive and enjoyable. I am grateful to Renee Jones at the St. Louis Public Library for locating the original publication of a Chopin story in the only repository for *St. Louis Life*; AnnaLee Pauls and Squirrel Walsh at Princeton University for helping me to track down a rogue attachment to one of Rawlings's letters; and Anne Causey's assistance with Ellen Glasgow's letters at the Albert and Shirley Small Special Collections

Library at the University of Virginia. In addition, I appreciate the support I received in obtaining images during a pandemic from Tomaro Taylor at the University of South Florida and Amber Kohl at the University of Maryland.

Throughout these years, I also benefited from the support of mentors and colleagues who served as readers, listeners, and the most ardent cheerleaders. Cynthia Patterson's recommendation to engage periodicals further (a recommendation foundational to connecting readings to archival findings) and her introduction to Katie Keene (the most patient editor) ensured that the project took shape, flourished, and found a publishing home. Discussions with Bryant Mangum continued to inform my thinking about authors and approaches to research. My work was propelled forward by his encouragement as well as by support from Marcel Cornis-Pope, Cristina Stanciu, David Wojahn, Gurleen Grewal, Steve Prince, and Kristin Allukian at Virginia Commonwealth University and the University of South Florida. Thank you especially to Meg Stowe, Amanda Stuckey, Haili Alcorn, Stephanie Lance, Neal Fischer, Mike Stowe, and Scott Neumeister, whom I can always count on.

Archival research and portions of the writing of this project were generously funded by a 2015–16 Frances S. Summersell Fellowship at the University of Alabama and a fellowship at the University of South Florida. When I faced obstacles in completing the book, my colleagues, especially Charlotte Rich, encouraged me to see it through. I am especially thankful for Melissa Vandenberg, who reminds me to privilege the space and time to create, and for the generosity of resources from the Department of English and the College of Letters, Arts, and Social Sciences at Eastern Kentucky University.

Finally, I cannot articulate fully the unwavering support I received from my husband and children. Marshall, Brendan, and Violet grew up as I wrote this book. I am grateful for their readings and especially their patience as they waited for me to finish "just one more sentence." And when I considered setting the project aside, Jamie prompted me to keep moving forward because, if I didn't, I would always wonder. Thank you for helping me to realize my capacity to know, not to wonder. Your care and patience are woven throughout these pages.

Arranging Stories

Introduction

Arranging Stories as a Frame for Social Commentary

In 1931, Ellen Glasgow invited a group of writers to participate in a southern writers' conference. She envisioned an annual event in which loosely defined "southern" writers would assemble to discuss their ideas, but it proved difficult to organize. Notables like William Faulkner and Allen Tate attended, but just as many others declined, including Thomas Wolfe, who served on the committee only to send his regrets a few days before the opening reception (Goodman 185–87). Glasgow delivered a memorable opening speech when the conference took place at the University of Virginia on October 23–24:

> When I was asked, as the only woman on this committee, to bid you welcome to Virginia, I modestly replied that women come before men only in shipwreck. But Mr. James Branch Cabell, who imposes his duty upon me, is constrained to illustrate his theory that after fifty the only thing worth doing is to decline to do anything. I, on the contrary, believe quite as firmly that the longer one lives in this world of hazard and disaster, the more reckless one should become—at least in the matter of words. (Raper, *Without* 90)

Glasgow begins her speech with a familiar trope—the call for women and children to disembark first in the event of a shipwreck—but then expands on this trope to illustrate her negotiation between sociocultural expectations for white southern women and the fact that her presence on the committee forces a reconsideration of these expectations. Charming her primarily white male audience with her wit, she guides her listeners toward comprehending that, depending on one's social position, reckless words wield either confining or liberating power.

Between the 1880s and the 1940s, opportunities for southern women writers like Glasgow increased dramatically, bolstered by readership demands for southern stories in northern periodicals and followed by these writers' acceptance into the southern literary canon during the Southern Renaissance movement, a period of literary production in the 1920s–30s that emphasized a romantic version of the South's antebellum past as emblematic of the region's modern identity. Yet it remained difficult for southern women writers to be reckless with words. Confined by magazine requirements and sociocultural expectations, writers often relied on regional settings and familiar southern themes to attract publishers and readers. Once a readership was established, these authors sought to publish a collection of stories separate from popular magazine contexts. This book offers critical insights about the sociocultural changes that led to the acceptance of four southern white women writers—Kate Chopin (1851–1904), Ellen Glasgow (1873–1945), Marjorie Kinnan Rawlings (1896–1953), and Katherine Anne Porter (1890–1980)—on both regional and national stages by examining how they selected and arranged previously published stories for their short story collections.

Their publications of short story collections span more than seventy years (1894–1965), a time when southern writers cultivated, established, and sustained an audience through publications in youth magazines, armed services editions, anthologies, and twentieth-century recovery efforts. Twenty-first-century readers remain familiar with many of these authors' stories. The collected stories examined in this book—Chopin's *Bayou Folk* (1894), Glasgow's *The Shadowy Third and Other Stories* (1923), Rawlings's *When the Whippoorwill* (1940), and Porter's The Old Order stories (1944, 1955, 1965)—were initially published during the first half of their authors' literary careers, even though Chopin, Glasgow, Rawlings, and Porter were in their mid-forties to early fifties when these collections were published. Whether the collections constituted an early career opportunity or resulted from an established reputation in southern letters, the writers' ages provided a vantage point for continued innovation and reflection. Each woman embraced her ancestral and geographically located connection to the American South, although none remained bound by southern geography and all attempted to circumvent southern ideologies that limited their voices.

This book examines short story collections that convey perspectives on the American South over time by examining how arrangement expands on or complicates narrative. Unlike stories published only once or serialized novels, short story collections indicate an author's ability to capture and maintain a loyal readership. Selecting and ordering magazine stories for these collections was neither arbitrary nor dictated by editors. Instead, southern white women writers contextualized stories by their proximity to other tales as a form of social commentary. By connecting individual stories to one another within an arranged narrative space, short story collections guide readers through a spatial experience in which both individual stories and the ordering of those stories become a framework for interpreting meaning.

Several years ago, I had the opportunity to ask poet Tom Sleigh about his selection and organization of poems about war-torn Lebanon for *Army Cats: Poems* (2011). He responded that a writer "might think about it in relation to four simple geometric shapes: is your book a line? a circle? a spiral? a vortex? . . . [W]hatever those concepts mean to you is sufficient."[1] Sleigh's use of geometric shapes makes arrangement visible in a way reminiscent of Michel Foucault's assertion in *The Order of Things* (1966) that "forms and arrangements must be described . . . by identification with geometrical figures, or by analogies that must all be 'of the utmost clarity,' [since] structure enables" what is not immediately discernable "to be transcribed into language" (153). How we order texts shapes intended meaning and reception. For instance, we regularly arrange books in a bookcase, groceries in a pantry, and items on a "to do" list. These arrangements reveal how we situate disparate information in context as well as facilitate our engagements with commonplace tasks and guide us through relationships between those tasks. In literature, the selection and arrangement of texts in a collection similarly expands on an individual story's content in relation to other texts in the volume. This relationship—between story-level narrative and collectively arranged narrative—acts as frame, purposely constructed and displayed to reveal a progression of meaning.

There is no narratological term specifically for the study of the selection and arrangement of texts in a collected volume. However, my use of *framing* to describe the process of selecting and arranging stories in collections by nineteenth- and twentieth-century women writers connects surface reading (a practice of critical description to locate patterns existing within and across texts) to feminist narratology (an engagement with interdisciplinary approaches and sociocultural contexts as part of a close reading practice). Surface reading focuses on the materiality of a book and "assumes that texts can reveal their own truths because texts mediate themselves" (Best and Marcus 10). By "locating narrative structures and abstract patterns on the surface as aggregates of what is manifest in multiple texts," we can "break down texts or discourses into their components . . . attend to what is present rather than privileg[ing] what is absent" (10). *Narrative Discourse: An Essay in Method*, Gérard Genette's seminal work in narrative theory, attends to what is already present by focusing on order, or the temporal sequence within a single text. Genette's analyses of paratexts (productions like prefaces, titles, and inscriptions that are designed to ensure a text's reception and consumption) and palimpsests (adaptations that alter an original text's content) integrate examinations of material contexts associated with a text and our readings of it (see Genette, *Paratexts*; Genette, *Palimpsests*). Even so, the collective arrangements examined in this book—primarily previously published magazine stories reprinted in a volume with minor revisions—are neither paratexts nor palimpsests. Suzanne Keen's review of narrative theory as a critical approach rightly points out that "the separation of a story from its context in a unified volume may matter to a critic," since stories serialized in magazines "differ from the stories deliberately grouped into a unifying volume form" (28–29). Nevertheless, this brief treatment remains tangential to Keen's larger argument about "relationships between genre and shapes of narrative" (19).

Feminist narratology extends these structuralist readings to consider relationships between texts and the historical and social contexts that influence their conception and production, "insist[ing] on contextualization as a means of understanding the interplay between gender and narrative form" (Ruth Page 14). Susan Lanser's seminal essay "Toward a Feminist Narratology" (1986) argues that a feminist narratological reading exposes a subtext voice in addition to a surface text voice, and it reveals itself as "a potentially subversive—hence powerful—tool" (349). Since this initial work, she has contributed further to feminist narratological readings by focusing on "intersectionality" and the connections between feminist and queer narrative theories.[2] In *Narrative Theory Unbound: Queer and Feminist Interventions* (2015), Robyn Warhol and Lanser contend that "generalizing about the oppression of nineteenth century women in the United States . . . makes no sense if race, region, and class are not part of the analysis" (7). Middle-class white women "lived so differently from their counterparts" who worked in factories or were enslaved (7). Drawing on queer theory's "recognition of the power of narrative," narratives are "critical to constructing, maintaining, interpreting, exposing, and dismantling the social systems, cultural practices, and individual lives that shape and are shaped by performative acts" (7–8). Functioning as textual, historical, and social content, form serves as "a methodological starting-point" that seeks "the intricacy of relations over interpretative depth," "reveal[s] the text's distinctions of privilege and priority [while] also grappl[ing] with ethical, political, and professional hierarchies that organize nontextual worlds," and "invites us to rethink effective political action" (Lanser, "Toward (a Queerer and)" 36; Levine 23, 111).

Mieke Bal's reflections on two separate visits to postmodern artist Ken Aptekar's exhibits in Washington, DC, and Soho, London, further visualize relationships between textual forms and nontextual worlds. In Washington, Bal recalls how Aptekar's exhibit began with an empty frame, or "ghost painting," that served to "open the other paintings up for framing by the audience" and guided the audience through a purposefully arranged experience ("Memories" 181). In Soho, her recollections focus on Aptekar's *I'm Six Years Old and Hiding* (1996). On sixteen panels of oil on wood, text is sandblasted onto glass and bolted an inch in front of the painting. Bal explains that the painting itself is simply a copy of François Boucher's *Allegory of Painting* (1765), but the gilded frame "casts strange shadows on portions of the painting and glass plates cover the visual work with words" (*Narratology* 66–67). "I read the text," Bal observes, "even though my reading was constantly interrupted by the painting that was looking back at me, nagging that I ought to look at it first" (68).

According to Bal, framing functions as cultural symbolism by completing the narrative vision ("Memories" 181). The frame's structure helps readers negotiate between surface and close readings and between text and the contexts that inform a text's reception. Bal's engagement with Aptekar's exhibits—ghost paintings, textual arrangements, copied primary text, overlay of words, shadow-casting frames, and retrospective telling—demonstrates how negotiations between texts and the framing of texts in visual art exhibits have the potential to inform our understanding of literary arrangements. In the case of a collection of written texts, each story is like a painting—or, more precisely, a copy of a painting, since, most stories examined in this book were published previously in magazines. Once the story becomes part of a collection, its meaning evolves to encompass both its individual content and its relationship to other stories in the same volume. Framing is the most suitable term for this process because it both comprises a performative act and, as part of this process, calls attention to this act to communicate a text's significance as part of a greater context.

However, I am not suggesting that only one possible interpretation exists for the cultural function of a particular frame used to aggregate a group of stories. Instead, a process of reading and rereading to locate patterns of story selection and arrangement, in conjunction with revelations of authorial intent from manuscripts and correspondence, determines a likely impetus for the narrative decisions pertaining to each collection of stories. The purpose is to further magnify a text's significance as one component within a frame, to situate literary interpretations of stories as informed by these frames, and to demonstrate relationships between individual and collective readings.

The textual histories of most short stories examined in this book began with the periodical press. This marketplace expanded significantly between the 1830s and 1890s as a consequence of technological advances in the printing press and of increased literacy rates among all classes. The 1890s in particular constituted a "revolution in magazine publishing and reading," ushered in by a demand for cheaper magazines, increased advertising, higher circulations, the development of libraries and social circles, and a "remarkably aggressive drive for self-improvement" in middle-class society (Mott, *History* 2:195–98, 209). Americans from the 1890s through the 1940s relied on economically accessible and consumable periodicals for information and entertainment. As a result, periodicals profited by responding to readers' demands and became a popular medium (Price and Smith 3; Smythe 123).

By publishing stories in magazines, emerging writers garnered a readership among patrons of specific periodicals. Three of the writers in this study—Chopin, Glasgow, and Rawlings—initially sought to publish their work primarily in northern "quality magazines"—elitist magazines produced for an audience "well above average in income and intellectual curiosity," such as *Scribner's Magazine*, *Harper's Monthly Magazine*, *The Century*, and the *Atlantic Monthly* (Peterson 2, 135, 357–61, 203–4). At the height of their popularity before World War I, quality magazines accompanied stories with artistically rendered illustrations, often printed them in color to capture a scene from the text. These illustrations—along with other paratexts associated with a particular magazine's editorial design, such as readers' associations about the "quality" of the magazine; the arrangement of selections in issues; authors included in issues; editors' introductory marks; and advertisements targeting a particular audience—sparked an audience's interest in a story.

When unable to place a story in a quality magazine, authors turned to magazines that targeted middle-class audiences. These magazines, such as *Vogue*, *Good Housekeeping*, and the *Saturday Evening Post*, did not print the pages of a text consecutively in the issue, included black-and-white illustrations, and often situated fiction alongside advertisements on the page. By the 1930s and 1940s, when Rawlings and Porter were primarily publishing their work in magazines, the surviving quality magazines had eliminated illustrations. "Little magazines," or eclectic periodicals like *Accent* and the *Southern Review*, were favored for their encouragement of emerging writers and networking opportunities (see Hoffman, Allen, and Ulrich).

Editors Aleta Feinsodane and Susan Alves borrow the first part of the title of their collection of essays about the relationship between women's literature and periodicals, *"The Only Efficient Instrument": American Women Writers and the Periodical, 1837–1916* (2001), from Margaret Fuller's essay "American Literature: Its Position in the Present" (1852), which contends that "the most important part of our literature, while the work of diffusion is still going on, lies in the journals, which monthly, weekly, daily, send their messages to every corner of this great land, and form, at present, the only efficient instrument for the general education of the people" (395). Feinsodane and Alves emphasize the periodical press's historical significance for American women seeking to become professional writers. Beginning in the 1880s, periodicals increasingly provided white southern women writers with opportunities to publish their work. As historian Jane Turner Censer examines in *The Reconstruction of White Southern Womanhood, 1865–1895* (2003), northern publishers eagerly considered submissions from these authors in response to readers' preoccupation with depictions of the South. Publishing provided new opportunities for southern white women to express themselves beyond the private sphere, and this shift compelled them to learn "to write for a larger audience" (233). They took advantage of these opportunities for a variety of reasons, including monetary compensation, public recognition, and interest in social reforms. The periodical evolved into "a social text, involving complex relationships among writers, readers, editors, publishers, printers, and distributors" (Price and Smith 3). From the late nineteenth century through the early twentieth century, southern white women writers sought to participate in the construction of this social text by cultivating a relationship with their readers to revise depictions of southern womanhood, even though it was often a "tumultuous relationship," as Censer describes Amélie Rives's experiences in "The Southern Lady and the Northern Publisher" and as discussed through Chopin's and Glasgow's experiences with the publishing industry in the first two chapters of this book.

Whether cultivated by northern publishers or by southern writers responding to historical and cultural change, the literature of the American South has been repositioning itself since its inception. As new southern studies scholars began to argue in the 1970s, the South is less a place than an idea sustained by narrative. The initial call for a distinctively southern literature originated in the late 1820s alongside the impetus to construct a national literature (see Hutchinson; Greeson). Following Reconstruction, the abundance of regional (often categorized as "local color" literature) in the 1880s constituted a response to northern depictions of the South. In the 1920s and 1930s, the Southern Renaissance sought to revise H. L. Mencken's 1917 essay, "The Sahara of the Bozart," and its damning assertion that most southern poetry and prose was "drivel." Modernist William Faulkner's response revised depictions of the plantation as dysfunctional in novels like *Absalom! Absalom!* (1936). Southern identity sustains itself, as Michael O'Brien contends in *The Idea of the American South, 1920–1941* (1979) and in *Placing the South* (2007), by its narrative response to crisis.

In *Inventing Southern Literature* (1998), Michael Kreyling situates this responsive revision as "cultural product," a "metanarrative, touching upon crucial moments when and where the official narrative is made or problematically redirected" (ix); a decade later, Scott Romine asserts in *The Real South: Southern Narrative in the Age of Cultural Reproduction* (2008) that the "fake" South becomes a "real" South through the intervention of narrative that perpetuates itself by selling its ideology. This "southernness" is maintained by a socially constructed relationship between memory, culture, and identity, even though the antebellum South was always an imagined South, or a geographic space that used its exceptionalism to contribute to the formation of an American literature (see Kreyling, *South*; Greeson). Examining the production of narratives, as K. Stephen Prince contends in *Stories of the South: Race and Reconstruction of Southern Identity, 1865–1915* (2014), illuminates how portrayals of the American South connect place and ideology within an ever-evolving narrative.

Depictions of southern womanhood in southern narratives evolved alongside the ideological concept of "true womanhood" in nineteenth-century America. If nineteenth-century women failed to embody piety, purity, submissiveness, and domesticity, "all was ashes" (Welter 152). They should unquestioningly accept the role of submissive caretaker, remaining by the fireside to keep a cheerful home, comfort others, engage in morally uplifting tasks like housework, master needlework, and possess an affinity for flowers (162–65). Embodied in archetypal figures like the "southern lady," southern women needed to reflect virtue to foster a sense of cultural stability (Scott 6).

The southern female body in particular represents a negotiation of this ideological power, a site that has been written and revised as part of responsive positioning through narrative. Multiple studies link southern female bodies to narrative production—bodies that are not static but part of a "never ending process of negotiating the boundaries between 'femininity' and 'masculinity' and between 'whiteness' and 'blackness'" (Donaldson and Jones 16; see also McPherson; Anne Goodwyn Jones; MacKethan). In *Dirt and Desire: Reconstructing Southern Women's Writing, 1930–1990* (2000), Patricia Yaeger calls for a new way of looking at southern female bodies, including the physical and psychological augmentation of the belle "miniature" to a figure of strength and the side-by-side positioning of Black and white southern women to demonstrate how "differing topographies of power" function within southern narratives (xi). Representations of the body in southern literature "serve as a window onto the pressing questions, challenges, and crises that face twentieth century regional and national culture" (Watson 27). By connecting the female body to a regional space, southern women writers use region as a "rhetorical construction" to locate and to magnify social injustices (Fetterley and Pryse 15, 114, 334). Framing previously published magazine stories, which capitalized on regional differences, in collected volumes exemplifies this rhetorical construction, since "the very notion of choice, of electing privileged or 'highly placed' scenes, of careful composition, and of arrangement brings into play a series of terms and concepts heavy with implications" (Caws 21). This book examines the implications of southern women writers articulating and at times revising the dominant narrative of white male supremacy over southern female bodies.

In contrast to the increasing possibilities for white southern writers in the late nineteenth century, Black southern women writers found significantly fewer opportunities to write themselves out of misogynistic and racist narratives. With the notable exceptions of poets Phillis Wheatley and Frances Ellen Watkins Harper, Black women writers often entered the literary canon through writing and publishing slave narratives.[3] Following Frederick Douglass's *Narrative of the Life of Frederick Douglass, an American Slave* (1845), African American women's slave narratives drew attention to the effects of sexual abuse and family division during slavery and post-emancipation servitude while using sentimental literary tropes to cultivate empathy and to convey the urgent need for social reform. Southern Black women were often viewed as either "jezebels" (an oversexualized image and site of reproduction) or "mammies" (the "ideal slave, ideal woman, and ideal symbol of the patriarchal tradition") (White 21). Writers such as Anna Julia Cooper sought to revise these representations in works like *A Voice of the South* (1892), urging readers to pursue "moral uplift" through education. "One of the most singular facts about the unwritten history of this country," Cooper argues, "is the consummate ability with which Southern influence, Southern ideas and Southern ideals, have from the very beginning even up to the present day, dictated to and domineered over the brain and sinew of this nation" (101). The southern Black woman's voice, Cooper contends, is best equipped to rewrite the plight of African Americans because her cause "is linked with . . . every wrong that needs a voice" (122).[4]

Southern Black women writers were writing and publishing short stories as regularly as Chopin, Glasgow, Rawlings, and Porter but lacked access to northern publishers, who controlled much of the periodical marketplace. Instead, writers like Alice Dunbar-Nelson (1875–1935) and Zora Neale Hurston (1891–1960) cultivated readers through African American periodicals like *The Crisis* and *Opportunity: A Journal of Negro Life*. Dunbar-Nelson found early career support from mentor Sylvanie Williams, the founder and president of New Orleans's Phyllis Wheatley Club. In Dunbar-Nelson's first collection of poems and stories, *Violets and Other Tales* (1895), Williams acknowledges the book's strengths and challenges, directing readers to support the author's early efforts: "May the energy displayed by one so young," Williams implores, "meet the reward it merits from an approving public" (5). Three of the volume's stories, set in New Orleans—"A Carnival Jangle," "Little Miss Sophie," and "Titee"—reappear in Dunbar-Nelson's short story collection, *The Goodness of St. Rocque* (1899).[5] Yet, "with few exceptions, the male editors who controlled white literary culture in Dunbar-Nelson's time—and whose choices have, until recently, delimited what remains in circulation since—refused to publish her submissions" (Adams, Zagarell, and Gebhard 218).

Publishing in African American magazines was "highly visible," but this visibility was confined to "a narrower readership" (Adams, Zagarell, and Gebhard 219). Hurston, praised for her novels, folk tale collections, autobiography, and depression-era ethnographic work for the Federal Writers' Project in Florida, published stories frequently in African American magazines. Nonetheless, her tales were not organized into a single-authored collection until *The Complete Stories* (1995), published thirty-five years after her death. In fact, much of Hurston's literary legacy remained dormant until Alice Walker's 1975 pilgrimage to locate her gravesite (and the essay that developed from this pilgrimage) renewed critical attention. In *In Search of Our Mothers' Gardens* (1983), Walker, who had "A Genius of the South" inscribed on Hurston's gravestone, shares that while attending college, she "heard not one word about early black women writers" despite "the richness of the black writer's experience in the South," which draws on "a compassion for the earth, a trust in humanity beyond our knowledge of evil, and an abiding love of justice" (9, 18, 21).

Both Dunbar-Nelson's and Hurston's legacies continue to benefit from recovery efforts and contemporary critical engagements.[6] Yet for the most part, the southern white women authors in this study did not explicitly champion the cause of racial injustice in their writings. Instead, their work often reinforced myths and does not use their position to disassemble oppression (Lewis 167–68). While feminist narratology recognizes the significance of intersecting oppressions within relationships between text and gender, the writers examined in this book often viewed these social categories as disparate sites of injustice. In particular, their limited engagements with race perpetuated the confining social narratives they sought to eliminate through much of their work. This book identifies the ways in which Chopin, Glasgow, Rawlings, and Porter address racial, gender, and class subjugation while also recognizing their complicit participation in racist ideologies through literary representations and absences of African American figures in their work.

These four authors drew on a tradition of nineteenth-century women writers publishing in popular magazines. These magazines provided opportunities for southern white women writers to publish their work but also limited an author's content through editorial prescriptions—from physical parameters, such as length or serialization policies, to sociopolitical agendas (see Morgan; Hardwig). Since collections were comprised of stories previously published in magazines, publishing a volume of collected stories enabled authors to revise their stories outside of magazines' requirements and provided the agency for authors to arrange individual stories into a collective narrative while earning income from their work.

In this book, *agency* refers to authorial control and the author's intent to use this control to convey social commentary, directly or subversively. However, since "narrative succeeds by covering the tracks of its own strategies" and since "those narrative strategies function as narrative content [so that] stories cannot even be apprehended unless we can read them as form," relationships between gender and narrative arrangements may remain "complex, subtle, and sometimes elusive" (Lanser, "Toward (a Queerer and)" 23). Therefore, as Lanser recommends, my engagements with special collections and archives assist toward "achiev[ing] a global and historical narrative knowledge" (31).

The biographical and textual research for this volume engages extensive archival sources—professional and personal correspondence, manuscripts, original periodical issues, and first editions of short story collections—in digitized and on-site repositories at the University of Alabama, University of Virginia, University of Florida, University of South Florida, University of Maryland, Princeton University, Missouri Historical Society, University of Michigan, State Library and Archives of Florida, and the St. Louis Public Library. These investigations located information about the extent to which writers made their own decisions about the selection and arrangement of stories for the collections and about their intentions to use these narrative decisions for conveying social commentary that unifies, expands on, or complicates readings of individual stories. In instances when authorial control appears limited or challenged, I analyze what a lack of agency might reveal about social positioning in relation to the other writers in this study. My archival research was not only crucial in determining *if* and *how* women writers gained agency through their narrative decisions but also contributed substantively to the contextual readings in this book.

These authors' lives and works were influenced by different, although often overlapping, historical and political events. The dates for this project—1894 to 1965—encompass the South's post–Civil War socioeconomic recovery, World War I, the Great Depression, World War II, the Cold War era, and the Korean War. Literary responses to these historical events include realism, naturalism, modernism, and postmodernism, although the authors in this study consistently and adamantly situated their work within the realist tradition to distance themselves from perceptions of women's literature as romantic and sentimental.

The late nineteenth century and early twentieth centuries marked a period of increased acceptance of women's voices in southern literature. During the 1880s–90s, northern periodicals frequently published southern stories in response to readers' demands for literature about the American South, while the Southern Renaissance, a movement initiated by a group of writers and critics who were associated with Vanderbilt University and called themselves Southern Agrarians, welcomed white women writers into the southern literary canon. However, as moderator Louis Rubin Jr. pointed out to a panel of southern writers (Porter, Flannery O'Connor, Caroline Gordon, and Madison Jones) at Wesleyan College in 1960, this "renaissance" initiated more misconceptions and unanswered questions than defining "the southern writer" (Porter, "Recent" 42). In response to Rubin's question about "who qualifies as a southern writer and on what grounds," panelists suggested writers' relationships with geographic location while simultaneously determining that southern literature is neither place-bound nor "full of [the] white columns and magnolias" preferred by northern publishers' romanticization of landscape (57). Instead, southern literature, as O'Connor determines, uses "the Southern situation" to "tell stories" universal to the human experience in "the whole western world, the whole edition of the present generation of people" (52–53). In other words, it is not the concept of southernness that made Chopin's, Glasgow's, Rawlings's, and Porter's stories popular as much as it is the writers' insistence on magnifying and rectifying the cultural expectations that defined their literary lives and production.

The authors and collections included in this book reflect these developments in literary and cultural history, using region to tell stories about relationships between places and people. Their "regional writing," a term I borrow from Judith Fetterley and Marjorie Pryse's *Writing out of Place: Regionalism, Women, and American Literary Culture* (2003) and intentionally use throughout the book, distinguishes between writers "who accept the assumptions of the regionalizing premise" (local color) and writers "who take exception to these assumptions" (regionalist writers) (Fetterley and Pryse 7). Chopin, Glasgow, Rawlings, and Porter come from diverse geographic locations within the regional microcosm of the American South, yet their narratives contain strikingly similar themes. Their tales continue to be represented in southern (and American) literature anthologies because their depictions of human experience transcend place and moment.

This project began with my readings of Porter's The Old Order stories and engagements with Porter's papers and artifacts at the University of Maryland's Hornbake Library. In response to a finding about Porter's involvement in the arrangement of her stories from archived professional correspondence, I worked backward chronologically to determine a trajectory of publishing experiences for southern white women writers. Authors and collections were selected for this study for their use of periodicals to garner and establish readership before publishing work in a collected volume; archival findings that demonstrated approaches to obtaining agency in a primarily male-dominated publishing industry; occurrences of personal and professional relationships between writers; and a longevity of readership spanning significantly beyond collections' initial publications. Each chapter focuses on one writer and her short story collection in historical, social, and political contexts. With the exception of chapter 4, which explores Porter's publication of a group of southern stories in three separate collections between 1944 and 1965, chapters are arranged according to publication date of the first edition of the collected volume. Chapter titles (mapping, advocating, preserving, reconstructing) emphasize an ongoing process of reading, or how framing—through the selection and arrangement of stories—conveys a social commentary meant to extend a reader's engagement with narrative.

Chapter 1, "Mapping Spatial Consciousness in Kate Chopin's *Bayou Folk* (1894)," traces the textual history of four stories—"Beyond the Bayou," "The Return of Alcibiade," "A Wizard from Gettysburg," and "Ma'ame Pélagie"—from their initial publications in periodicals to their inclusion in Chopin's first short story collection, *Bayou Folk* (1894). A prolific writer often associated by contemporary readers with her novel, *The Awakening* (1899), Chopin's publications in magazines like the *Youth's Companion*, *The Century*, and *Vogue* capitalized on readers' interest in southern regional literature to cultivate a national audience. These four stories portray the aftermath of the Civil War in

Louisiana between the 1860s and 1890s. When read together, they demonstrate a progressively deteriorating landscape, strategically revising northern magazine editors' positioning of the South as sentimental and exotic to magnify the social concerns that continued to envelope a nation recovering from war. Chopin challenges geographic boundaries through her narrative representations of them to develop a reader's spatial consciousness about relationships between dominant power structures and regional exceptionalism.

Like Chopin's deconstruction of the sentimental to expose social concerns, chapter 2, "Advocating for Social Justice in Ellen Glasgow's *The Shadowy Third and Other Stories* (1923)," demonstrates how Glasgow repurposes sentimental narratives to make visible injustices toward women. Glasgow refused to concede to a patronizing publishing culture, and in the first four stories of *The Shadowy Third*—"The Shadowy Third," "Dare's Gift," "The Past," and "Whispering Leaves"—she situates deceased wives and mothers, ancestral plantations, and African American caretakers as ghostly characters, capable of disrupting tyranny. The ordering of these stories according to their original magazine publication dates, in conjunction with their alternating settings between New York and Virginia, suggests that they were written sequentially. Each story's ghost functions as a representation of gender and racial oppression, exposing how romanticized versions of sociocultural narratives maintain and perpetuate this oppression. In the only short story collection published during her lifetime, Glasgow does not confine critique to the South but magnifies injustices across topographical boundaries by systematically alternating between northern and southern geographic locations.

Chapter 3, "Preserving the Hammock in Marjorie Kinnan Rawlings's *When the Whippoorwill* (1940)," also examines an author's only collection of short stories published during her lifetime. The tales in *When the Whippoorwill* fictionalize Rawlings's experiences living in the rural Florida Cracker community of Cross Creek during the 1930s. Writing from the perspectives of both participant (resident at Cross Creek) and observer (a writer depicting a region's culture to convey universal meaning), Rawlings envisions herself as an ethnographer, determined to portray a way of life through literary representations that convey its beauty to readers. Her selection and arrangement of four previously published magazine stories progressively positions the female Florida Cracker character's voice—represented by Drenna in "A Crop of Beans," Florry in "Jacob's Ladder," Mattie Syles in "Gal Young Un," and Quincey Dover in "Cocks Must Crow"—at the center of a community's interdependence and resiliency. These stories convey Rawlings's efforts to preserve the Florida scrubland and its inhabitants, a vestige of the waning American frontier.

Chapter 4, "Reconstructing Memory in Katherine Anne Porter's The Old Order Stories (1944, 1955, 1965)," considers the arrangement of a group of six (ultimately seven) stories, first submitted for publication in 1932 and eventually published together in three separate collections—*The Leaning Tower and Other Stories* (1944), *The Old Order: Stories of the South from The Leaning Tower, Pale Horse, Pale Rider, and Flowering Judas* (1955), and *The Collected Stories of Katherine Anne Porter* (1965). The Old Order stories depict protagonist Miranda's childhood memories of postbellum South but only tangentially engage the inherently problematic social issues related to gender and race that permeate her memories. Porter does not edit the stories' content between publications but in subsequent volumes rearranges the stories from a chronological to an anachronistic portrayal of fictional events. Instead of revising the content of Miranda's memories, Porter (re)contextualizes their significance by their reordering to demonstrate Miranda's ongoing critical engagement with the past.

Arranging Stories explores how stories are constructed and how stories are told. The textual histories of these collections provide an overview of the changes in the periodical marketplace and demonstrate how southern white women used this marketplace to both garner readership and resist the prescribed demands of a male-dominated publishing industry. Short story collections, unlike other genres, allowed a writer to transcend popular magazine contexts to construct her own narrative framework. These collected volumes convey their authors' intentions regarding a single text in relation to a larger oeuvre. Isolating and magnifying a process of narrative production in a regional microcosm of the United States from the late nineteenth to mid-twentieth century informs future critical engagements with relationships between texts and contexts. Chopin, Glasgow, Rawlings, and Porter wrote to challenge the oppressive narratives that confined them, and their insistent selection and arrangement of stories for their collections constitutes a context designed to convey social commentary.

I

Mapping Spatial Consciousness in Kate Chopin's *Bayou Folk* (1894)

Kate Chopin, portrayed by early biographers Daniel Rankin and Per Seyersted as a conventional nineteenth-century woman, is described as more flamboyant than traditional in contemporary accounts of her life.[1] Her Cloutierville, Louisiana, neighbors even recalled an anecdote about how she used her riding crop to whip an elderly male relative in the street when he attempted to admonish her behavior (Toth, "Shadow" 290). Chopin's husband, Oscar, was originally a cotton merchant in New Orleans but moved the family to Cloutierville after a series of poor cotton crops plunged him into debt. He died of malaria in 1883, leaving his widow to raise six children on a limited income. Like women before her, Kate Chopin sought to supplement her income by publishing her writing. A prolific writer, she published two novels, poetry, essays, translations, one play, and nearly one hundred short stories during a career that lasted slightly longer than a decade (Ewell, "Kate Chopin" in *History*; Chopin, *Kate Chopin's* 126; Toth, *Unveiling* 78–100). However, as evidenced by surviving account books, these publications did not earn enough to support her household. Instead, she relied on income from inherited property.[2]

Fig. 1.1 Kate Chopin in her riding hat (perhaps with the infamous lavender plume), 1876, a little more than a decade before she began her career as a professional writer. Courtesy of the Missouri Historical Society, St. Louis.

Chopin's life and work expose the paradox between the forced dependence of domestic ideology and the intellectual independence required to financially support a family. In her essay "On Certain Brisk, Bright Days" (1899), she responds to the question, "When do I write?," by telling readers, "I write in the morning, when not too strongly drawn to struggle with the intricacies of a pattern, and in the afternoon, if the temptation to try a new furniture polish on an old table leg is not too powerful to be denied" (Chopin, *Complete* 721–22). On the one hand, Chopin cultivates the appearance of "true womanhood" (nineteenth-century sociocultural expectations for women that included piety, domesticity, purity, and submissiveness) by explaining that she wrote only when she became uninterested domestic tasks.[3] On the other hand, she refused to be confined by prescribed definitions of feminine behavior, scandalously wearing "dashing riding habits and hats with lavender plumes" (figure 1.1), attracting male attention by showing her ankles, and smoking Cuban cigarettes (Toth, "Shadow" 290–92; Toth, *Unveiling* 82–100). As Mary Papke rightly points out, it was a "schizophrenic prescription" (13).

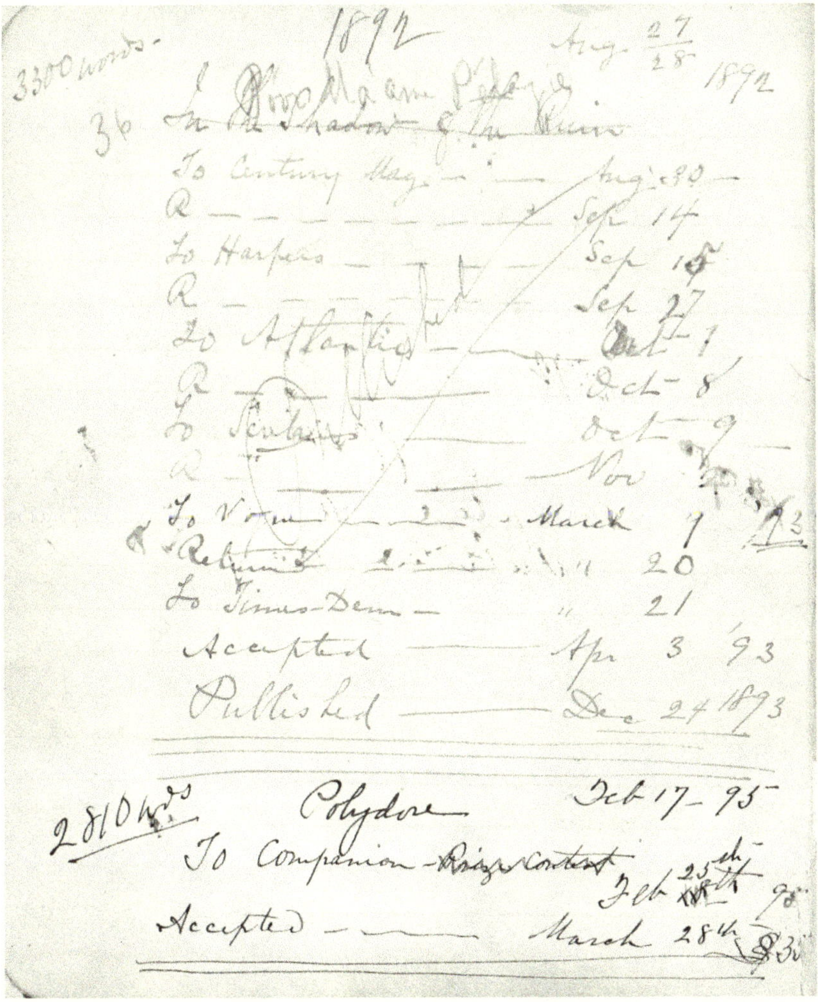

Fig. 1.2 Kate Chopin's account book recording the history of submissions for "Ma'ame Pélagie." Courtesy of the Missouri Historical Society, St. Louis.

Contrary to her claim of indifference, Chopin's account books reveal a systematic approach to publishing her work.[4] She dutifully recorded the history of each manuscript—dating its completion, first submission, returns and resubmissions, first and subsequent publications, and associated financial earnings (figures 1.2 and 1.3). Her account books also demonstrate a submissions' hierarchy, or progressive pattern of placement from "quality" magazines to local magazines and newspapers, as figure 1.2 shows. While many of her

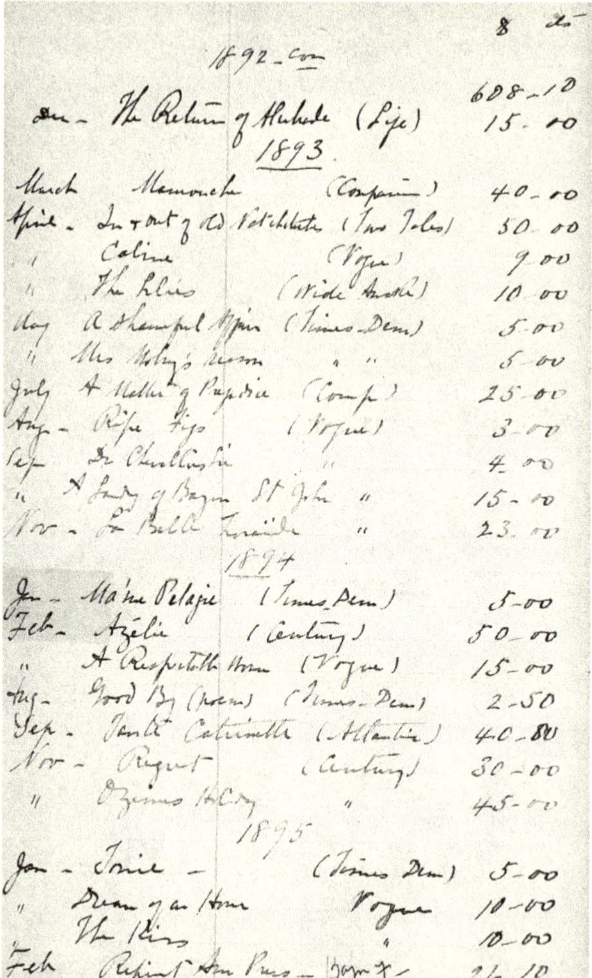

1892 – con

			608 – 10
Dec –	The Return of Alcibiade	(Life)	15 – 00

1893

March	Mamouche	(Companion)	40 – 00
April –	In & Out of Old Natchitoches	(Two Tales)	50 – 00
"	Caline	(Vogue)	9 – 00
"	The Lilies	(Wide Awake)	10 – 00
May	A Shameful Affair	(Times-Dem)	5 – 00
"	Mrs Mobry's Reason	" "	5 – 00
July	A Matter of Prejudice	(Comp)	25 – 00
Aug –	Ripe Figs	(Vogue)	3 – 00
Sep	Dr Chevalier's Lie	"	4 – 00
"	A Lady of Bayou St John	"	15 – 00
Nov –	La Belle Zoraïde	"	23 – 00

1894

Jan –	Ma'me Pélagie	(Times-Dem)	5 – 00
Feb –	Azélie	(Century)	50 – 00
"	A Respectable Woman	(Vogue)	15 – 00
Aug –	Good By (poem)	(Times-Dem)	2 – 50
Sep –	Tante Cat'rinette	(Atlantic)	40 – 80
Nov –	Regret	(Century)	30 – 00
"	Ozème's Holiday	"	45 – 00

1895

Jan –	[illegible] –	(Times Dem)	5 – 00
"	Dream of an Hour	Vogue	10 – 00
	The Kiss	"	10 – 00
Feb	Reprint Am Press –	Bayou F–	21 – 10
"	A Dresden Lady in Dixie	(Home Jl)	60 – 00
Mar	Her Letters	Vogue	25 – 00
April	Polydore	(Comp)	35 – 00
"	Cavanelle	(Am. Jewess)	10 – 00
Aug	Bayou Folk	(Collection)	1 – 75
Oct	The Unexpected	(Vogue)	10 – 00

1896

Jan –	A Sentimental Soul	Times Dem	10 – 00
Feb –	Ma'me Martel's Christmas –	Comp	50 – 00
			1247 – 45

Fig. 1.3 Kate Chopin's account book listing the *New Orleans Times-Democrat*'s payment for "Ma'ame Pélagie" as well as several other stories' original publications. Courtesy of the Missouri Historical Society, St. Louis.

stories were submitted and accepted for publication in the *Youth's Companion*, several first were submitted to quality magazines such as *The Century*, *Scribner's Magazine*, *Harper's Monthly*, and the *Atlantic Monthly*.[5] If the work was rejected by a quality magazine, Chopin then sent it to magazines like *Vogue* and *Ladies' Home Journal*. If they too refused the story, she placed the work in local magazines and newspapers, where she had cultivated relationships with editors and was assured of publication (Toth, *Unveiling* 121–47). Furthermore, Chopin "manipulated fictional formats," such as "dramatizing her concerns within familial settings and various age readers . . . to maximize her marketing potential" (Shaker, "Kate Chopin" 88). Whether a work was published in Chopin's first or last preference, the account books reveal her determination to submit her work to periodicals until all completed manuscripts were published.

Kate Chopin wanted to establish herself as a recognized, professional writer, but this process often proved wearisome. In a series of six essays, published under the title "As You Like It" in *The Criterion* between February 13 and March 27, 1897, Chopin recalls her experiences with two editors whose opinions varied widely about the same submission.[6] A New York editor returned a story because the public was "getting tired of that sort of thing" (*Complete Works* 2:717), but a Boston editor accepted it enthusiastically. Chopin then submitted a second story to the Boston publication, which rejected it; however, the New York editor deemed it "clever and excellent" (717). As Chopin concludes, "Editors are really a singular class of men; they have such strange and incomprehensible ways" (717).

Her professional negotiations with that "singular class of men" began in 1888 with the publication of her poem "If It Might Be" and the writing of "Euphasie," a story that was eventually published in *The Century* and in her first short story collection, *Bayou Folk* (1894), as "A No-Account Creole." The following year, she published two stories, "A Point at Issue" and "Wiser Than a God," and by 1890, she had self-published her first novel, *At Fault*. After 1891, she devoted herself to writing "southern stories" because they sold quickly (Ewell, "Kate Chopin," in *History* 212). She earned $787 from her magazine publications, "a sum that makes up more than one-third of her lifetime's literary income of $2,300" (Shaker, "Kate Chopin" 81).

In the late nineteenth century, magazines sought southern stories, and the South's geographic (and cultural) exoticism was exploited to garner northern readers' interest in the region. Depictions of Louisiana in particular were valued for their sense of exoticism, and magazines capitalized on readers' perceptions of regional differences by printing stories and photographs from the South alongside stories and photographs from international destinations such as the Middle East and Europe (Hall 202). Northern editors used southern stories as a political tool to reunify northern and southern geographies (and people) into a cohesive nation (Hardwig 16). Opportunities emerged for southern white women writers, but these opportunities remained confined to editors' prescriptive expectations for southern stories.[7] These expectations, as Thomas Morgan contends, required "a pleasant ending with a positive moral message" to connect middle- and upper-class readers to "the quaint and picturesque lower-class groups" in the South, who were "documented for [readers'] enjoyment" (136, 144). Writers were "curtained by the social and political conformity expected by *Atlantic*-group editors," who controlled both the periodical short story market and access to publishing a collection (164).

Chopin was aware of this opportunity and its subsequent limitations. First, she capitalized on northern readers' interest in regional literature by strategically cultivating a national audience through her publications in the *Youth's Companion*, *The Century*, and *Vogue*. Then, she traveled to Boston and New York to pitch her collection of these stories, originally called "Collection of Creole Stories." During her visit, Chopin obtained an audience with the *Century*'s editor, Richard Watson Gilder, who initially seemed interested. Ultimately, however, she did not find a publisher until her fourth attempt, when Houghton Mifflin accepted it in 1893 (Toth, *Unveiling* 133–47; Vanlandingham 161; Rankin 136).

Chopin was forty-three years old when she finally signed the contract for *Bayou Folk*, which contains twenty-three stories and sketches written between 1891 and 1894. All of the tales were published previously in magazines except for "In Sabine," "Old Aunt Peggy," "Madame Célestin's Divorce," and "A Gentleman of Bayou Têche." They depict Louisiana's landscape and culture while simultaneously addressing social issues like marriage, interracial children, and poverty. Upon publication, *Bayou Folk* received several favorable reviews, but Chopin lamented that they showed "no feeling for the spirit of the work, the subtle genius which created it" (*PP* 187). For Chopin, "spirit" and "subtle genius" embodied more than descriptions of Louisiana's landscape and regionally inspired characters. "Virtually all of the stories," as Emily Toth asserts, "contained some kind of social criticism that was just as applicable to St. Louis or Boston—as it was to Louisiana" (*Unveiling* 150). Chopin was able to publish this social criticism only because reviewers failed to recognize that her critique extended beyond the Louisiana bayou setting of the tales.

In the same way that "mapping the literary and social relations found in her stories" (Morgan 144) exposes the logic that influenced nineteenth-literary production, the four Civil War stories in the collection—"Beyond the Bayou," "The Return of Alcibiade," "A Wizard from Gettysburg," and "Ma'ame Pélagie"—reveal a spatial relationship that links images of a changing landscape to deteriorating architectural spaces and thus revises the sentiment that northern publishers cultivated in their selections of southern stories for magazine publication. "Beyond the Bayou," the most anthologized story among the four stories examined here, depicts Jacqueline La Folle, a freed African American woman who continues to demonstrate self-sacrificing love for P'tit Maître's son, Chéri. When Chéri shoots himself in a hunting accident, La Folle must conquer her fear of crossing the bayou to save him. In "The Return of Alcibiade," Jean Ba fears that his son, Alcibiade, may never return after fighting in the Civil War. Refusing to give up hope, the elderly patriarch mistakes Fred Bartner for Alcibiade, and all the characters become players in an elaborate reenactment of the celebratory Christmas dinner of Jean Ba's imagination. In "A Wizard from Gettysburg," Bertrand Delmandé returns to his plantation, Bon-Accueil, but a head injury acquired at Gettysburg means that he cannot remember his relationship to it. Bon-Accueil's geographic landscape temporarily awakens his memory. Finally, in "Ma'ame Pélagie," Pélagie saves money with her sister, Pauline, to rebuild their destroyed home. The Valmêt ruins embody Pélagie's sense of identity, but once removed from the landscape, Pélagie begins to age rapidly, and her deteriorating body resembles the removed architectural ruins.

In *Writing out of Place: Regionalism, Women, and American Literary Culture* (2005), Judith Fetterley and Marjorie Pryse demonstrate that regionalist writers' use of constructed "space" imparts an "alternate vision . . . inviting readers to immerse themselves in the 'open exception' regionalists take to the very power structure that has 'regionalized' their characters and their writing" (24). Like her systematic approach to periodical publications, Chopin's selection and arrangement of previously published stories indicate a strategic move to revise periodical editors' positioning of the South as sentimental and exotic and thus inform readers of the social concerns that enveloped a nation still recovering from war. *Bayou Folk* establishes her as a professional writer on a national stage and includes four Civil War stories that portray Louisiana from Reconstruction through the early 1890s.[8] Chopin's selection and arrangement of these stories demonstrates the tension between perpetuating and dismantling antebellum sociopolitical boundaries during the period of instability following the Civil War.

If we think of a story as a map that depicts physical and psychological boundaries within representational borders, then a short story collection gathers and orders these maps into a single volume. By connecting individual stories to one another within an arranged narrative space, Chopin's collection guides readers through a spatial experience in which both individual stories and the ordering of those stories become a framework for interpreting meaning. Examining these relationships, as geographer Edward Soja argues in *Postmetropolis: Critical Studies of Cities and Regions* (2000), "cannot only enrich our understanding of almost any subject but [has] the added potential to extend our practical knowledge into more effective actions aimed at changing our world for the better" (2).[9] Chopin's use of region allows the reader to visualize how sociopolitical narratives are constructed and potentially deconstructed over time. Prior to Edna Pontellier's fateful swim in *The Awakening* (1899), Chopin's *Bayou Folk* stories cultivated a critical awareness of social injustice by mapping spatial consciousness.

CHOPIN'S CIVIL WAR

Rankin and Seyersted contend that historical fiction was not Chopin's forte, yet the Civil War stories in *Bayou Folk* depict Chopin's treatment of social issues, or stratifications of race, class, and gender, magnified by recovery from the war. Her stories build upon traditions in nineteenth-century women's writings, while also allowing her to confront her childhood memories of the war.

Biographical evidence suggests that Chopin suffered from war-induced trauma, perpetuated indefinitely by the South's insistence on repositioning Confederate defeat by reinstating antebellum social hierarchies. According to Toth, Chopin earned the moniker "littlest rebel" as a young girl living in St. Louis, Missouri, during the Yankee occupation and was widely known for her daring pro-Confederate antics, such as ignoring soldiers' threats and hiding a Union flag they hung on her porch. Her half-brother, George, who had enlisted in the Confederate Missouri Mounted Infantry, was captured, imprisoned, and released, only to die of tuberculosis contracted in prison before returning home. The condition of other returning Confederate soldiers made an indelible impression on the young Chopin. Chopin witnessed "ragged, even naked" men whom one of her neighbors described as "look[ing] as if they had been stolen out of a graveyard" and heard stories about how "some had eaten their own horses" and wallpaper to survive. Toth contends that Chopin "never found the words" to express her grief (*Unveiling* 28–29).

The trauma that Chopin and others experienced produced a visceral, enduring response that is evident in multiple Confederate memoirs. Veterans describe experiences with starvation, mutilation, and death that echo Chopin's childhood observations.[10] Jessie Gilley, for instance, recalls that General James Longstreet's soldiers were forced to march without shoes so that "the trail made by the soldiers through the ice and snow was so bloody as though skinned beef had been dragged over it."[11] John West and the Reverend Joshua Morbut explain how fire often consumed wooded battlefields. Unable to reach a soldier crying out for help, Morbut recounts that even though the "occurrence was many a long years ago," "that cry for help appeals to me yet."[12] Surely, as West concludes, "war is hell."[13] In the words of the anonymous editor of these memoirs, these accounts came from a small, non-slaveholding community in Calhoun County, Alabama, that sent sixty soldiers to fight for the Confederacy and had fewer than twenty return.[14]

The long-term trauma highlighted in these accounts provides context for Chopin's Civil War stories that can be used as a lens for contemporary wartime responses. Adam Kotlarczyk links Chopin's Civil War stories to contemporary soldiers' experiences with post-traumatic stress disorder, arguing that Chopin's writing "reflects an acute and perhaps ahead-of-its time consciousness of the debilitating mental and emotional impact war has on combatants and non-combatants alike" and identifying six stories written between 1891 and 1897 that deal either with the veteran figure or with characters who have lost a loved one due to war (23).

Chopin's Civil War stories evoke the traditions of southern literary nationalism and nineteenth-century women's literature to depict war's lingering trauma. The South, as literary historian Coleman Hutchinson explains, incorporated its sociopolitical views, such as justifications for slavery, throughout the antebellum construction of a national (and southern) literature, which reached its first height in the mid-nineteenth century with Confederate propaganda literature. Confederate literature was a response to the need quickly to invent a literary tradition with a "future-oriented" emphasis (8). Chopin uses the same tensions that Hutchinson identifies in Confederate literary works—urgency, timeliness, and aspiration—to situate her Civil War stories within an 1890s context (7–17). Simultaneously, she borrows from nineteenth-century women's literature's sentimental tradition to evoke sympathy for characters who continue to deal with wartime trauma, though she eschews sentiment's didacticism. Like Confederate propaganda author Augusta Jane Evans Wilson in *Macaria, or Altars of Sacrifice* (1863), Chopin introduces the political into a seemingly domestic narrative in the Civil War stories found in *Bayou Folk*. Her organization of these stories in *Bayou Folk* concludes with an almost all-female cast of characters in "Ma'ame Pélagie." Through her arrangement of literary representation, Chopin argues for southern white women's positioning at the forefront of a transitioning South. She sought to participate in the South's (re)writing of a southern nationalist literature.

Chopin's Civil War stories in *Bayou Folk* consistently subvert antebellum southern social hierarchies and repurpose the sentimental tradition to connect readers to an evolving southern body politic—one that the New South, a term referring to the South's transition from an agricultural-based economy to an industrial-based economy, must embrace despite its reluctance to do so.[15] Southern white women writers during and after Reconstruction, as Sarah Gardner contends, were preoccupied with the war and entered the public national debate through writing "as a way to exorcise their demons" (112–13). This exorcism occurred both publicly and privately, through publications and readings of nonpublished works. For example, expanding on the mission of the ladies' memorial associations to provide proper burials for Confederate soldiers after the Civil War, members of the United Daughters of the Confederacy (UDC) built monuments, educated children through pro-southern textbooks, and were encouraged to pen romanticized narratives from the antebellum South as part of a sociopolitical movement to rewrite defeat as a rightful cause (see Cox; Janney). Although the evidence is scant, Chopin likely was a member of the UDC.[16] But while sentimentalized antebellum themes are present in her early work, Chopin does not allow them to replicate southern nationalist initiatives.

Chopin's selection and arrangement of the four Civil War stories in *Bayou Folk* illustrates how literary representations of the Civil War and its long-term effects on the nation remain historically, politically, and socially relevant. More than a century later, popular audiences continue to be captivated by films that depict aspects of the war, such as Steven Spielberg's *Lincoln* (2012) and Nate Parker's *The Birth of a Nation* (2016); television series such as *North and South* (1985–94) and *Mercy Street* (2016); and long-running documentaries like Ken Burns's *The Civil War* (1990). Perspectives on the Civil War and Reconstruction continue to be analyzed and (re)written. The South's defeat, as historian Richard Harwell asserts, created "political solidarity, and an even deeper sense of self-consciousness" (22–23). This "political solidarity" and "sense of self-consciousness" certainly maintain their hold on the national imagination.

Remapping the National Imagination

Among the stories examined here, "Beyond the Bayou" has received the most critical attention for its social commentary. It provides a map for how to read the other three Civil War stories. Like many of Chopin's stories, "Beyond the Bayou" was published in the *Youth's Companion*.[17] The *Youth's Companion* consistently printed work by emerging women writers, whose contributions upheld its mission to "provide moral and religious guidance for children" (Mott, *History* 2:263). Each issue included moral anecdotes, four to six poems, and illustrated stories. By the 1880s, the twelve-page magazine contained articles by famous statesmen, scientists, and explorers such as Theodore Roosevelt and Booker T. Washington (267–83).

Chopin's account books confirm that she submitted "Beyond the Bayou" solely to the *Youth's Companion* on November 7, 1891, and that it was readily accepted on December 11, 1891, although it was not published until June 15, 1893 (*PP* 153, 169). The delayed publication was in keeping with the magazine's standard policy (Shaker and Pettit 387–89). The June 1893 issue contained four extra pages; all advertisements were relegated to the end. In addition, the issue lacked a table of contents. Chopin's roughly one-page story appears near the beginning of the issue and is printed in four newspaper-like columns without illustrations.

Of the four Civil War stories (and of all the stories in *Bayou Folk*), only "Beyond the Bayou" begins with a topographic description of geographic space. "The bayou," says the narrator, "curved like a crescent moon around the point of the land on which La Folle's cabin stood" (99).[18] In the narrative, the land is as much a protagonist as Jacqueline La Folle, so much so that a reader, as Dara Llewellyn suggests, could sketch it (figure 1.4). For La Folle, the bayou represents a definitive boundary, a "shape [that] encloses the world where the character La Folle lives" (Llewellyn 255). There is the bayou and

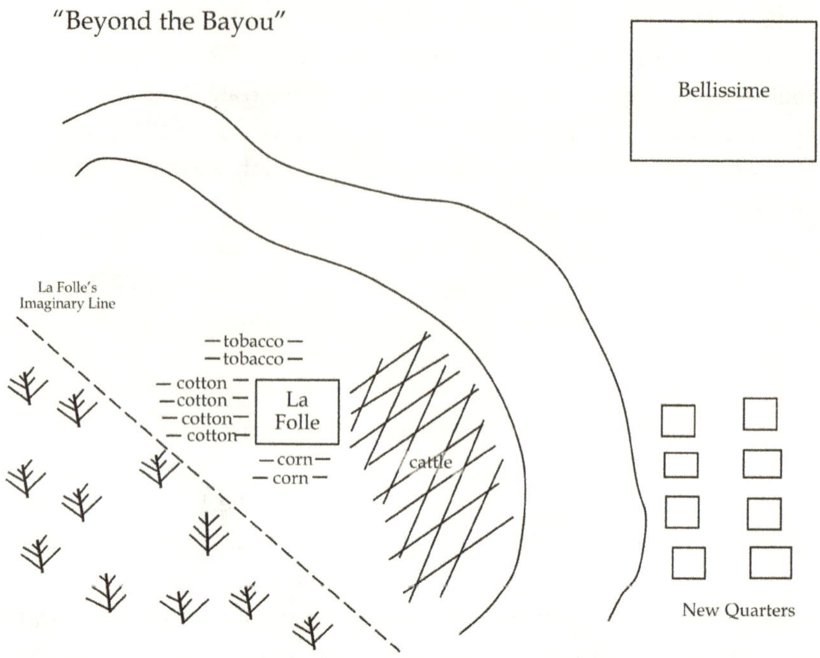

Fig. 1.4 The geographic space in "Beyond the Bayou," originally published in Fox, "Mapping," 112.

"yonda, beyon' de bayou," a world that La Folle designates as located on the other side of her "imaginary line" (100, 99). La Folle refuses to relocate to the "new quarters," choosing to live alone in her "solitary cabin" even though "the rest of the quarters had long since been removed" (100). Her geographic anxiety constitutes "the form of her only mania," a mania that relegates her body to a liminal space (99).

La Folle's situated "mania" continually links past experience to present moment and in doing so extends topographical mapping into a social space.[19] Imbued in the social and spatial, La Folle's geographic confinement, as the narrator suggests, stems from a traumatic childhood experience during the Civil War, but it must also be examined in relation to the larger sociohistorical context, or the geosocial design of the antebellum plantation as a space for the construction and maintenance of racial injustice. La Folle's cabin remains where the slave cabins once stood and most likely is the same cabin as her mother's cabin—the one from which P'tit Maître entered "black with powder and crimson with blood" after a skirmish in the woods (99). The cabin continually evokes memories of the racial confinement that bound

La Folle's mother and previous generations to the institution of slavery. La Folle's "obsession with 'place,'" as James Nagel contends, "was occasioned by fear, not by fantasy or depression" (133). The identified source of trauma in the story therefore cannot be limited to one moment, since architectural structures situated within the plantation's landscape perpetuate trauma-inducing sociohierarchies of power.

Bellissime's geographic and architectural divisions perpetuate slavery in the absence of slavery, positioning La Folle as a Black mammy archetype—a character who is nonthreatening to white readers and who "legitimize[s] black enslavement" (Shaker, *Coloring* 72). After carrying the injured Chéri across the bayou and placing him in P'tit Maître's arms, La Folle sees a world that appears red and then suddenly black, the same as when P'tit Maître entered her mother's cabin during the war and "stunned her childish reason" (107, 99). Eliminated from the version of the story in *Bayou Folk*, additional descriptions of "flaming red" and "aflame with blood color, alternating with black" appear in the *Youth's Companion* version, emphasizing the significance of these images. Repetitions and variations on red and black occur within the narrative's present time frame (the telling of the story) and retrospective time frame, which also infuse La Folle's memories of experience. In both versions of the story, these red-black images merge and conclude with La Folle's collapse at the foot of Bellissime's stairs. The narrator's implication that La Folle cannot ascend the stairs because of physical and psychological exhaustion after crossing the bayou does not consider the symbolically charged sociohistorical space embedded in the plantation's architectural structure. In the same way that Tante Lizette's cabin in the new quarters only exchanges one side of the bayou for the other, Bellissime represents the maintenance of a physical and psychological barrier.

The closer La Folle's body moves in geographic proximity to the plantation home—a static representation of racial tyranny—the more her body appears to resemble an animal rather than a human. Mapping her physical movements after Chéri's accident, La Folle stands at the bayou's edge and cries out for help, but her cries remain either "unheard or unheeded" (104). She then "clasp[s]" Chéri against her chest, shuts her eyes, and "plunge[s]" through the trees, with only "instinct . . . to guide her" (105). Moving past the new quarters and closer to Bellissime, La Folle's face becomes so "distorted" that by the time she reaches the house, "her eyes [appear] bloodshot and the saliva had gathered in a white foam on her black lips" (106). Finally, La Folle's heavy breathing resembles "a tired ox" (106). When La Folle confines herself to her cabin and the geographic area that immediately surrounds it, the narrator compares her physical strength to that of a man, but once she moves beyond her geosocial confinement, she evolves into an ox-like figure.

In *Race and Nature: From Transcendentalism to the Harlem Renaissance* (2008), Paul Outka argues that slave masters sought social justification for the treatment of slaves by rewriting Black bodies as animal bodies (55–59). In this light, the narrator's description of La Folle's first journey across the bayou and her physical proximity to Bellissime reduces her from human subject to silenced animal and further justifies her marginalization. As La Folle traverses the bayou for the first time, the surface of her body carries sociocultural ideology bolstered by nineteenth-century ethnographic arguments that classified African Americans as more beast than human.

To rewrite the body, Chopin rewrites the geographic space that confines it, using La Folle's first journey to locate sources of oppression and her second journey to demonstrate the possibility of revision. Critics read the landscape in both journeys as an extension of racial injustice (see Shaker, *Coloring*; Nixon), but the landscape actually suggests emancipation during her second journey. Instead of considering why Chopin "chooses a marshy, sluggish body of water as the real and symbolic boundary for the story world" (Llewellyn 255), we should consider that this nearly static body of water has almost entirely receded by the latter half of the story. In another *Bayou Folk* story, "Désirée's Baby," Désirée enters the bayou with her infant son, presumably never to return. She seeks its refuge after her husband blames her for their child's mixed race. In contrast, "the water ran so low" in "Beyond the Bayou" "that even the little children at Bellissime were able to cross it on foot" (109). La Folle emerges from it.

With a geographic boundary diminished, La Folle's social confinement also recedes. Nature—or more precisely, natural changes in the landscape—provides La Folle with geographic access to Bellissime.[20] Therefore, her engagement with nature during her second journey should not be read as a "pathetic fallacy."[21] Her eyes are open; she feels the "springy turf" of the lawn near the house; and she smells the "thousand blue violets," "the big waxen bells of the magnolias," "the jessamine clumps," and the "roses without number" (109). La Folle engages nature as human observer, not animal participant.

La Folle's newfound relationship with nature foreshadows her social resistance. As geographer Tim Cresswell asserts in *In Place/Out of Place:*

Geography, Ideology, and Transgression (1996), "a powerful ideological strategy is to 'naturalize,' or to hide and obfuscate the social and the historical" through normalized behaviors (165). Distinguishing between two out-of-place behaviors, he defines transgressions as replacing "normal" behaviors with unexpected behaviors (such as La Folle's crossing of the bayou to save Chéri) and resistance as the repetition of a transgressive behavior (such as La Folle's second journey to Bellissime). Repeated transgressions, or acts of resistance, question dominant power structures, which use normalization to dictate in-place behavior (Cresswell, *In Place* 9–10, 166). La Folle's movements during her second journey to Bellissime map her progression from transgression to resistance: She "slowly and cautiously mount[s] the many steps that led up to the veranda." She "turn[s] to look back at the perilous ascent." She "rap[s] softly" on the door, but when asked to leave, she refuses. She speaks directly to Chéri's mother, "*Non*, madame. I'm goin' wait yair till Chéri wake up" (109–10). Who controls the discourse is important because it "says something about who gets to participate in the construction and dissemination of meanings for places and thus places themselves" (Cresswell, *In Place* 60). For the first time in the story, La Folle's voice replaces the narrator's voice. Moreover, her refusal to leave Bellissime revises her spatial relationship to its static representation. Her conscious decision to wait for Chéri resists unconscious, normalized behavior.

As Chéri's mother's attempt to "dissemble her astonishment" (110) makes clear, La Folle's resistance constitutes her out-of-place awareness at the end of the story. Physically located at the topmost stair of Bellissime's veranda, she refuses to leave this contested space, thereby challenging the plantation's "socialized geography of (in)justice."[22] In a reading of "Désirée's Baby," Cynthia Griffin Wolff asserts that the existence of an illusive, territorial "barrier of insurmounted proportions" was built to appear "clear and inviolable" to separate race in social spaces (128). But in "Beyond the Bayou," Jacqueline La Folle crosses this barrier and thus becomes capable of seeing "the new, the beautiful world beyond the bayou" (110). During her "perilous ascent" of the stairs, she looks back and sees the river "bending like a silver bow"; in this moment, the geographic and the social merge, and "exultation possess[es] her soul" (110). In the span of only two days, La Folle transgresses and resists geosocial boundaries designed to separate, dominate, and oppress African Americans in the absence of slavery. She learns to view the world from beyond its imposed but imaginary lines.

When isolated from the rest of Chopin's oeuvre, this reading of "Beyond the Bayou" cannot fully represent her definitive response to racial injustice. In an unpublished sketch "A Free Little Mulatto," written in 1892 between the magazine publication of "Beyond the Bayou" and the appearance of *Bayou Folk*, the narrator ponders young Aurélia's unhappiness and determines that since she cannot fit in with "the white children up at the big house" or "the little darkies who frolicked all day long as gleefully as kittens before their cabin doors," it would be best for her to live in "paradise," L'Isle des Mulâtres, where she and her family can "breathe an atmosphere which is native to them."[23] According to Susan Castillo, even though "A Free Little Mulatto" is not included in *Bayou Folk*, its resolution "by special containment and racial apartheid" (70) parallels Chopin's treatment of race throughout much of her fiction. The fact that Chopin includes animalistic portrayals of La Folle despite her expressions of resistance at the end of the story furthers Castillo's argument. In the same way that biographers disagree about the significance of Chopin's representations of African American figures in her fiction (Seyersted 79–80; Toth, *Unveiling* 125), readers are left "in doubt as to her opinions," since "like her characters, Chopin seems caught in the shifting tides of racial change and not entirely certain of her course [even though] she does not shy away from dealing openly with this volatile issue" (Castillo 70; Bonner 143). Ultimately, her sociopolitical opinions cannot be known.

The second Civil War story, as ordered in *Bayou Folk*, replicates the racial stereotypes featured in late 1880s popular magazines at the same time that it overturns romanticized depictions of settings in fictional accounts of the antebellum South. Written after "Beyond the Bayou" but published prior to it, "The Return of Alcibiade" demonstrates another approach to how nineteenth-century women writers garnered readership. As Chopin's account books reveal, she also utilized local periodicals as a component of her diversified portfolio in the periodical marketplace.

"The Return of Alcibiade" was originally published in *St. Louis Life*, which was edited by Sue Moore, one of the growing number of women who worked as editors for local periodicals by the 1880s (Mott, *American* 489–500). This progression opened up new possibilities for women writers to introduce their work to a local market, either before or simultaneously with national submission attempts. Unlike Chopin's experiences with patronizing male editors in New York and Boston, female editors often sought relationships with local women writers, cultivating and maintaining them primarily through social circles. Once these relationships had been established, local periodicals provided an almost guaranteed venue for publishing women writers' work.

In fact, Chopin wrote "The Return of Alcibiade" after Moore requested a Christmas story for the December 1892 issue of *St. Louis Life* (*PP* 217).[24] The magazine's cover was embellished with ornate red calligraphy, cherubs holding instruments, and scrolls and other adornments (figure 1.5). The issue includes short selections of fiction, minimal advertising, and numerous detailed sketches, such as the three illustrations for "The Return of Alcibiade," which feature characters framed by ribbons and flowers or standing beside a column with flowing vines (figure 1.6). Organized in two columns, Chopin's story appears near the beginning of the issue and spans two and a half pages. The issue lacks a table of contents.

In "The Return of Alcibiade," Monsieur Jean Ba, an aging patriarch, anxiously awaits his son's return after the Civil War and fixates on Alcibiade's promise to come home in time for Christmas dinner. Each year, Jean Ba orders Alcibiade's favorite dishes in preparation for his impending arrival, and each year, Alcibiade does not return. But this year, a man arrives, and the senile Jean Ba mistakes Fred Bartner, a commission merchant from New Orleans, for Alcibiade. To fulfill her grandfather's desire, Esmée implores Bartner to perform the ruse for Christmas dinner.

The Christmas dinner becomes a stage for exposing the tensions between a static past and a changing present, a space that connects the social, the spatial, and the temporal. Living in a house less grand than Bellissime from "Beyond the Bayou," Jean Ba appears "small" and "shrunken" at the top of the stairs, framed by the home's "grotesquely" long structure and "faded green" shutters (114–15).[25] During the dinner, Bartner expresses discomfort akin to "paralysis," while "two '*grif* boys," "a big black woman," "a little mulatto girl," and especially the vestige belle figure, Esmée, enact the past "as seriously as her grandfather" (119–20). Outside the home, an audience of "little black and yellow faces [kept] bobbing up constantly above the window-sills" observes the three diners (119–20). By positioning the elderly Jean Ba at the top of the stairs of a physically deteriorating house, Chopin uses the relationship between architecture and body to suggest a declining (fictional) world (see Punday 11, 157). Flanked by Jean Ba and Esmée at either end of the dining table, Bartner is neither patriarch nor belle. The "bobbing" faces transform a potentially dramatic scene into a comical one. Like Bartner, the scene, its actors, and even the audience are out of place, so that Jean Ba's anachronistic

Fig. 1.5 Cover of *St. Louis Life* 7, no. 131 (December 10, 1892). Kate Chopin first published "The Return of Alcibiade" in this issue. Courtesy of the St. Louis Public Library.

6 ST. LOUIS LIFE.

THE RETURN OF ALCIBIADE.

Mr. Fred Bartner was sorely perplexed and annoyed to find that a wheel and tire of his buggy threatened to part company.

"Ef you want," said the negro boy who drove him, "we kin stop yonda at ole M'sié Jean Ba's an' fix it; he got de bes' black smif shop in de pa'ish on his place."

"Who in the world is old Monsieur Jean Ba," the young man enquired.

"How come, suh, you don' know old M'sié Jean Baptiste Plochel? He ole, ole. He sorter quare in he head ev' sence his son M'sié Alcibiade got kill' in de wah. Yonda he live'; whar you sees dat che'okee hedge takin' up half de road."

Little more than ten years ago, before the "Texas Pacific" had joined the cities of New Orleans and Shreveport with its steel bands, it was a common thing to travel through miles of Central Louisiana in a buggy. Fred Bartner, a young commission merchant of New Orleans, on business bent, had made the trip in this way by easy stages from his home to a point on Cane river, within a half-day's journey of Natchitoches. From the mouth of Cane river he had passed one plantation after another—large ones and small ones. There was nowhere sight of anything like a town, except the little hamlet of Cloutierville, through which they had sped in the gray dawn. "Dat town, hits ole, ole; mos' a hund'ed year' ole, dey say. Uh, uh, look tu me like it heap ol'er an' dat" the darkey had commented. Now they were within sight of Monsieur Jean Ba's towering Cherokee hedge.

It was Christmas morning, but the sun was warm and the air so soft and mild that Bartner found the most comfortable way to wear his light overcoat was across his knees. At the entrance to the plantation he dismounted and the negro drove away towards the smithy which stood on the edge of the field.

From the end of the long avenue of Magnolias that led to it, the house which confronted Bartner looked grotesquely long in comparison with its height. It was one-story, of pale, yellow stucco; its massive wooden shutters were a faded green. A wide gallery, topped by the overhanging roof, encircled it.

At the head of the stairs a very old man stood. His figure was small and shrunken, his hair long and snow-white. He wore a broad, soft felt hat, and a brown plaid shawl across his bent shoulders. A tall, graceful girl stood beside him; she was clad in a warm-colored, blue stuff gown. She seemed to be expostulating with the old gentleman, who evidently wanted to descend the stairs to meet the approaching visitor. Before Bartner had had time to do more than lift his hat, Monsieur Jean Ba had thrown his trembling arms about him and was exclaiming in his quavering old tones: "*a la fin! mon fils! a la fin!*" Tears started to the girl's eyes and she was rosy with confusion. "Oh, escuse him, sir; please escuse him," she whisperingly entreated, gently striving to disengage the old gentleman's arms from around the astonished Bartner. But a new line of thought seemed fortunately to take possession of Monsieur Jean Ba, for he moved away and went quickly, pattering like a baby, down the gallery. His fleecy white hair streamed out on the soft breeze, and his brown shawl flapped as he turned the corner.

Bartner, left alone with the girl, proceeded to introduce himself and to explain his presence there.

"Oh! Mr. Fred Bartna of New Orleans? The commission merchant!" she exclaimed, cordially extending her hand. "So well known in Natchitoches parish. Not *our* merchant, Mr. Bartna," she added, naively, "but jus' as welcome all the same, at my grandfather's."

Bartner felt like kissing her, but he only bowed and seated himself in the big chair which she offered him. He wondered what was the longest time it could take to mend a buggy tire.

She sat before him with her hands pressed down into her lap, and with an eagerness and pretty air of being confidential that were extremely engaging, explained the reasons for her grandfather's singular behavior.

Years ago, her uncle Alcibiade, in going away to the war, with the cheerful assurance of youth, had promised his father that he would return to eat Christmas dinner with him. He never returned. And now, of late years, since Mons. Jean Ba had begun to fail in body and mind, that old, unspoken hope of long ago had come back to live anew in his heart. Every Christmas day he watched for the coming of Alcibiade.

"Ah! if you knew, Mr. Bartna, how I have endeavor' to distrac' his mine from that thought! Weeks ago, I tole to all the negroes, big and li'le 'if one of you dare to say the word, Christmas-gif', in the hearing of Monsieur Jean Baptiste, you will have to answer it to me.'"

Bartner could not recall when he had been so deeply interested in a narration.

"So, las' night, Mr. Bartna, I said to grandpère, 'pépère, you know to-morrow will be the great feas' of la Trinité; we will read our litany together in the morning and say a *chaplet*.' He did not answer a word; *il est malin, oui*. But this morning at daylight he was rapping his cane on the back gallery calling together the negroes. Did they not know it was Christmas day, an' a great dinner mus' be prepare for his son Alcibiade, whom he was especting!"

"And so he has mistaken me for his son, Alcibiade. It is very unfortunate," said Bartner, sympathetically. He was a good looking, honest faced young fellow.

The girl arose, quivering with an inspiration. She approached Bartner and in her eagerness laid her hand upon his arm.

Fig. 1.6 First illustrated page from "The Return of Alcibiade," *St. Louis Life* 7, no. 131 (December 10, 1892): 6. Courtesy of the St. Louis Public Library.

warning about not selling slaves to Robert MacFarland near the end of the story only confirms what the spatial relationships in the story have already established—a narrative space that resembles "a dream which clothes the grotesque and unnatural with the semblance of reality" (120).

This farcical performance within a geographically and chronologically defined social space magnifies the presence of illusion, which extends beyond Christmas dinner. Southern studies scholars like Jennifer Rae Greeson argue that the South is not a located place but an imaginative one, and while Greeson does not examine "The Return of Alcibiade" in *Our South: Geographic Fantasy and the Rise of National Literature* (2010), the story's portrayals align with Greeson's observations from other literary representations. Geographic exceptionalism is waning by the end of the nineteenth century. In a sequence narrated retrospectively, Bartner travels approximately 260 miles from New Orleans to (almost) Natchitoches by horse and carriage. However, the narrator informs readers that the Texas and Pacific Railroad will join New Orleans to Shreveport within twelve years, meaning that the story takes place around 1870.[26] In addition, Bartner's physical presence as a commission merchant traveling within Louisiana's rural landscape and Esmée's familiarity with his name suggest that authority is moving away from the plantation patriarch and toward the business merchant. The landscape described in "The Return of Alcibiade" no longer exists by the time the narrator tells the story.

The performance of the past at Christmas dinner and Bartner's conversations with Esmée seem to disrupt time, but this transgression can only be temporal. As the story maps characters' physical movements after dinner, this tension between past and present time becomes the site of spatial consciousness, which is ultimately articulated by Bartner: Jean Ba sits comfortably alone on the gallery, "with the sun warming his feet and old shrunken knees" (121). Esmée and Bartner walk in the garden among the same flowers—magnolias, violets, and roses—that awakened La Folle's senses in "Beyond the Bayou." But their perfume remains more "subtle" than intoxicating. Picked for an arrangement, the gathered flowers are described as "broken," a brokenness that immediately precedes Bartner's words to Esmée. "You know," Bartner begins, "I can't stay here always. . . . [Y]our grandfather will discover that we have been deceiving him,—and you can see how cruel that will be" (121). Simultaneously, the receding sunlight spotlights Jean Ba's body. His passing eliminates the possibility of maintaining the illusion of belonging to a previous time. Within the narrative frame of the story, Jean Ba's death signifies the end of his waiting for Alcibiade's improbable return. Alcibiade's body, absent from the text except in Jean Ba's imagination, further emphasizes the impossibility of returning to the antebellum past.

The final lines of "White Oaks," a poem written by Chopin in 1898 but never published, lament, "O! that tomorrows were far away / And all 'forever' a long 'to-day' / When the world stands still and the soft winds blow / In the beautiful land where the white oaks grow."[27] Despite this poem's longing for stagnancy, tales like "The Return of Alcibiade" reveal the futility of the desire to recapture a romanticized version of the antebellum South. By the end of the story, no one remains. Jean Ba passes away, Bartner leaves for Natchitoches, and Esmée relocates to New Orleans with her aunt. The ancestral plantation home serves as a relic within the landscape, an ever-deteriorating reminder of previous social structures. In this way, the story employs both the spatial and the temporal, inviting readers to observe how the spaces between geographic locations are lessening over time. It maps the progressive replacement of the South's exceptionalism with the late nineteenth century's movement toward the South's reassimilation into the nation. By ending the story with "the shrill whistles of steam cotton gins" (124) instead of a romantic conclusion between Esmée and Bartner, "The Return of Alcibiade" positions the narrative as forward-thinking and not mired in the past. Chopin's realism rewrites the sentiment associated with southern stories published for northern magazines.

Sarah E. Gardner argues in *Blood and Irony: Southern White Women's Narratives of the Civil War, 1861–1937* (2004) that "the movement of people to towns and cities exacerbated the breakdown of the household structure and social hierarchy" and that "conflicting images of the South—that of a phoenix rising from the ashes or conversely of the landscape irreparably damaged by war—shaped literature written by southern women" (77–78). Applying this idea to *Bayou Folk*, La Folle's spatial consciousness begins with topographical change but evolves into social change from her new perspective. In contrast, Jean Ba's senility renders him incapable of (re)envisioning the landscape and his relationship to it. Further, Jean Ba's mental trauma cannot be defined as senility alone but also suggests postwar mental illness (Kotlarczyk 26–27). Chopin's depiction of his deterioration, alongside his insistent waiting for the return of his Confederate veteran son when the possibility has long passed, suggests that her writing of the story extends beyond her exorcism of wartime trauma. Alcibiade does not return, and the story's ending eliminates the possibility of returning to an antebellum past.

Chopin wanted to distance herself from the sentimental and domestic fiction tradition because she viewed it as impeding her ability to be recognized as a "serious" writer (see Bonner; Nancy A. Walker 58). And yet "A Wizard from Gettysburg" begins with familiar elements from sentimental plots: an amnesic Confederate soldier wanders home decades later, digs up buried treasure, and is reunited with his family. Despite scholarly debate about the contributions of this story to Chopin's oeuvre, in the context of the four Civil War stories published in *Bayou Folk*, "A Wizard from Gettysburg" extends relationships between geographic place and social positioning in narrative to further illustrate the futility of reenvisioning the past.[28]

In "A Wizard from Gettysburg," young Bertrand Delmandé helps a "tramp" tend to his wounds on the road. Bertrand brings the man to his familial plantation, Bon-Accueil, only to discover that he is Bertrand's grandfather, also named Bertrand Delmandé, who was injured at Gettysburg. Bon-Accueil is in a state of financial ruin, so it is advantageous that the elderly Delmandé regains his memory long enough to recall where he buried money during the war. This money allows Bertrand to return to school, but the act of locating the funds does not permanently reinstate the elderly Delmandé's recognition.

Chopin completed "A Wizard from Gettysburg" on May 26, 1891 (the same year she composed "Beyond the Bayou") and submitted it only to the *Youth's Companion*, which accepted the story on June 15, and paid her thirty-five dollars. The magazine published it in its July 7, 1892, issue (*PP* 171). Chopin's work is listed as the second feature in the issue's "Leading Articles," which include nine tales, a "children's page," and a small selection of poems (figure 1.7). The story, divided into four columns, comprises a little over one page. The only illustration, located at the center of the text, portrays the elderly Delmandé sitting in his rocking chair on the porch and speaking with his grandson, though at this point in the narrative, neither character is aware of the familial connection (figure 1.8).

Unlike the previous stories examined in this chapter, "A Wizard from Gettysburg" explicitly describes two landscapes at odds with one another: the world within Bon-Accueil plantation (a replica of an antebellum plantation like Bellissime) and the world outside Bon-Accueil (which includes the Battle of Gettysburg, war and postwar hospitals, and industrial factories). The borders between these locations are geographically delineated by "the great tangled Cherokee hedge that marked the boundary line and that twinkled with multiple white roses," a gate, and a "dark green hedge [that] towered like a

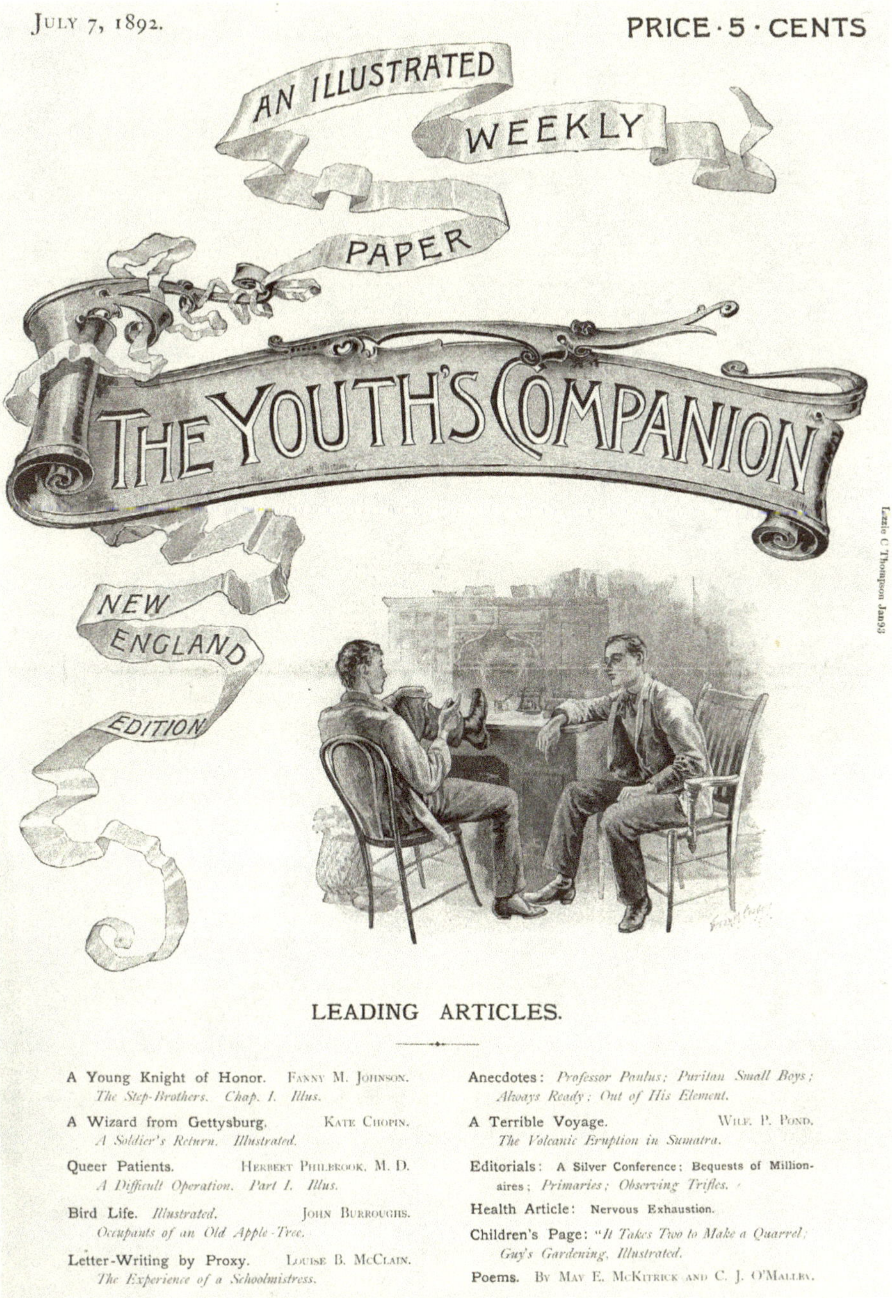

JULY 7, 1892. PRICE · 5 · CENTS

AN ILLUSTRATED WEEKLY PAPER

THE YOUTH'S COMPANION

NEW ENGLAND EDITION

Lizzie C Thompson Jan93

LEADING ARTICLES.

A Young Knight of Honor. FANNY M. JOHNSON.
The Step-Brothers. Chap. I. Illus.

A Wizard from Gettysburg. KATE CHOPIN.
A Soldier's Return. Illustrated.

Queer Patients. HERBERT PHILBROOK, M. D.
A Difficult Operation. Part I. Illus.

Bird Life. *Illustrated.* JOHN BURROUGHS.
Occupants of an Old Apple-Tree.

Letter-Writing by Proxy. LOUISE B. MCCLAIN.
The Experience of a Schoolmistress.

Anecdotes: *Professor Paulus; Puritan Small Boys; Always Ready; Out of His Element.*

A Terrible Voyage. WILF. P. POND.
The Volcanic Eruption in Sumatra.

Editorials: A Silver Conference; Bequests of Millionaires; *Primaries; Observing Trifles.*

Health Article: Nervous Exhaustion.

Children's Page: "*It Takes Two to Make a Quarrel; Guy's Gardening. Illustrated.*

Poems. BY MAY E. MCKITRICK AND C. J. O'MALLEY.

Fig. 1.7 Cover of the *Youth's Companion* 65, no. 27 (July 7, 1892). Courtesy of Special Collections, Tampa Library, University of South Florida.

346 THE YOUTH'S COMPANION. JULY 7, 1892.

For the Companion.

A WIZARD FROM GETTYSBURG.

Fig. 1.8 First page of "A Wizard from Gettysburg," *Youth's Companion* 65, no. 27 (July 7, 1892): 346. Courtesy of Special Collections, Tampa Library, University of South Florida.

high and solid wall on one side" and psychologically delineated by the tramp's loss or recovery of memory (231–32).[29] On the one side of the hedge, there is the euphoric past, agriculturally driven and defined by social hierarchies of class and race; on the other side, there is a world in which a person is doomed to wander aimlessly and without identity, a place of cruel anonymity. While depicted in the story as seemingly adjacent, these landscapes cannot converge physically. They can only intertwine psychologically through the tramp's memories, since his mind is incapable of existing wholly in either world.

When the young Bertrand first sees the tramp along the road, he is out of place in the landscape, but once he settles into his old rocking chair, his physical positioning within the landscape awakens his spatial consciousness. He locates himself within the state of Louisiana and addresses young Bertrand as "'St. Agne,' not once, but every time he had spoken to him" (231–32). He does not gaze absentmindedly into the garden. Instead, he moves where he can observe the plantation's day-to-day operations:

> If he had turned partly around, he would have faced the flower garden, with its graveled walks and trim parterres, where a tangle of color and perfume were holding high revelry this April morning; but he liked better to gaze into the back yard, where there was always movement: men and women coming and going, bearing implements of work; little negroes in scanty garments, darting here and there, and kicking up the dust in their exuberance. (237)

Through his observations, the elderly Bertrand Delmandé participates in the landscape, and through this act of participation, he begins to map connections between located place and dislocated identity.

As with a reader's ability to draw the bayou in "Beyond the Bayou," the reader becomes geographically positioned in the landscape through Bertrand Delmandé's memories of it and can sketch its geospatial significance (figure 1.9). After observing Bon-Accueil, Bertrand Delmandé begins to retrieve his identity through the act of geographically locating and retrieving the buried money. Bon-Accueil's landscape, coupled with overhearing that young Bertrand might not be able to return to school due to lack of money, awakens the old man's spatial awareness. He (re)discovers "pleasant avenues" lined with peach, pear, apple, and plum trees and the pomegranate hedge against the fence. At the center of the orchard, he locates the pecan tree, which is

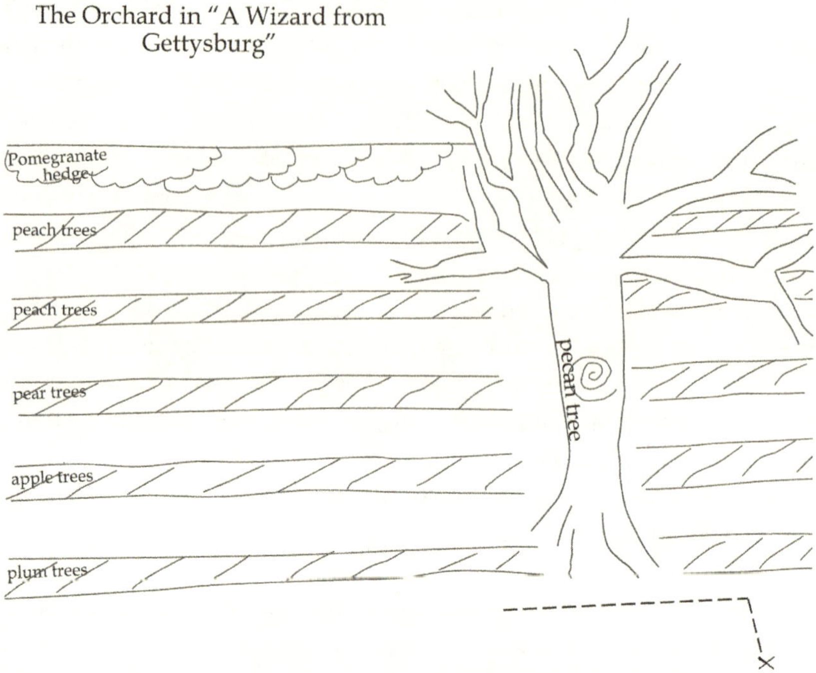

Fig. 1.9 The geographic space in "A Wizard from Gettysburg," originally published in Fox, "Mapping," 121.

"twice the size of any other . . . seeming to rule like an old-time king" (239). He recalls the exact location of the money, buried before he left to fight in the Civil War and still located within fifteen paces of the pecan tree.

The act of physically engaging the landscape to locate and unearth the money builds a bridge for Bertrand Delmandé's remembered experiences so that he begins to recall his patriarchal identity. Instead of using a "quavering" voice, he speaks "with quick authority": "St. Ange, you must go to school! . . . The war's over. . . . Don't let the negroes see us. Get a spade—the little spade that Buck Williams was digging his cistern with" (238). But once Madame Delmandé recognizes the old man, he returns to the identity of the injured soldier, incapable of merging one identity (patriarch of Bon-Accueil) with another (Gettysburg soldier). Bonnie James Shaker argues that since "maintaining the father figurehead . . . preserved the financial economy but also an economy of race and gender relations that valued the white male patriarch," Chopin's ending "justifies the absolute power invested in antebellum masters by portraying the elder Delmandé as the 'wizard' who restores privilege to the next generation of his patrilineal line" (*Coloring* 39–40). When read sequentially in *Bayou Folk* after "The Return of Alcibiade," however, the ending of the story replaces the romantic possibility of recovering the past through memory with the realistic portrayal of the ongoing effects of Bertrand Delmandé's physical injury.

In the summer of 1892, when "A Wizard from Gettysburg" was published in *Youth's Companion*, Francis Bellamy was likely writing the Pledge of Allegiance, which appeared in the magazine's September 8, 1892, issue honoring Columbus Day. The magazine would have been aware of Bellamy's forthcoming work at the same time as Chopin's submission, and this knowledge may have initiated the decision to include "A Wizard from Gettysburg," not for its social commentary on war trauma, but for the story's patriotic content. In the story, the narrator describes "the awfulness of Gettysburg" using sentimental rhetoric, and northern readers would have equated gestures such as "a human hand stretched out . . . in kindness" (236) as emblematic of reconciliation efforts. This may account for the delayed publication of "Beyond the Bayou," which was accepted for publication within a few months of the appearance of "A Wizard from Gettysburg." Chopin's sympathetic account of a returned Confederate veteran figure who was irrevocably damaged and no longer posed a threat to national unity would have appealed more than a story that portrays racial injustice, whether or not it was recognized explicitly by readers.

Read from a contemporary perspective, Chopin's story neither cultivates patriotism, as the *Youth's Companion* may have desired, nor restores the patriarchy. Instead, it depicts the process of socioeconomic restructuring that began in the war and continued through the late nineteenth century. Before Reconstruction, Confederate conscription laws exacerbated class inequities during the war. The first year of the war, as Confederate veteran J. W. Pater explains in his memoir, "robbed many a home of its promising youth," but by 1862, husbands and fathers were also subject to the draft unless they owned at least ten slaves. According to Pater, the "ten negroes" rule protected "the very men [who were] most vitally interested in the results of the war." Southern aristocratic men "were exempt from all of the dangers and hardships," and this discriminatory practice marked "the beginning of the end of the Confederacy."[30]

It is difficult to know whether the fictional Bertrand Delmandé volunteered or was conscripted for war. However, Delmandé's participation in the Battle of Gettysburg (1863), even though the initial descriptions in the story suggest that Bon-Accueil was (and always had been) a prosperous plantation, suggests that he was not an aristocratic landowner who owned more than ten slaves. Reading "The Return of Alcibiade" (as representative of early Confederate conscription laws) in conjunction with "A Wizard from Gettysburg" (as representative of Confederate conscription laws beginning in 1862) provides a progressive depiction of the long-term effects of war policies familiar to Chopin. While her biographical material does not specifically mention the "ten negroes" rule, Chopin's family, the O'Flahertys, would have been directly affected by these conscription policies. According to the 1860 census, the O'Flaherty family owned six slaves, and Kate and her mother, Eliza, were the only caretakers who remained on the estate during much of the war (Toth, *Unveiling* 9–33).

The characters in "A Wizard from Gettysburg" replicate Gardner's list of politically powerless figures—the southern belle, the infirm, the ineffectual Confederate veteran, and the local freedman. These characters were readily found in stories to suggest to readers that no one could oppose national reintegration (Gardner 91). After Chopin's anonymous tramp begins to remember his past identity as patriarch and Confederate veteran, he then starts to forget, signifying its irrelevance in the current era. Delmandé remains a politically powerless figure not because he accepts reconciliation but because his remembered experiences are necessary only to help the next generation obtain an education or to reintegrate within the nation's body politic. Thus, while Bertrand Delmandé's head injury seems like a sentimental trope, his amnesia demonstrates how insistent reliance on past memory to inform present experience precludes the ability to sustain connections between identity and place. In the narrative, he is powerless because his existence remains out of place chronologically or geographically, without the possibility of connecting the two.

Similarly, in the final Civil War in *Bayou Folk*, the protagonist does not suffer physical injury but remains incapable of reconciling the past with the present. In "Ma'ame Pélagie," which directly follows "A Wizard from Gettysburg," memory enables Pélagie to relocate herself imaginatively to a previous time and place—among the ruins of Valmêt mansion.

Like "The Return of Alcibiade," "Ma'ame Pélagie" was initially published in a special Christmas issue—in this case, the December 24, 1893, issue of the *New Orleans Times-Democrat*, which featured one of Chopin's stories at Christmas for four years (Rankin 135). However, according to Chopin's account books, she first attempted to publish the story under the title "In the Shadow of the Ruin" in quality magazines. *The Century* and *Scribner's Magazine* were obvious choices, since they frequently ran stories on the American South. *Century*'s editor, Richard Watson Gilder, published a three-year Civil War series on "Battles and Leaders." According to Mott, the magazine's huge success with southern stories "did much to invite that flood of dialect fiction which characterized the decade centering on 1890" (*History* 2:471–73). Nonetheless, the magazine rarely published women writers (Gardner 81–84). *Scribner's* published "The Great South," a series of articles by Edward King. And both magazines published many southern writers who remain familiar to contemporary audiences, including James Branch Cabell, Joel Chandler Harris, Thomas Nelson Page, and Grace King (Mott, *History* 2:457–65). But despite *The Century*'s and *Scribner's Magazine*'s interest in southern stories, Chopin's attempts to publish "Ma'ame Pélagie" met with almost monthly rejections. Beginning in August 1892, *The Century*, *Harper's*, the *Atlantic Monthly*, *Scribner's*, and even *Vogue*—where she had a personal relationship with the editor—returned the story (*PP* 154–55; Toth, *Unveiling* 172–73).

Ultimately, "Ma'ame Pélagie" was accepted for publication in the *New Orleans Times-Democrat* on April 3, 1893, as a consequence of Chopin's social connections to the editor (Toth, *Unveiling* 172–73). The story earned only five dollars (*PP* 154–55). A narrative written in four parts, it occupied four columns of a single page, without illustration. Chopin's story begins beneath an illustrated poem in the first column and ends in the fourth column, prior to the illustration for another author's poem that appears approximately a third of the way down the page.

"Ma'ame Pélagie" illustrates Chopin's resolve to publish her work and provides a model for her approach to submissions. She might have preferred to have the story appear in a quality magazine and tenaciously attempted to reach that goal, but she was willing to have it appear in a local periodical. In fact, several of her first stories were published in St. Louis newspapers, contributing to her "local celebrity" and widening "her intellectual circle" (Nancy A. Walker 55). Whether a quality magazine, juvenile magazine, or local periodical, Chopin benefited from readership, since "just as the line between newspapers and literary journals as venues for serious writers was not as firmly drawn as it would be later, so the distinction between authors who wrote for children and those who wrote for adult readers was by no means firm" (55).

The story depicts two sisters, Ma'ame Pélagie and Mam'selle Pauline, residing in a three-room cabin "almost within the shadow of the ruin of the Valmêt mansion" and sipping coffee on its "ruined portico" (246).[31] However, while both Pélagie and Pauline are geographically located in close proximity to the ruin, their memories of it are not the same. Pauline remembers only "a faint gleam here and there" from the state of "half-consciousness" and a "confusion ending in fire and flame" (247). For Pélagie, the ruins physically represent the remnants of her life before the Civil War and, in particular, the last time she saw her fiancé, Félix. She returns to the ruins to remember, a physical remnant of the psychological presence she refuses to forget.

Pélagie's dreams of reconstructing the mansion constitute a mythical space. Mythical spaces, as place theorist Yi-Fu Tuan explains, imaginatively extend known or familiar spaces that are incapable of reproducing reality. The memorialization of the past, mythical spaces are created as "a response of feeling and imagination to fundamental human needs" and develop over time into a "primary text for handing down a . . . view of reality" (174, 86, 112). Since the Valmêt mansion no longer exists as an intact architectural structure like the plantation homes in "Beyond the Bayou," "The Return of Alcibiade," and "A Wizard from Gettysburg," Pélagie must return to its remnants instead of living within a progressive state of deterioration. By continuing to replay the night soldiers destroyed her home, she memorializes the past. And by planning to construct another Valmêt mansion out of the ruins, she attempts to educate Pauline about the symbolic significance of this mythical space.

Chopin's depiction of Pélagie challenges readers' sympathies and asks us to observe the relationship between constructed, collective identity and mythical space. We are both sorry for her loss and sorry for Pauline, who must relive Pélagie's trauma as if it were her own. Thus, while Mary Papke describes Pélagie as both "selfish" and a "tyrant," a character who controls her sister and "chooses to live alienated and alienating to the very last . . . stand[ing] alone . . . just on the edge of this new world" (57–59), this portrayal feels too harsh. People look to the past "to acquire a sense of self and of identity," and their "passion for preservation arises out of the need for tangible objects that can support a sense of identity" (Tuan 186, 197). Pélagie's understanding of herself remains bound to the ruins of the Valmêt mansion. During the fire, Pélagie attempts to resist; she "wants to show them how a daughter of Louisiana can perish before her conquerors" (257). But when "little Pauline clings to her knees in an agony of terror," Pélagie remembers her parents' warning: "*Il faut pas faire mal à Pauline* [We must not let Pauline get hurt]" (257). This mantra informs Pélagie's future decisions (and newfound martyrdom). Pélagie must preserve the past by rebuilding the ruins and adhering to her parents' last instructions. She would have preferred martyrdom by fire.

The geographic boundary between Pélagie's sense of identity and potential loss of it is less of an imaginary line when defined by the geographic space between the cabin and the ruin. In part III of the story, Pélagie crosses the permeable border for the last time "to dream her dreams; to see the visions that hitherto had crowded her days and nights, and to bid them farewell" (254). In addition to mapping Pélagie's physical movements, this story narratively positions the reader within an ongoing negotiation between the physical and the psychological that form Pélagie's spatial consciousness: Pélagie crosses the distance between the cabin and the ruins with "hurried and agitated" steps (253). She recalls being late to a social gathering at her home and sits on the bench in the ruins. She thinks about her observations of individual guests and then notices the white crape myrtle growing in the ruins. She remembers how Félix's uniform buttons hurt her chest when he held her against him and how she planned to reconstruct the room where she last saw him, where she "had meant all along, for thirty years, to lie there upon [the sofa] some day when the time came to die" (253–57). Pélagie's physical and psychological movements converge within the same geographical landscape (the ruins), blending boundaries of place and chronological time at the site of her body.

Different from La Folle's receding bayou in "Beyond the Bayou," the boundary between geographic and social spaces in "Ma'ame Pélagie" is in the process of closing, limiting Pélagie's mythic constructions of reality. By granting Pauline's desire to construct a modern home so La Petite will remain at Valmêt, Pélagie relinquishes her ability to traverse the space between her cabin and the ruins. In losing the located source of her mythically constructed space, Pélagie also loses the source of her mythically constructed identity. The possibility of constructing Valmêt's mansion dies as a potential reality and can only be replaced by an illusion of its continued existence—which is what it always has been.

By closing the possibility of traversing mythical boundaries and arranging the story near the end of the collection, Chopin writes La Folle's newly acquired perspective on spatial consciousness into the narrative landscape of "Ma'ame Pélagie." Both the cabin and the ruins of the Valmêt mansion disappear, replaced by "a shapely structure fashioned from woods that the forests of the State had furnished" (259). By removing the remaining physical remnants of a site of social injustice in the final *located* story of the *Bayou Folk* collection, Chopin positions the present over the past and relegates geographic fantasies to a permanently imaginative space. The architecture of the Valmêt mansion's replacement merges with a regional landscape. Its distinction is its assimilation.

Unlike La Folle's resistance, Pélagie's resistance separates her from Pauline, La Petite, and her brother, Leandré. At the end of the story, Pélagie suddenly "grow[s] very old"; similar to the aging bodies of Jean Ba and Bertrand Delmandé, "years instead of months seemed to pass over her since the night she bade farewell to her visions" (260). In the absence of the ruin, Pélagie embodies its shadow. As a spectator of the present, she becomes like the Valmêt mansion—a remnant of the past.

Spatial Consciousness

The four parts of "Ma'ame Pélagie" serve as a map for Chopin's selection and arrangement of the four Civil War stories in *Bayou Folk*. Part I (like "Beyond the Bayou") portrays how Pélagie and Pauline unsuccessfully attempt to live within the past's relics. Part II (like "The Return of Alcibiade") conveys the difficulty of living in the present when memorializing the past. Part III (like "A Wizard from Gettysburg") emphasizes trauma's role in romanticizing the past. Finally, part IV (as depicted by the ending of "Ma'ame Pélagie") offers the possibility for a future that emerges from past trauma whether or not the characters choose to embrace it.

It is difficult to know whether Chopin was thinking of spatial awareness as a lens to facilitate readers' perspectives when selecting and arranging her stories for *Bayou Folk*, since much of Chopin's correspondence has been lost or destroyed.[32] Writing to Chopin on December 19, 1893, her publisher, Houghton Mifflin, requested only that she keep the "Santien boys" together, which she does by grouping "A No-Account Creole," "In and Out of Old Natchitoches," and "In Sabine" as the first three stories of the collection.[33] Toth concludes that the rest of the stories were arranged "for variety" (*Unveiling* 150–51).

Chopin's revisions between the magazine and collected versions of the Civil War stories provide some insight into the significance of their arrangement in *Bayou Folk*. In a letter to Waitman Barbe on October 2, 1894, Chopin writes that "it is either very easy for me to write a story, or utterly impossible; that is, the story must 'write itself' without any perceptible effort on my part, or it remains unwritten. There is not a tale in 'Bayou Folk,' excepting the first, which required longer time than two, or at most three sittings of a few hours each" (*PP* 205). Her revisions between the magazine and collected versions of "The Return of Alcibiade" and "A Wizard from Gettysburg" support her letter's assertion: she made only twenty revisions, all of them punctuation or dialect changes. However, the content revisions between the periodical and collected versions of "Beyond the Bayou" and "Ma'ame Pélagie" indicate a holistic approach to revision that connects the stories to one another and may have required more than a few sittings.

These revisions emphasize relationships between chronological time, regional settings, and characters. For instance, as published in the *New Orleans Times-Democrat*, the narrative in "Ma'ame Pélagie" began "thirty years ago"; in *Bayou Folk*, however, Chopin situates the story historically with "When the war began." In another example, Chopin repeats the red and black imagery from "Beyond the Bayou" in the description of Pélagie slapping the Yankee soldier: "the stigma stands out red as blood" (257). She also revises the original name of Pélagie's brother from *Alcibiade* to *Leandre* in *Bayou Folk*. On the one hand, this revision avoids the confusion of having two characters named *Alcibiade* in the collection, but on the other hand, her revision, coupled with the arrangement of tales in the collection, eliminates the possibility of reintroducing the memory of a Confederate veteran into the final story. Finally, Chopin eliminates a description in part IV of "Ma'ame Pélagie" that would have constructed the newly built Cote Joyeuse out of materials from the ruin: "There was more of that brick to be seen about the place; a cabin here and there to shelter the workers [*illegible*] and the foundations of cisterns. Not a brick of the ruin had gone to waste."[34] In *Bayou Folk*, the narrator explains that "one would have looked in vain for the ruin; it was no longer there; neither was the log cabin" (259). Neither the ancestral plantation home nor the slave cabin remains.

Spatially, all four stories depict a geographical and chronological landscape located between New Orleans and Natchitoches and occurring (sometimes within multiple narrative time frames in the same story) between approximately 1862, when Union forces took the Port of New Orleans, and the early 1890s, as provided by textual clues in the narration of the four stories (table

1.1). "Beyond the Bayou" follows the "Santien boys" stories and a short sketch, "A Very Fine Fiddle," near the beginning of the collection. "The Return of Alcibiade" is separated from "Beyond the Bayou" by a one-page sketch, "Old Aunt Peggy." Equidistantly positioned five stories from the end of the collection in the same way that "Beyond the Bayou" and "The Return of Alcibiade" are positioned approximately five stories from the beginning of the story, "A Wizard from Gettysburg" and "Ma'ame Pélagie" are adjacent to one another. This emphasis on a liminal geographic and chronological space situates the stories during a period of political and economic transition in which the urban industrial reshapes the rural agricultural landscape in the late-nineteenth-century South.

When read together, these stories describe a deteriorating landscape, signaled by environmental and architectural changes, such as the bayou drying up, discarded and irreparable ancestral plantation homes, and invasive technological advances like the railroad and cotton gin. The arrangement of these stories does not reflect their original composition or publication dates, but textual clues map settings chronologically and historically by referencing familiar phases of the Civil War and Reconstruction. For instance, in "Beyond the Bayou," La Folle was a child when she resided in her mother's slave cabin during the war, but in the narrative's setting, the war is over, her mother is deceased, and the original slave cabins (except hers) are now vacant. "The Return of Alcibiade" is set in approximately 1870. In "A Wizard from Gettysburg," Bertrand Delmandé fought at Gettysburg in 1863, returning home approximately twenty years later, as contextualized by Judge Parkerson's death. And in "Ma'ame Pélagie," Pélagie saves money for the reconstruction of Cote Joyeuse for thirty years after it was destroyed in Louisiana's early battles of the Civil War, which occurred in 1862.

Chopin further complicates the tensions between geography and historical time by writing archetypal characters who cling to the past even as the narrative dismisses the possibility of the past's return. The African American oppressed by the remnants of slavery, the cotton merchant from New Orleans, the southern belle, the senile aristocratic patriarch, the Confederate veteran who cannot place his identity, the martyred southern matriarch, and the emerging figure of the "new" woman are all present in these stories, representative of the nation's reconfigured body politic.

Chopin's surviving correspondence with Houghton Mifflin demonstrates that she was integrally involved in each step of *Bayou Folk*'s publication

Table 1.1: Publication History of Stories and Sketches in Kate Chopin's *Bayou Folk* (1894)

Title (page numbers)	Original Magazine Publication
"A No-Account Creole" (1–50)	*The Century* 47, no. 3 (January 1894): 382–93
"In and out of Old Natchitoches" (51–77)	*Two Tales* 5, no. 57 (April 8, 1893): 103–14
"In Sabine" (78–95)	not published previously
"A Very Fine Fiddle" (96–98)	*Harper's Young People* 13, no. 630 (November 24, 1891): 79
"Beyond the Bayou" (99–110)	*Youth's Companion* 66, no. 24 (June 15, 1893): 302–3
"Old Aunt Peggy" (111–12)	not published previously
"The Return of Alcibiade" (113–25)	*St. Louis Life* 7, no. 131 (December 10, 1892): 6–8
"A Rude Awakening" (126–42)	*Youth's Companion* 66, no. 7 (February 2, 1893): 54–55
"The Bênitous' Slave" (143–46)	*Harper's Young People* 8, no. 642 (February 16, 1892): 280
"Désirée's Baby" (147–58)	"The Father of Désirée's Baby," *Vogue* 1 (January 14, 1893): 70–71, 74
"A Turkey Hunt" (159–62)	*Harper's Young People* 8, no. 642 (February 16, 1892): 287
"Madame Célestin's Divorce" (163–69)	not published previously
"Love on the Bon-Dieu" (170–92)	*Two Tales* 2, no. 20 (July 23, 1892): 148–56
"Loka" (193–206)	*Youth's Companion* 65, no. 51 (December 22, 1892): 670–71
"Boulôt and Boulotte" (207–9)	*Harper's Young People* 13, no. 632 (December 8, 1891): 112
"For Marse Chouchoute" (210–22)	*Youth's Companion* 64, no. 34 (August 20, 1891): 450–51
"A Visit to Avoyelles" (223–29)	"The Lover of Mentine," *Vogue* 1 (January 14, 1893): 74–75
"A Wizard from Gettysburg" (230–44)	*Youth's Companion* 65, no. 27 (July 7, 1892): 346–47
"Ma'ame Pélagie" (245–60)	*New Orleans Times-Democrat*, December 24, 1893
"At the 'Cadian Ball" (261–79)	*Two Tales* 3, no. 33 (October 22, 1892): 145–52
"La Belle Zoraïde" (280–90)	"La Belle Zoraïde: A Tragedy of the Old Régime," *Vogue* 3 (January 4, 1894): 2, 4, 8–10
"A Gentleman of Bayou Têche" (291–303)	not published previously
"A Lady of Bayou St. John" (304–13)	*Vogue* 2 (September 21, 1893): 154, 156–58

Note: The stories examined in this chapter are shaded.

process. Discussions about *Bayou Folk* began as early as September 26, 1893, and through January 6, 1894, Houghton Mifflin requests a set of sheets for "A No-Account Creole," which was in press with *The Century*, urging Chopin to provide as much of the collection's manuscript as possible (*Miscellany* 108–10). On December 19, 1893, Houghton Mifflin notes that "a list of the stories and sketches" that the publisher had already received accompanies the letter and requests that Chopin settle on a name for the collection (*Miscellany* 110–11). A January 6, 1894, letter references Chopin's December 28, 1893, request that the publisher replace "A Romantic Attachment" with "Ma'ame Pélagie" and revise the title of "The Lover of Mentine" to "A Visit to Avoyelles" (*Miscellany* 111). According to one of Chopin's account books, "A Romantic Attachment" was submitted to *Youth's Companion* on February 27, 1893, and accepted March 23, 1893, for forty dollars. Whether Chopin replaced it for aesthetic reasons or due to an arrangement with *Youth's Companion* is unclear. However, its title was changed to "Mamouche," and approximately one month after the publication of *Bayou Folk*, it appeared in the April 19, 1894, *Youth Companion* (*PP* 157). The story was later included in Chopin's second short story collection, *A Night in Acadie* (1897). Houghton Mifflin granted her requests.

Whether or not she was aware of their difficulties, Chopin's correspondence with Houghton Mifflin coincided with the publishing house's increasing financial struggles, which began in the 1880s. Lynne Shackelford identifies the 1890s as "a critical period" (214) for Houghton Mifflin, since many of its authors, among them James Russell Lowell, John Greenleaf Whittier, Oliver Wendell Holmes, and Harriet Beecher Stowe, had died. With copyrights expiring, Houghton Mifflin published new illustrated editions of its standard authors and followed "a conservative policy" (216) to survive the Panic of 1893. The fact that *Bayou Folk* was accepted for publication on August 11, 1893, and published on March 24, 1894—between the onset of the Panic of 1893 (February 20, 1893) and Henry Oscar Houghton's death (August 25, 1895)—suggests that the publishing house was confident of the collection's success.[35]

Daniel Rankin, Chopin's first biographer, rightly contends that the "distinctive power [of her early stories] was not fully recognized until scattered illustrations of it were brought into a collective whole" in *Bayou Folk* (138). While earlier southern women writers like Augusta Jane Evans Wilson used writing as both an aesthetic and political conduit for change, Chopin's work does not overtly argue for social reform. Nonetheless, her authorial voice in *Bayou Folk*, while perhaps most recognized in "the awakening" of Edna Pontellier, insistently exposes social injustices embedded in southern landscapes and culture.

Chopin uses spatial relationships to trace a transitioning regional landscape over three decades. By challenging geographic boundaries through narrative representations of them, her stories reveal how dominant power structures are constructed, maintained, and often hidden within the frame of regional exceptionalism. *Bayou Folk* stories dry up semi-stagnant bayous, shrink geographic distance and chronological time, unearth buried treasure, and replace symbols of tyranny with modern homes. By opening previously impermeable spaces and mapping relationships among place, time, and body, Chopin cultivates spatial consciousness at the end of the nineteenth century.

2

Advocating for Social Justice in Ellen Glasgow's *The Shadowy Third and Other Stories* (1923)

Like Kate Chopin, Ellen Glasgow, a white daughter from a prominent Richmond, Virginia, family, benefited from her social position. The Glasgow family owned and operated Tredegar Iron Works, a Richmond business that relied on slave labor for its production prior to and during the Civil War. Near the end of the war, it was one of few businesses to survive the burning of the city. According to Glasgow's biographer, Susan Goodman, Tredegar survived during Reconstruction by selling cotton to England and accepting federal contracts (12–13). The Glasgows profited from the factory's continued production during a time when many southern aristocratic families confronted financial ruin.

Despite her wealth and status, however, Glasgow was not able to tap into the networks of professional female editors who guided and sustained Kate Chopin's early writing career. In part, geographic location, social expectations, lack of formal education, familial tragedies, and physical illnesses (especially progressive deafness; see Kornasky) contributed to Glasgow isolation. As Glasgow writes in her posthumously published autobiography, *The*

Woman Within (1954), her experiences were indicative of the systematic exclusion of women writers from the American literary canon. For example, she describes an invitation to a meeting of the self-elected "Forty Immortals of the American Academy," who "constituted the only critical judgment," in hopes of obtaining publishing advice. These male authors permitted Glasgow to observe but not to participate in their literary establishment.[1] On another occasion early in her career, she paid a visit to Macmillan critic Price Collier, who refused to read her manuscript. Instead, he explained that his "best advice" was "to stop writing, and go back to the South and have some babies [since] the greatest woman is not the woman who has written the finest book, but the woman who has had the finest babies" (*WW* 107–9). Years later, Macmillan president George Brett admitted that this decision constituted one of his two mistakes as a publisher (Goodman 110). According to Glasgow, "I stood alone. I stood outside" (144). In the face of what later became known as the glass ceiling, only tenacity and perseverance could enable Glasgow to infiltrate a patriarchal literary culture that sought to exclude women writers.[2]

The most revealing statements about Glasgow's (and other women writers') limited access to publishing opportunities are conveyed in her publishers' memoirs. In *A Publisher's Confession* (1905), Walter Hines Page devotes much of a chapter, "Are Authors an Irritable Tribe?," to his experiences working with American women. Although he describes Glasgow as "one of our most successful novelists," he declares that women writers are difficult to work with because they "like to have everything explained in great detail" and their "imaginations are more easily excited by the hope of success" (46–48). Page's partner, Frank Nelson Doubleday, was less generous in *The Memoirs of a Publisher* (1972). In "The Lady or the Tiger," a chapter dedicated to Glasgow, the "one lady who has greatly distressed me," Doubleday recounts how her letters infuriated him. After one such letter, he required her to sign an agreement that read, "I will be good. You manage my book in the way you think best and I won't interfere until you prove that you have not done the proper thing, so help me Bob" (186–87). Doubleday laments that Glasgow's adherence was short-lived: "At times I am fond of her when she does not have her claws out," he concludes, but "when she does have them out, I would rather face a wild tiger" (187–88). Male publishers "patronized [Glasgow] as neurotic because they resented her independence" (Goodman 67). Characterized as "neurotic" because she dared to write and to take ownership of her work, she demanded agency at every stage of the publication process.[3] Glasgow refused to concede to the patronizing publishing culture that sought to define her as lady or tiger. She determined to be both.

Glasgow worked to obtain and maintain agency throughout her literary career, an ambition fueled by her social initiatives to secure justice for women. While she used her professional and social influence throughout her life to eliminate cruelty and to provide opportunity, such as her founding of the Society for the Prevention of Cruelty to Animals and her vocal resistance to library censorship in her hometown (see Glasgow, *Five Letters*), her first involvement with reform evolved from experiences with Great Britain's suffragist movement (figure 2.1). In 1909, Glasgow traveled to England and met with suffragist and writer May Sinclair. She accepted Sinclair's offer to march with the suffragists, and upon returning to Richmond, became a spokeswoman for the Virginia League for Woman Suffrage (later called the Equal Suffrage League of Virginia). Ellen and her sister, Cary, attended suffragist meetings on Franklin Street until Cary's death in 1911 (Goodman 112–22; *WW* 87).

In 1913, Glasgow published two essays on suffrage and feminism developed from her experiences with Sinclair and the Virginia League. "No Valid Reason against Giving Votes to Women," published in the *New York Times* on March 23, calls the burgeoning southern suffragist movement an "inspiring . . . battle cry" and argues that the world would benefit from women's freedom, since women "are less casual in their attitude toward evil" (SM 11). In "Feminism," published in the *New York Times* on November 30, 1913, she argues that women have a "hunger for freedom" (656). "It is foolish to talk of [feminism as] a revolt against nature as if, by taking thought, one could change the principle of one's being," Glasgow writes, "and it is not without deep significance that woman's long endeavor to exist artificially, instead of mutually, should result in the violent position of the present" (656).

Glasgow also encouraged other women writers who were addressing resistance to suffrage and feminism. Between the publication of her two essays in the *Times*, she wrote to writer, literary critic, and suffragist Edna Kenton to praise her essay published in the November 1913 issue of *The Century*.[4] Introduced by *The Century*'s editor as an explanation of feminism, Kenton's "The Militant Women—and Women" dispels misinformation that situates feminism as a militant movement and commends suffragists' efforts in England. Kenton argues that women "must refuse to accept the old ideals of the relations between men and women [and] decline to be dependent longer, economically and spiritually, upon men" (17–20). Glasgow wrote to Kenton almost immediately after reading

Fig. 2.1 Ellen Glasgow, 1930. Courtesy of the University of Michigan.

her article and emphatically supported her views: "It seems impossible that any woman could read [your essay] unmoved or unconvinced."[5]

Glasgow's participation in the suffragist movement waned by 1916, by which time she had endured the deaths of her mother, Anne Jane Gholson Glasgow; her lover, Gerald B.; her brother, Frank Glasgow; her sister, Cary Glasgow; and her father, Francis Thomas Glasgow (Goodman 112–22). She then turned to writing short stories, which were published in a collection, *The Shadowy Third and Other Stories* (1923). All the collection's stories except "A Point of Morals," which appeared in the May 1899 issue of *Harper's New Monthly Magazine*, were written and initially published in magazines after 1916. The title story, the first in the volume, originally appeared in December 1916.

Though *The Shadowy Third* was published less than three years after the Nineteenth Amendment gave US women the right to vote, Glasgow by this time possessed less faith in politically wrought change, which seemed futile while men maintained social and political power. As she reflects decades later, neither "woman's acknowledged intuition" nor "woman's unacknowledged intelligence would change so much as an atom in man's practical politics. . . . [S]o long as the serpent continues to crawl on the ground, the primary influence of woman will remain indirect" (*WW* 187). Instead of direct engagement with politics, Glasgow harnesses the "primarily indirect influence" of women by cultivating a readership sympathetic to the nexus between her causes—alleviating cruelty and righting injustice.

Like Chopin, Glasgow became one of the most prolific American women writers of her time, publishing nineteen novels, a collection of poetry, a collection of short stories, and a collection of essays. Critics labeled her early publications "a social history of Virginia."[6] Glasgow was recognized primarily as a novelist, but she wrote poetry before fiction (Meeker 3). Her first poem, "The Freeman," published in the December 1897 issue of the *Atlantic Monthly*, launched her collection, *The Freeman and Other Poems* (1902), but it sold few copies. She did not write verse after 1920 (Meeker 3). Most scholars agree that the second half of her career, particularly her novel *Barren Ground* (1925), represents her best work. *The Shadowy Third* constitutes the only short story collection published during her lifetime, transitionally located between these two phases of her oeuvre.

Unlike late-nineteenth-century southern women writers whose short stories ushered their work onto a national stage, Glasgow's stories remained supplementary to her novels and were published only during the first half of her career. Page and other advisers discouraged her from writing stories on the grounds that "seriousness required bulk" (Meeker 3–4). In a May 12, 1900, letter, often cited as evidence for Glasgow's disinterest in writing short stories, Glasgow thanks Page for warning her against publishing stories and confirms that she has not accepted *Harper's Magazine*'s offer to serialize *The Battle-Ground* (Glasgow, *Letters* 32). None of her novels were serialized, despite offers, and only a few of her poems were published in magazines (Colvert). By 1925, ten of the twelve short stories she wrote were placed in periodicals such as *Harper's Magazine*, *Scribner's Magazine*, and *Good Housekeeping*.[7] Glasgow selected six of these tales for *The Shadowy Third*, adding the previously unpublished "Jordan's End."

Since Richard Meeker's lament about the lack of scholarly engagement with Glasgow's short stories in his introduction to *The Collected Stories of Ellen Glasgow* (1963), her stories (and novels) have received further critical attention, but none of these readings considers *The Shadowy Third* stories' original magazine publications alongside their collective arrangement. Previous examinations attribute story selections to Glasgow's biographical tragedies as well as to cultural influences such as Darwinism and Edgar Allan Poe.[8] While these influences may have contributed to individual stories, their selection derives from the collection's shape, or how Glasgow conveys meaning through her grouping of these stories. The stories are primarily arranged into two groups by alternating narrative settings between New York and Virginia. She establishes this pattern with the first four ghost stories ("The Shadowy Third," "Dare's Gift," "The Past," and "Whispering Leaves") and ends the collection with this pattern in the final two stories ("The Difference" and "Jordan's End"). The fifth, centrally located story, "A Point of Morals," provides a transition between the ghosts in the first four stories and the lack of mysticism in the last two stories. Structured as a frame narrative with a setting within a setting, the story's narrator, who is traveling by ship, tells of his experiences on a train between Glasgow, Scotland, and London, England. When read as part of the collection, "A Point of Morals" alerts readers to differentiate between the first four stories, which focus on social injustices, and the last two stories, which thematically engage perspectives on morality related to infidelity and suicide.

This chapter focuses on *The Shadowy Third*'s first four ghost stories. Glasgow's writing of these stories, narratively connected by apparitions and alternating settings, also ushers her personal transition from direct engagements with political causes to indirect approaches that garner readers' sympathies for reforming social injustices. The first story in the collection, "The Shadowy Third," is narrated by Miss Randolph, a nurse living in New York City. Miss Randolph realizes that Mrs. Maradick is not a patient suffering from hallucinations but a wife who is ruthlessly confined by her doctor-husband after the death of her daughter, Dorothea. The second story, "Dare's Gift," written in two parts, links the narratives of Meredith Beckwith and Lucy Dare by geographic location and ending despite being set twenty years apart. The tale's apparition, neither Beckwith nor Dare, reveals itself at the site of the ancestral plantation home. "The Past" portrays how the apparition of Mr. Vanderbridge's first wife haunts the home until the narrator, Miss Wrenn, discovers letters that reveal the first wife's infidelity. Finally, "Whispering Leaves" depicts Mammy Rhody as a "faithful slave," capable of protecting her young charge, Pell, even from beyond the grave. To save Pell from an unfeeling stepmother and deteriorating plantation, Mammy Rhody haunts the narrator, Effie, a distant relative from New York, when she visits Virginia.

The ghost stories' collective arrangement by original publication date suggests that they were written together and purposely grouped together. Each story's apparition embodies one representation of gender and racial injustice, and together they expose how romanticized versions of sociocultural narratives maintain and perpetuate tyranny. Moreover, by systematically alternating between New York and Virginia settings, Glasgow does not confine her critique to the South but demonstrates the presence of injustices toward women across regional boundaries. She uses familiar tropes, such as the ghost story, and genres, such as sentimental fiction, to educate readers about social constructions of narrative and place with the goal of deconstructing and eliminating their marginalizing power. In her selection and arrangement of stories for *The Shadowy Third*, Glasgow compels readers to exchange oppressive ideology for intellectual independence.[9] Disenchanted with political causes and distraught from personal challenges, Glasgow wrote ghost stories that magnify the serpent that continues to crawl on the ground to rectify the historical subjugation of women in American society.

Ghosts and Serpents

In *The Woman Within*, Glasgow remembers her "earliest sensation" as a comfortable rocking movement in her mother's arms that suddenly became terrifying when she noticed her reflection in the window as a face without a body: "One minute, I was not; the next minute, I was. I felt. I was separate. I could be hurt. I had discovered myself [and] the universe apart from myself" (3–4). Glasgow's Lacanian-like beginning links her first recognition of self-identity with the supernatural, observing herself as "a bodiless apparition, distorted, unreal, yet more real to [her] than either [her]self or the world" (3–4).

This memory may have engendered her use of the ghost story genre in the first four stories of *The Shadowy Third*. Like Chopin, Glasgow insistently distanced her work from the sentimental and romantic traditions associated with nineteenth-century women's literature, even as she used these traditions to guide readers through her retelling of a story without a romanticized ending.[10] Glasgow's realism combines William Dean Howells's emphasis on "truthful treatment" in *Criticism and Fiction* (1891) with Henry James's psychological development in novels like *Daisy Miller* (1878) and *The Turn of the Screw* (1898). She defines her approach to realism as "not reality," "not modeled in clay," or "not even dough, to be twisted and pinched into artificial perfection" (*WW* 124). If twisting is present, "it must not be visible; it must remain always below the surface of art" (124). Realistic fiction "must contain not only the perfection of art, but the imperfection of nature" (125). Reminiscent of Marianne Moore's line from "Poetry" (1919)—"imaginary gardens with real toads in them" (33)—Glasgow's realism seeks to make universal truths visible.[11]

In "The Shadowy Third," "Dare's Gift," "The Past," and "Whispering Leaves," Glasgow's ghosts are visible to some characters but not others, neither completely real nor entirely illusion. They enact fictional identities that remain suspended in place by their imposed marginalization. The stories arrange their ghostly protagonists by age, replicated by their placement in the volume according to original magazine publication dates. The apparition in "The Shadowy Third" is a young child, whereas the one in "Whispering Leaves" is an older, deceased caretaker. As a whole, this arrangement guides the reader through a trajectory of maturation. In representation, each ghost serves as a metaphor for female victims confined by socially constructed narratives at different stages of life. "Through them," as Gwen M. Neary argues, Glasgow sought to replace a pattern of society she "hated" with "humane and honest values" (8). In *The Shadowy Third and Other Stories*, not the ghost but the narrative that confines the ghost must be deconstructed to release its haunting. Ghosts disappear from each story when characters refuse to maintain or perpetuate oppressive narratives.

Likely written between June and July 1916, "The Shadowy Third" was originally published in the December 1916 issue of *Scribner's Magazine*. *Scribner's* was smaller than the other three quality magazines—*The Century*, the *Atlantic Monthly*, and *Harper's Monthly*—so that it had a lower subscription rate, though its illustrations and content targeted a similar upper-middle-class audience. The magazine primarily devoted its pages to fiction and poetry through the early twentieth century but increasingly included war pieces after 1914 (Mott, *History* 4:717–18, 727).

Glasgow's short story appeared at the end of 1916, as World War I continued and America's noninterventionist policies and commitment to neutrality were eroding. *Scribner's* December 1916 issue mirrors the nation's preoccupations, including war-themed poetry and fiction, such as Henry Van Dyke's "War Music" and Mildred Cram's "The Victory." Readers encountered advertisements that encouraged financial investments over commodities purchased with disposable income. Essays also sought to evaluate conflicting perspectives on the feminist movement, such as Robert Grant's "Feminism in Fiction and Real Life," which warns against feminism in the context of World War I. "The Shadowy Third" is the issue's fourth selection, introduced by Elenore Plaisted Abbott's illustration of a mother and daughter's embrace. The caption reads, "I saw her lift her little arms, and I saw the mother stoop and gather her to her bosom." Glasgow chose the same illustration for the frontispiece (and only artwork) in the first American edition of *The Shadowy Third* seven years later (figure 2.2).

The illustration's intimate scene induces the reader's sympathy before reading the story and suggests that the tale will convey sentiment. Early twentieth-century readers would have been familiar with sentimental literature, primarily written by female authors and designed to evoke an emotional response from its audience. Particularly in the mid- and late nineteenth century, sentimental novels were published serially, read widely, and constituted America's first bestsellers (Tompkins 150). These serializations provide significant insights into an evolving American culture, "tell[ing] stories about how—and whether—individuals can come together to form a society" and about the "forging [of] an idea of a group, a society, a nation" (Okker 4–7). Designed to instruct young women about morality, plots prescribed self-discipline over resistance in the face of cruelty.

"The Shadowy Third" initially mirrors this model through its depiction of a widow, Mrs. Maradick, a widowed woman whose second husband, Doctor

Fig. 2.2 Elenore Plaisted Abbott's illustration for "The Shadowy Third," *Scribner's Magazine* 60, no. 6 (December 1916): 658. This illustration was also chosen for the frontispiece of the first American edition of *The Shadowy Third and Other Stories* (1923). Courtesy of Special Collections, Tampa Library, University of South Florida.

Maradick, has inherited her family home as a result of their marriage. He cannot access further monetary inheritance because her first husband secured it in a trust for his daughter, Dorothea.[12] When she becomes ill and dies under Doctor Maradick's medical care, Mrs. Maradick accuses him of murder. In a plot twist reminiscent of Charlotte Perkins Gilman's short story, "The Yellow Wallpaper" (1892), Doctor Maradick reconfigures Mrs. Maradick's accusation as a hallucination, confines her to her bedroom, and then arranges for her to be sent to an asylum, where she dies. Gilman's story appeared in *New England Magazine* decades before Glasgow wrote "The Shadowy Third," and she may have been familiar with it. Perkins's narrator is prescribed Dr. Weir Mitchell's "rest cure," which was designed for nervous conditions and was primarily prescribed for women. Goodman confirms that Glasgow uses Mitchell as a model for Doctor Maradick (146).

Throughout the story, Mrs. Maradick demonstrates the self-discipline possessed by sentimental fiction's heroines, including strict adherence to her husband's/doctor's orders even when she determines that he is responsible for her daughter's death. As Mrs. Maradick prepares herself for institutionalization, Dorothea's ghost runs into the room and embraces her mother for the last time. Mrs. Maradick and the narrator, Miss Randolph, are the only characters who claim to see the apparition. Abbott's illustration captures the final moment between mother and daughter.

Glasgow's story initially follows the conventions of sentimental literature by connecting readers to characters' plights through sympathy and by instructing (female) readers using fictional figures as models of self-sacrifice and piety. The final scene between mother and daughter in "The Shadowy Third" echoes a scene in Susan Warner's best-selling sentimental novel, *The Wide, Wide World* (1850), in which a mother is also confined to her room due to illness and forcibly separated from her daughter by her husband. In both texts, husbands limit physical and emotional connections between mothers and daughters, using geographic separation and prescribed narratives of illness or madness to isolate and control wives. Unable to escape, maternal characters pass away quietly and stoically, leaving their daughters to navigate the world alone.

Most sentimental novels are told from a third-person omniscient perspective. However, in Glasgow's story, readers receive a first-person account of narrative events through Miss Randolph as Dorothea's ghost guides the narrator toward the child's silenced narrative. When Miss Randolph first enters the home and is left alone in the hallway, she sees a child's red and blue rubber ball and follows it into a room. Dorothea subsequently appears in her mother's room and in hallways, prompting Miss Randolph to observe and eventually to inquire about Dorothea's identity. Miss Randolph narrates the events in the story for the reader, but Dorothea guides the narrative vision. Consequently, the more informed Miss Randolph becomes about Doctor Maradick's history of tyranny over mother and daughter, the less Dorothea appears. In the presence of the ghost, Miss Randolph enacts the role of observer, but as the story continues, Dorothea increasingly positions the narrator as a replacement, a participant in the girl's vision for the story's unfolding. The final mother-daughter scene marks both the absence of Dorothea (until the end of the story) and the transfer of the narrative vision from Dorothea to Miss Randolph.

The ability to see Dorothea does not free characters from Doctor Maradick's narrative control. Old Gabriel, the elderly African American butler from South Carolina, also sees Dorothea. His observations are dismissed because, as the day nurse, Miss Peterson, remarks, "Nobody pays attention to anything he sees. [He is] supernatural by instinct" (23).[13] Miss Randolph sees Dorothea's ghost but decides that since others cannot (or choose not to) see her, "it was useless to tell them" (35). In a final example, Miss Peterson recognizes the consequences of seeing the apparition and resolutely responds to Miss Randolph's inquiry by "setting her lips tightly" and declaring "I never see anything" (22). Seeing Dorothea also allows Miss Randolph to convey to readers the story's subtext—a subversive narrative different from Doctor Maradick's construction—even though her capacity to tell Mrs. Maradick's and Dorothea's story to other characters becomes limited after Doctor Maradick suspects that she sees the ghost and sympathizes with his wife. Furthermore, Doctor Maradick continues to employ Miss Randolph when her night nurse services are no longer required. Because she is confined to his Fifth Avenue home, she cannot return to the hospital to share her observations. When characters' perspectives diverge from Doctor Maradick's prescriptive narrative, they are rendered incapable of telling their versions of the story.

Glasgow emphasizes Doctor Maradick's role in constructing narrative to perpetuate injustice. Between the magazine and collected versions of the story, her revisions focus on descriptions of Doctor Maradick's power. In the *Scribner's* version of the story, for instance, Miss Randolph describes Doctor Maradick's social position as godlike: "Fate had selected him for the rôle, and it would have been sheer impertinence for a mortal to cross wills with the invisible Powers."[14] The collected version replaces this sentence with "he was, I suppose, born to be a hero of women" (6). By revising "invisible Powers" as "heroic," Glasgow repositions the romanticized, invisible power of a godlike figure as the socially constructed, visible power wielded by one character. Removing the supernatural from Doctor Maradick's description makes his cruelty visible.

In "The Shadowy Third," Glasgow rewrites sentimental conclusions as cruel and in need of vindication. By negotiating between the illusion of sentiment and the "nostalgic aspects" of its "literary heritage," Glasgow connects with readers while simultaneously developing a "critique [of] the conventions accompanying sentimentality and the danger and violence that such systems produce" (Lear, "Ellen Glasgow" 27). Sentimental novels portray how continual self-sacrifice leads to a prosperous conclusion (often depicted as marriage), even if obtained through the loss of independence and self-expression, but "The Shadowy Third" makes it clear that submitting to a prescriptive narrative leads to either psychological or physical death. After Mrs. Maradick's death, Doctor Maradick can inherit her money, sell her family home, and marry the woman who once rejected him for his lack of wealth. While Dorothea's ghost does not reappear, Miss Randolph notices a "loosely coiled" child's skipping rope on the stairs moments before Doctor Maradick trips and falls to his death at the bottom of the stairs. In a direct address to the reader, she concludes that "it may have been, as the world believes, a misstep in the dimness, or it may have been, as I am ready to bear witness, an invisible judgment" (43). Doctor Maradick's death resembles Mr. Hale's demise in Susan Glaspell's *Trifles* (1916), a play that was first performed prior to the story's publication. And both Glasgow's "Dare's Gift" and Glaspell's "The Hearing Ear" appeared in *Harper's Monthly Magazine* in 1917, less than a year after the first publication of "The Shadowy Third" and the first performance of *Trifles*.

Northern magazines promoted romanticized representations of the South, such as Thomas Nelson Page's *In Ole Virginia, or Marse Chan* (1895), a practice Glasgow disliked, especially because they contributed to the perpetuation of the Lost Cause," or citizens' work toward revising inaccurate portrayals of the South through memorialization and vindication campaigns. One of her most recognized assertions is that the South needs blood and irony to remedy its "sentimental decay" (Glasgow, *Certain Measure* 28). In "The Novel in the

South," a four-part essay published in the December 1928 issue of *Harper's Monthly*, Glasgow argues that the sentimental literature associated with the South emerged from the "political expediency" to "defend the lost" by conveying a nostalgic southern past in response to Reconstruction's occupation (95). "What had begun as an emergency measure," Glasgow argues, "matured into a sacred and infallible doctrine" (100). The second ghost story in *The Shadowy Third*, "Dare's Gift," responds to these ill-conceived "doctrines," situating northern and southern perspectives on the South in the same story.

"Dare's Gift," was first published as two parts in the February and March 1917 issues of *Harper's Monthly Magazine*. Like *Scribner's*, considered the oldest of the quality magazines, *Harper's* was beautifully illustrated and benefited from a significant circulation among socially elite readers. Mott contends that "no other magazine can be shown to have been markedly superior to it in literary quality, variety, illustration, and physical appearance" (*History* 2:400). *Harper's* February and March 1917 issues included mostly short fiction and a few poems, as well as a scientific essay and an essay on immigration. In 1917, well-known realist writer and critic William Dean Howells returned to the magazine to write the "Editor's Easy Chair" column. By publishing "Dare's Gift" in *Harper's Monthly*, Glasgow strategically positions her work within the realist tradition.

A compilation of two narratives, "Dare's Gift" deconstructs the Lost Cause narrative to problematize its romanticized perpetuation. In part I, Howard Beckwith, a lawyer (and the story's narrator), confides to his wife, Mildred Beckwith, about evidence that would expose the Atlantic and Eastern Railroad's issuance of illegal rebates to the American Steel Company, a narrative reminiscent of Henry Demarest Lloyd's "The Story of a Great Monopoly," published in the March 1881 issue of the *Atlantic Monthly* to expose ongoing corporate corruption between the railroads and the Standard Oil Company. Antitrust laws such as the Sherman Act (1890), the Clayton Act (1914), and the Federal Trade Commission Act (1914) eventually remedied this corruption. In the first part of "Dare's Gift," however, Mildred shares the evidence with Herbert Tremaine, a corporate corruption investigator, and her husband loses the case. When Harold questions Mildred, she responds, "I had to do it. I would do it again" (103).[15] Part II looks backward in time to tell the story of Lucy Dare, conflicted between her loyalty to the Confederate cause and her personal feelings for her Yankee fiancé, recently escaped from a prisoner-of-war camp. Lucy Dare's decision to reveal his location leads to his murder.

Fig. 2.3 C. E. Chambers's illustration for "Dare's Gift: Part I," *Harper's Monthly Magazine* 134, no. 801 (February 1917): 329. Courtesy of Special Collections, Tampa Library, University of South Florida.

Fig. 2.4 C. E. Chambers's illustration for "Dare's Gift: Part II," *Harper's Monthly Magazine* 134, no. 802 (March 1917): 521. Courtesy of Special Collections, Tampa Library, University of South Florida.

She explains to Dr. Lakeby, the narrator in part II, "I had to do it . . . I would do it again" (116). Pairing Mildred Beckwith's story with Lucy Dare's story appears to indict femininity and the narratives' common setting at the ancestral plantation, Dare's Gift, as sites of betrayal. As in "The Shadowy Third," predictable relationships between tales must be deconstructed to reveal truth.

C. E. Chambers's illustrations of both parts of the story in *Harper's Magazine* reinforce the similarities between Mildred Beckwith's and Lucy Dare's narratives. The illustration in part I features Harold and Mildred, with a caption quoting Mildred Beckwith's words to her husband: "'I wish you would leave me alone,' she replied in a shaking voice" (figure 2.3). Part II's illustration portrays Lucy Dare with her Yankee fiancé in the shadows of a doorway behind her. The caption describes Lucy Dare's thoughts as she contemplates her decision: "I can never see him again. I do not wish to see him" (figure 2.4). Both women are seated at a small table in the garden and positioned with their right elbows on the table and their right hands supporting their heads.

They appear similarly lost in contemplation, oblivious to the men nearby. The excerpts printed beneath the illustrations confirm the female characters' resolves to distance themselves from the male characters.

Like Mrs. Maradick in "The Shadowy Third," Mildred Beckwith cannot narrate her own story. Instead, Harold Beckwith conveys it to the reader, situating, as his friend Harrison points out, his reading of her thoughts as a replication of his own (56–57). Yet her relative silence does not indicate her complacency in the narrative's construction. When Mildred does speak in the text, her words contradict Harold's idealized image of Dare's Gift. As depicted in Chambers's illustration of Harold Beckwith's arrival at Dare's Gift (which appears as the frontispiece for the February 1917 *Harper's*; figure 2.5), Harold's descriptions of the plantation draw on sentimental representations of the antebellum South. The illustration's soft lines depict a gate opening up to a misty, utopian setting as the plantation home comes into Harold view. Quoting from the story, the caption reads, "The Old World charm of the scene held me captive."[16] In contrast to Harold's captivation, Mildred sees the home's "architectural absurdities"—its "cramped and poorly lighted" rooms, "broken pieces of the queer mullioned window," and mantle detail work "blurred by recent disfigurements" (61–62). Harold's vision of "memories of the old river" and "the garden . . . falling gently from its almost obliterated terraces to the scalloped edges of the river" situates the ancestral plantation as a romanticized depiction of the antebellum South and erroneously contributes to his conclusion that Dare's Gift never changed (48).

While Glasgow made few revisions between the *Harper's Monthly* and *The Shadowy Third* versions of "Dare's Gift," her replacement of the magazine version's passive voice to describe the plantation with past-tense verbs further supports this reading. At the beginning of the story in *Harper's*, Harold recollects that "while I had climbed the rough road, and passed more slowly between the marvelous walls of box—of box which had the majesty and permanence of history—I had told myself that the place must be Mildred's and mine at any cost."[17] The collected story's version revises "had told" to "I told myself" (49). The change moves Harold from a distant observer to an active constructor of the narrative.

Unable to move beyond his romanticism and in the absence of an explanation for Mildred's behavior that fits into his narrative vision, Harold looks for a ghost at Dare's Gift and is frustrated when Dr. Lakeby cannot provide him with one. Dr. Lakeby describes Lucy Dare as the quintessential southern

Fig. 2.5 C. E. Chambers's illustration for "Dare's Gift: Part I," *Harper's Monthly Magazine* 134, no. 801 (February 1917): frontispiece. Courtesy of Special Collections, Tampa Library, University of South Florida.

Fig. 2.6 C. E. Chambers's illustration for "Dare's Gift: Part II," *Harper's Monthly Magazine* 134, no. 802 (March 1917): frontispiece. Courtesy of Special Collections, Tampa Library, University of South Florida.

lady, "ordinary, submissive, feminine, domestic" (83), a portrayal reinforced by Chambers's statue-like depiction of her that accompanies the story in *Harper's* (figure 2.6). The illustration portrays Lucy Dare standing near a conversation between her Confederate soldier cousin and colonel father, as she overhears their words, quoted in the caption: "And the Confederacy is lost, you say, if he escapes?"

Lucy reveals where her fiancé has hidden. Despite her static depictions in Chambers's illustrations, she cannot be the ghost who caused Mildred Beckwith's "illness"; as Dr. Lakeby explains, Lucy is alive. Instead, the doctor concludes, the idea of Lucy's act, not her body, continues to haunt Dare's Gift: "The act dies; it decays like the body, but the *idea* is immortal" (77). The ghost in "Dare's Gift" is metaphysical, representing the embodiment of an idea.

The male narrators in the two parts of "Dare's Gift" are actively engaged in constructing the idea of a ghost through their romanticized tellings of Mildred Beckwith's and Lucy Dare's stories. But the stories are not actually the same. Lucy perpetuates the ideology that confines her, while Mildred disrupts (albeit temporarily) her husband's patriarchal narrative control. Mildred's resistance betrays Harold's master narrative, represented by corporate corruption in the early twentieth century and her husband's use of his social and professional position of power to attempt to conceal this corruption. In contrast, Lucy remains a stagnant archetype, portrayed as holding her knitting yarn in both youth and old age so that she appears unaffected by change. By ordering the two parts of "Dare's Gift" anachronistically, Glasgow invites a subversive reading of the narrators' portrayals, privileging Mildred's twentieth-century exposure of corruption over Lucy's nineteenth-century perpetuation of the Lost Cause narrative to expose the misconceptions embedded in romanticized versions of the past.

Uncharacteristically, Glasgow published the third ghost story, "The Past," in the October 1920 issue of *Good Housekeeping* instead of in a quality magazine. Described by Mott as "scrapbookish" and "lower class," *Good Housekeeping* printed readers' work until 1910, when it began to publish more prominent authors. Mott specifically mentions "The Past" as one of the most "notable short stories" the magazine published (*History* 5:125–34).

Aimed at an audience of female homemakers, *Good Housekeeping* features articles on home economics rather than short fiction and poetry. A one-page article, "The Business of Housekeeping: Good Food and Its Relation to Success," precedes Glasgow's "The Past": in it, Emma Gary Wallace argues that "food and progress are linked together" (63). To illustrate her assertion, Wallace compares two fictional married couples, John and Sue and Ralph and Eunice. While Sue gets her feelings hurt easily and thinks that her husband is critical, Eunice "delight[s] in "see[ing] to it that Ralph should always feel a pleasant expectation of what the next meal would present" (63). As a result, Ralph is promoted to partner at his manufacturing plant, whereas John is not. Wallace's article suggests that a woman's best fulfillment lies in her usefulness to her husband, an argument that explicitly contradicts Glasgow's insistence on women's intellectual independence.

In another difference between Glasgow's previous magazine publications and "The Past," *Good Housekeeping* divides short fiction among nonconsecutive pages in the issue, and fiction shares the page with advertisements. While the largest incremental increase of magazine advertisements occurred after World War I, Ellen Gruber Garvey's *The Adman in the Parlor: Magazines and the Gendering of Consumer Culture* (1996) contends that *Good Housekeeping* sought to cultivate a "reader as consumer" ideology through advertisement competitions and associating advertisements' information with "consumer power" (67–69, 150, 164; see also Peterson 19). *Good Housekeeping* generally grouped together the first two or three pages of a story near the front of an issue and then mixed the remainder with ads on the pages near the end. The October 1920 issue of *Good Housekeeping* follows this model, ending the first section of "The Past" (in the middle of a sentence) on page 66 and resuming it on page 155. Furthermore, the latter half of the story's text encompasses only one-third of a page, sharing print space with distracting advertisements for commodities such as face powder, furniture, shower sprays, clothes dryers, and women's undergarments. Given Glasgow's insistence that her novels not be serialized, it seems strange that she permitted physical fragmentation to impede the continuity of this story.

Only one surviving letter from this era sheds light on the matter. On September 17, 1920, Glasgow writes to the president of the Equal Suffrage League of Virginia, Lila Hardaway Meade Valentine, to reminisce about her work with her sister, Cary, on behalf of the league (*Perfect Companionship*, 65). Glasgow may have written the letter because of her pending publication in *Good Housekeeping*, which published work by well-known suffragist leaders such as Mary Chapman Catt, Alice Carpenter, Elizabeth M. Gilmer (under the pseudonym Dorothy Dix), Emmeline Pankhurst, and Rose Emmet Young.[18] For example, the magazine printed nine feminist articles by Young between 1913 and 1915, with subjects that included women's leadership in politics to career possibilities for women (outlined in an ongoing column, "Your Daughter's Career"). In "What is Feminism," published in February 1914, Young includes "higher education for women, economic opportunity for women, rights of persona and property for women" with "political enfranchisement for women" (679). Glasgow likely would have felt that her work was in good company. Cary Glasgow's efforts, along with Ellen's, established the League of Virginia, and in "The Past," published less than three months after the ratification of the Nineteenth Amendment and ten years after Cary's death, Ellen Glasgow seems preoccupied with these memories.

Set in New York, "The Past" features Mr. Vanderbridge, who remains bound to his memories of his first wife and the guilt he feels over her death during childbirth. In the story's only illustration (figure 2.7), Mr. Vanderbridge slumps in his chair, looking toward the floor and unaware that the ghostly presence of his first wife stands directly before him. The narrator, Miss Wrenn, watches from a distance in disbelief. The caption, borrowed from Miss Wrenn's narration of the story, describes the significance of this portrayal: "Mr. Vanderbridge came in and sat down in one of the big velvet chairs before the wood fire. He had not noticed me, for one of his moods was upon him, and I was about to slip out as noiselessly as I could, when I saw that the Other One was standing in the patch of firelight on the hearth-rug." The apparition represents Mr. Vanderbridge's all-consuming memories and haunts all the characters in the story. The hauntings continue until Miss Wrenn discovers letters that expose the first wife's infidelity. In doing so, she rewrites Mr. Vanderbridge's romanticized versions of his first wife's life and death.

Like the South's perpetuation of "the Lost Cause" portrayed in "Dare's Gift," the characters in "The Past" perpetuate the ghost's appearances and narrative by maintaining a role in its construction. The second Mrs. Vanderbridge, Miss Wrenn, and the housemaid, Hopkins, all contribute their own associations to the apparition. Hopkins names the ghost "the Other One." Miss Wrenn gives physical qualities to the apparition's metaphysical existence, noting that she appears "quite young . . . though she was not really beautiful"; that she "was the most graceful creature"; and that "she appeared so much frailer, so much more elusive, as if she would vanish if you touched her" (120–21).[19] Finally, Mrs. Vanderbridge refers to the first wife's ghost as "her" and "she," personifying and attributing power to it.

Fig. 2.7 Lejaren A. Hiller's illustration for "The Past," *Good Housekeeping* 71 (October 1920): 65. Courtesy of the University of Michigan.

In the same way that Dorothea guides Miss Randolph's narration of "The Shadowy Third," the only way to eliminate the first wife's hauntings is to reposition their significance within the narrative vision. When Miss Wrenn finds old letters exchanged between the first wife and her lover during her marriage to Mr. Vanderbridge, Mrs. Vanderbridge burns the letters instead of showing them to her husband. In doing so, she frees herself from the ghost's appearances. As Miss Wrenn observes, Mrs. Vanderbridge "had won. . . . She had changed the thought of the past, [and] in that lay her victory" (139). Mrs. Vanderbridge revises the past's narrative not by destroying the text that confines her but by destroying its hold over her. In this story, Glasgow continues her initiative to expose how narratives can perpetuate romanticized versions of reality and how this perpetuation might be controlled.

Glasgow adds pages of copious description and dialogue to the collected version of "The Past," and it is the only ghost story in the collection that for which critics have explored the revisions between the versions. However, some of this older scholarship requires clarification. For instance, in his 1966 article, R. H. W. Dillard misdates *Good Housekeeping*'s publication of the story to July–August 1920, even though Richard Meeker had identified the correct date (October 1920) three years previously in an editor's note in Glasgow's *Collected Stories* (246, 139). But although Meeker asserts that Glasgow made fewer revisions between the magazine and collected versions of "The Past" than she did for any other story (Glasgow, *Collected Stories* 139), Dillard points out that more than 190 "extensive and significant" revisions occur in three broad categories: spelling and punctuation (reflecting Glasgow's preference for English spellings); single-word changes for "precision of meaning"; and larger revisions "to heighten suspense and to increase the reader's awareness" of tensions between characters (246–47).

I found only ninety-nine revisions, but differences between Dillard's method of counting revisions and my own may account for the discrepancy. Even so, both findings demonstrate a significant increase in revisions compared to "The Shadowy Third" (ten revisions) and "Dare's Gift" (twenty-five revisions). In "The Shadowy Third" and "Dare's Gift," most changes consist of verb tense corrections or converting American spellings to English spellings; the revisions to content primarily eliminated text for the collection. In "The Past," significant amounts of text are added.

Dillard contends that Glasgow's revisions in "The Past" demonstrate that she was "conscious of her art and determined to develop it" (250). This remark implies the existence of critical doubt regarding the quality of Glasgow's lesser-known short stories in the 1960s. His scholarship, which first demonstrates the extent of her revision process, puts this doubt to rest. Echoing Dr. Lakeby's assertion in "Dare's Gift" that the ghost is the embodiment of an idea rather than a representative of a deceased physical body, Glasgow's revisions between the magazine and collected versions of "The Past" rewrite the ghost as a metaphor, or "visible manifestation" (Dillard 248), of Mr. Vanderbridge's preoccupation with the past. Glasgow's replacement of "apparition" in *Good Housekeeping* (162) with "the past" in *The Shadowy Third* (146) supports this conclusion. As Dillard argues, "By the change of one word, Glasgow emphasiz[es] that the past rather than the ghost must be exorcized. Miss Glasgow made the psychological significance of the ghost, as well as the meaning of the story, clearer" (248).

Further extending Dillard's argument, Glasgow's meticulous revisions in "The Past," as part of her insistent narrative decisions throughout her oeuvre, provide additional confirmation of her agency in the publication process of *The Shadowy Third*. Highlighting another Glasgow revision, previous textual scholarship does not call attention to her replacement of Miss Wrenn's "handkerchief" in *Good Housekeeping* with Hopkins's "ball of yarn." In the *Good Housekeeping* version of the story, Hopkins "stoop[s] to pick up [Miss Wrenn's] handkerchief which had dropped by [her] chair" (158), whereas in the collected version of the story, Hopkins "stoop[s] to pick up the ball of yarn which had rolled under [Miss Wrenn's] chair" (126). Independent of the stories' arrangement in the collection, this revision appears insignificant, but in context, it links "The Past" to the previous two ghost stories using similar objects—Dorothea's red and blue rubber ball in "The Shadowy Third" and Lucy Dare's ball of yarn in "Dare's Gift"—as further evidence of Glasgow's narrative vision for her grouping of the stories.

Meeker writes in his editor's note to the "The Past" that "its symbolism is all too obvious" (Glasgow, *Collected Stories* 139), but this is not a defect. Glasgow's intentional revision of the handkerchief in "The Past" creates continuity between the first three stories, using similarly shaped objects to guide readers. The child's ball in "The Shadowy Third" leads the narrator away from Doctor Maradick's construction of Mrs. Maradick's illness narrative and toward Dorothea's and Mrs. Maradick's victimization narrative. In "Dare's Gift," the first description of Lucy Dare holding yarn immediately follows Dr. Lakeby's assertion about the Confederacy: "We were, one and all, victims of an idea—of a divine frenzy" (96). As Dr. Lakeby portrays it, Lucy Dare continuously holds her ball of yarn throughout the fifty-year span of the narrative, symbolic of her stagnation. And in "The Past," Hopkins stoops to pick up her ball of yarn after confiding her fear of the ghost to Miss Wrenn. Each interaction signals a revelation about the past that informs the story's telling.

The volume's fourth story, "Whispering Leaves," does not contain a ball of yarn, but its ghost is perhaps the most culturally recognized figure among *The Shadowy Third*'s apparitions. Modeled after Glasgow's childhood mammy as described in *The Woman Within*, Mammy Rhody haunts the deteriorating plantation, Whispering Leaves, and Effie, the distant cousin and the story's narrator, visiting from New York.[20] Both Mammy Rhody and her mistress have died prior to Effie's arrival at Whispering Leaves, but Mammy Rhody continues to watch over Pell, her mistress's son. Readers are introduced to her ghostly figure as she rescues Pell from falling out of a tree in the first of four illustrations drawn by Elizabeth Shippen Green for *Harper's Monthly Magazine's* publication of "Whispering Leaves." The caption—"Her features were irradiated by a passion of tenderness"—furthers her portrayal as apparition caretaker (figure 2.8).

"Whispering Leaves" was published in two parts in *Harper's Monthly Magazine*'s January and February 1923 issues, alongside such writers familiar to twentieth-century readers as Sherwood Anderson and Frederick L. Allen. Four years after the end of World War I, the selections in these issues of *Harper's Monthly* include more nonfiction than the 1917 issues that contained "Dare's Gift." There are essays on immigration, patriotism, courtship, calories, and business relationships. Several of the short fiction pieces engage foreign and domestic explorations. Edward S. Martin replaces William Dean Howells in the "Editor's Easy Chair." Glasgow's publication of "Whispering Leaves" occurs during a period of transition for *Harper's*. By September 1925, *Harper's* had eliminated its illustrations except for each issue's frontispiece and repositioned itself as "a journal of diversified opinion, written by the leading thinkers of the new day" (Mott, *History* 4:404), and by the 1930s it printed little to no serialized fiction.

More indicative of the fiction produced during Howells's tenure with the magazine than its future emphasis on "diversified opinion . . . by leading thinkers," "Whispering Leaves" develops its tale by drawing on the faithful slave narrative tradition, an archetype used to romanticize and to justify antebellum slavery and postbellum servitude. Like other sociocultural narratives

Fig. 2.8 One of Elizabeth Shippen Green's illustrations for "Whispering Leaves: Part I," *Harper's Monthly Magazine* 146, no. 872 (January 1923): 149. Courtesy of Special Collections, Tampa Library, University of South Florida.

produced to enforce white male supremacy, mammy narratives are fictionalized accounts of southern Black women caring for white children, but the dissemination of these stories was purposefully constructed as nonfiction. In fact, stories written by southern white women about their Black female caretakers in the late nineteenth and early twentieth centuries provide strikingly similar accounts of Black women devoted to white children.[21] Julia Neely Finch's handwritten sketch, "An Old-Time Southern 'Mammy.' (A Picture from Real Life.)," for example, provides a late-nineteenth-century account of her relationship with her Black caretaker almost identical to Glasgow's depictions of Mammy Lizzie Jones in *The Woman Within*.[22] A writer from Alabama, Finch creates a portrait of a virtuous woman, well kempt, pious, and content to stand "many years [over] a cradle" for generations of white children.[23] Just as Glasgow's pines for Mammy Lizzie, Finch concludes sentimentally, "But ah! I pity the children that are not to know it and knowing, to love! . . . But in our hearts she hath this 'old time Southern mammy' monument and memory perpetual."[24]

In *Black Feminist Thought* (1990), Patricia Hill Collins rightly indicts the perpetuation of stereotypical images of Black women, such as mammy narratives, asserting that "elite groups, in exercising power, manipulate ideas about Black womanhood . . . by exploiting already existing symbols, or creating new ones" (76). Glasgow scholarship suggests that her fiction employs these racial stereotypes, and textual evidence from "Whispering Leaves" supports these arguments.[25] Uncle Moab describes African Americans as superstitious. The second (white male) carriage driver explains Mammy Rhody's faithfulness by saying, "Darkeys are like that, I reckon. A vow's a vow" (162–63).[26] Effie contemplates that as she is "beginning to discover, time and space are the flimsiest abstractions in the imagination of the negro" (154). And Glasgow replaces Mammy Rhody's white handkerchief in the magazine version of the story with a red turban in *The Shadowy Third*, invoking nineteenth- and early twentieth-century portrayals that exaggerate stereotypical representations of African Americans.

By writing Mammy Rhody as a ghost, however, Glasgow leaves a space to revise archetypal constructions of the quintessential mammy to make visible racial and gender injustices. Mammy Rhody's character embodies both the supernatural and racial Other.[27] Unable to speak, Mammy Rhody uses alternate forms of communication such as the gaze order to construct an "inaudible language" in which to communicate with Effie (172). Mammy

Rhody intervenes to save Pell's puppy, Wop, when his stepmother, Mrs. Blanton, sends him to be drowned. Finally, the ghost saves Pell from the fire that destroys Whispering Leaves (figure 2.9). In *Figures of the Hero in Southern Narrative* (1987), Michael Kreyling asserts that the construction of southern narrative relies on a familiar "hero," or the white male figure who acts as "the linchpin of [the] powerful social, historical, and psychological myth" of the Old South (11). However, Glasgow's novels, Kreyling contends, dismantle this heroic narrative—an argument applicable to a collective reading of her stories (76–79).

In "Whispering Leaves," Glasgow writes Mammy Rhody's Otherness as visible, heroic power. The story begins as a romanticized plantation scene, drawing on the faithful slave narrative tradition, and ends in the annihilation of the plantation home by fire and Mammy Rhody's emancipation from its landscape. The fire destroys both the plantation home (a symbol of slavery) and the mammy figure (an archetype for enslaved Black women), even though Mammy Rhody's disappearance into a spiral of smoke, as portrayed in the fourth illustration of the story in *Harper's Magazine*, does not indicate a physical death because she was always phantasmal. She resembles more "shape," as the caption describes Effie's observations of Pell's rescue, than human figure. Her disappearance forces the socially constructed narrative, produced and perpetuated to maintain racial tyranny, to conclude. Both the symbol of oppression and its archetype are eliminated from the collective narrative vision in the final ghost story of *The Shadowy Third*.

Glasgow's elimination of Mammy Rhody's symbolic existence in "Whispering Leaves" cannot speak for the author's views on race, which were more complex than the ending of the story implies. Influenced by the sociocultural constructions regarding expectations of Black-white relations in the South, which continued to assume racial inferiority and prescribed a fixed place for African Americans in society (see Williamson 5–7), her position may have been benevolent, but it did not champion equality. In December 1925, Glasgow describes to her friend Cabel Tutwiler her recent charity visit to the Afro-American Home for Old Folks. She brought a large Christmas turkey roasted by her African American servant, James, and thought "it was so pathetic to see those old colored people and they have so little done for them, and are not in the Community Fund. They sang for us, some of them over ninety, and all the old school."[28] While *pathetic* conveys sympathy, *old school* indicates that this sympathy was reserved for Black men and women

Fig. 2.9 One of Elizabeth Shippen Green's illustrations for "Whispering Leaves: Part II," *Harper's Monthly Magazine* 146, no. 873 (February 1923): 341. Courtesy of Special Collections, Tampa Library, University of South Florida.

who continued to embrace an attitude of servitude. Glasgow also mentions that the grave of her caretaker, Lizzie Jones, is unattended and that she has employed a man to put a marker on it. Glasgow does not regularly frequent the Afro-American Home for Old Folks or Jones's grave; they represent geographic boundaries defined by racial difference—boundaries that Glasgow refuses to traverse except in charity, even when these places include her beloved Jones. Glasgow may sympathize with African Americans' plight in the 1920s, but she does so only as long as they follow "old school" societal expectations and from a distance.

In "Whispering Leaves," Mammy Rhody's disappearance from the text represents a permanent absence, without possibility of (supernatural) resurrection. On the one hand, this emancipates her representative body from the master narrative that confines her to servitude in both life and death. On the other hand, the story's ending suggests that the source of Mammy Rhody's apparitional power derives from her faithful protection of Pell. If it is no longer necessary for Mammy Rhody to enact her role, the story implies that it is better for her not to exist at all.

Her presence positions the reader as a witness to her suffering, but her permanent disappearance does not signal the end of her perpetual construction, since Mammy Rhody's removal from the narrative does not constitute emancipation from subjection. Being oppressed, as bell hooks points out, means "the absence of choices" (5). Manipulating ideas about Black womanhood, such as portraying African American women figures with "mythical power and strength" and "exploiting already existing symbols or creating new ones," draws on stereotypes as a form of power gained through exploitations (hooks 5, 13; Collins 76).

Glasgow's arrangement of these stories deconstructs sentiment and romanticism to give white women access to intellectual independence. A ghostly character or idea embodies the imponderable and possesses the power to reside within and outside of the shadows. These shadows provide spaces for supernatural (and nonsupernatural) characters to disrupt the tyranny of prescriptive narratives. Feminist geographer Gillian Rose contends that these kinds of spaces are paradoxical, created to overcome distinctions between mind and body, to distinguish between real and metaphorical, and to resist the separation of experience from emotion in the interpretation of places (258–59). Paradoxical space constitutes a "position of being both prisoner and exile, both within and without," which may or may not remain emancipatory (271–72). The ghosts in *The Shadowy Third* orchestrate their own appearances and disappearances, allowing them to permeate sociospatial boundaries that transcend political confinement.

Apparitions' movements between life and death represent the ability to negotiate descriptive delineations of geography, meaning that these ghosts control not only their visibility but also their self-constructed spaces. In "The Shadowy Third," Dorothea relies on Miss Randolph's narrative presence to tell her story, but even if she finds vindication in Doctor Maradick's death, she cannot escape the victimization that rendered her a ghost. In "Dare's Gift," Mildred Beckwith's resistance remains contextually bound to a narrative of betrayal that is maintained by her husband's and Dr. Lakeby's control of the story. In "The Past," Mrs. Vanderbridge and Miss Wrenn denounce the first wife's ghostly presence by burning her letters, but the story does not indicate whether Mr. Vanderbridge abandoned his preoccupation with a romanticized past. Finally, in "Whispering Leaves," Mammy Rhody emancipates herself by delivering Pell to Effie during the fire, but Pell's father remains the patriarch of the remnants of the Whispering Leaves plantation.

"Whispering Leaves" ends with the destruction of the plantation home but not with Mammy Rhody's ability to articulate injustice. When she disappears from the setting (and the text), she relinquishes her apparition status. No longer a ghost, she ceases to occupy this paradoxical space. Instead, we witness the removal of her apparitional body as well as her resistance. Even as Glasgow magnifies gender inequality in *The Shadowy Third*, white supremacist ideology remains embedded in her stories because she does not deconstruct the intersecting oppressions of race and class that inform this inequality.

Places for Shadows

Scholars have devoted little attention to the question of how Glasgow selected and organized the seven stories for her collection. Some observers argue that she included only stories that had been published previously in quality magazines. Both Meeker and James Colvert argue that Glasgow strategically chose magazines for her work: she "knew from the very beginning precisely what she thought about her talent, the medium best suited to it, and the kind of audience she wanted for it. Proper audience . . . meant an intelligent, discriminating audience. [This] govern[ed] a number of her opinions and decisions" (Colvert 177–78). Glasgow's focus on quality magazines may account for exclusion of her first published story, "Between Two Shores" (which appeared in *McClure's Magazine* in February 1899), "Thinking Makes It So" (*Good Housekeeping*, February 1917), and "The Artless Age" (*Saturday Evening Post*, August 25, 1923, though the latter may not have been completed until *The Shadowy Third* was in press. But this argument does not account for the inclusion of "The Past," which had appeared in *Good Housekeeping*.

McClure's, like *Good Housekeeping*, included copious amounts of advertising and focused on domestic-related nonfiction more than poetry and fiction. *McClure's* began as one of the "cheap class periodicals" and eventually prospered with serializations. The early *McClure's* was known for Ida M. Tarbell's serialized investigative journalism, which led to her publication of *The History of the Standard Oil Company* in 1904; its scientific articles; its emphasis on locomotives in stories and features; its articles on wild animals and exploration; and its stress on personalities (Mott, *History* 4:590–92). In 1902, *McClure's* editorial positioning changed, and it became known for its articles on corruption, such as the oil industry and labor union "rackets" (597–98). "Between Two Shores" was published right before the magazine's focus shifted.[29]

Meeker considers it "odd" that Glasgow did not publish "Jordan's End," the final story in the collection, in a magazine and speculates that she may have been "too absorbed in *Barren Ground* and *The Shadowy Third* collection to publish it elsewhere first" (Glasgow, *Collected Stories* 216). This conjecture aligns itself with scholarship maintaining that *The Shadowy Third* was a literary exercise for writing *Barren Ground* (Raper, "Invisible" 66–90; Goodman 159).

Correspondence demonstrates that Glasgow thought of her collection as more than an exercise and that she lobbied to include stories from it in a future compilation of her works. According to Meeker, only two letters survive that explicitly reference *The Shadowy Third*. The first letter was written to Joseph Hergesheimer on January 7, 1924, and sent to him with a copy of the American first edition of *The Shadowy Third* (Meeker 8). Meeker discovered the second letter pasted in a copy of *The Shadowy Third* at the University of Virginia's Alderman Library. In this letter, Glasgow writes to Mrs. Robert C. Taylor on February 8, 1924, "it makes me happy that you love my Shadowy Third stories. They are very near to my heart, those stories, and I lived in that atmosphere when I was writing them" (qtd. in Meeker 8). I have located a third letter, written on August 19, 1937, and archived at the University of Florida in the Marjorie Kinnan Rawlings Papers. Glasgow requests that Maxwell Perkins, the editor of the *Virginia Edition of the Works of Ellen Glasgow* at Charles Scribner's Sons, include "several good short stories" from *The Shadowy Third*.[30] While Perkins declined, citing Scribner's preference for including novels, this letter complicates prior assumptions about her lack of long-term interest in the collected stories. Moreover, it provides another example of her insistent authorial control.

Glasgow and Perkins corresponded frequently during the production of the *Virginia Edition*, particularly regarding the selection and ordering of texts. Perkins first suggests the possibility of reprinting a collection of Glasgow's novels on August 18, 1937, with the idea that they would be issued in chronological order, that each volume would include a preface and frontispiece, and that they would be called either the Old North State or the Virginia edition."[31] Glasgow accepts Perkins's offer in her August 19, 1937, letter but revises his suggestions, including how she would like the volumes organized.[32] Between August and November 1937, Glasgow chose the title, selected all of the frontispieces, wrote prefaces, designated the edition to be used for reprinting, ordered the arrangement of volumes, commented on editing mistakes, and insisted on correcting her own proofs.[33] "*It will be necessary*," she stresses, "*for me to see the proof of the prefaces*."[34] Despite the fact that the early volumes of the collection either were in press or had already been issued, she changed the arrangement of the novels, writing to Perkins on October 26, 1937, that she was "inclined to think that [she] might have a better arrangement of the volume."[35] Perkins agreed, albeit reluctantly since the decision delayed production.[36] These letters collectively support Meeker's assertion that Glasgow usually "had her way" with her publishers and editors (7).

While a dearth of definitive evidence testifies to Glasgow's selection and organization of *The Shadowy Third*, Glasgow's correspondence with Perkins about the *Virginia Edition* demonstrates her business acumen and insistence of agency in each step of the publishing process that would not have been isolated to this publication.[37] In the prefaces written for her *Virginia Edition* novels (1938) and collected in *A Certain Measure: An Interpretation of Prose Fiction* (1938), Glasgow writes that "the right arrangement of parts may bring out latent and unsuspected possibilities in the simplest scene or situation" (17). The "right arrangement" was integral to Glasgow's design of *The Shadowy Third* (table 2.1).

Table 2.1: Publication History of Stories in Ellen Glasgow's *The Shadowy Third and Other Stories* (1923)

Title (page numbers)	Original Magazine Publication
"The Shadowy Third" (3–46)	*Scribner's Magazine* 60, no. 6 (December 1916): 659–71
"Dare's Gift" (47–106)	Part I: *Harper's Monthly Magazine* 134, no. 801 (February 1917): 322–30 Part II: *Harper's Monthly Magazine* 134, no. 802 (March 1917): 515–24
"The Past" (107–50)	*Good Housekeeping* 71 (October 1920): 64–66, 155, 157–64
"Whispering Leaves" (151–200)	Part I: *Harper's Monthly Magazine* 146, no. 872 (January 1923): 147–57 Part II: *Harper's Monthly Magazine* 146, no. 873 (February 1923): 334–43
"A Point in Morals" (201–24)	*Harper's New Monthly Magazine* 98, no. 588 (May 1899): 976–82
"The Difference" (225–64)	*Harper's Monthly Magazine* 147, no. 877 (June 1923): 28–42
"Jordan's End" (265–91)	not published previously

Note: The first four stories are examined in this chapter.

The first four stories feature ghosts and supernatural events, connecting the physical and metaphysical to expose injustices toward women. Their chronological ordering according to their magazine publication dates suggests that they were written sequentially. The only illustration in the collection, Dorothea's ghost from the title story, positions the reader to witness her victimization. Each story's ghost increasingly resists prescriptive narratives, so that by the conclusion of "Whispering Leaves," Mammy Rhody's struggle allows her to rescue Pell from the cruelty that afflicted Dorothea in "The Shadowy Third."

The New York and Virginia settings reinforce this arrangement by alternating primary geographic locations between stories while also integrating relationships between these settings within each of the four stories. In "The Shadowy Third," most of the story takes place at Doctor Maradick's home, on New York City's Fifth Avenue. Miss Randolph is a nurse from Richmond, Virginia, and her cousin, Miss Hemphill, is the supervising nurse at the New York hospital where Doctor Maradick is a surgeon. "Dare's Gift" is set on the ancestral planation by that name near Richmond, while Harold and Mildred Beckwith are from New York. "The Past" is set in New York, but both Miss

Wrenn and the second Mrs. Vanderbridge are originally from Richmond, and she hires Miss Wrenn as her secretary based on the counsel of a friend from Richmond. Finally, in "Whispering Leaves," Effie travels from New York to Richmond, where she discovers that she can visit her mother's childhood home, Whispering Leaves, by taking a train and carriage to Rappahannock, Virginia.

Most of Glasgow's fiction portrays this geographic movement between New York and Virginia, but no other example features such systematic ties between the two settings as *The Shadowy Third*. One explanation for her choice of settings is biographical. Raised in Richmond, Glasgow traveled to New York when she "needed a place to breathe . . . where she could lose herself in the crowd" (Goodman 122). Her progressive deafness eliminated the option of expatriation like other American writers. New York became her "compromise, a place close to Richmond by train but a world apart" where she could be "an exquisite stranger" living in self-imposed exile (Goodman 122). After her father's death in early 1916, she returned permanently to Richmond's 1 West Main Street.

As a southern writer drawing on her experiences in Virginia and New York, Glasgow understood the power of social constructions of place to either perpetuate or deconstruct narrative. Social constructions of place, according to geographer Tim Cresswell, connect one's sense of identity to geographic location in ways that both "make the world meaningful" and assume a "context of power" from this meaning (*Place* 19). Approximately fifty years before new southern studies scholars would argue similarly, Glasgow viewed place as more idea than geography. In *The Shadowy Third*, she alternates northern and southern settings to make injustice universally visible while incorporating a chronological narrative framework to blend rather than magnify geographical distinctions.

Early critics comprehended the significance of the collection's arrangement. An October 28, 1923, *New York Times* review asserts that Glasgow's emphasis on visibility as a device makes "the dead who continue to live in the memory assume at times a visual form" (Scura 227). Two months later, the *Greensboro Daily News* describes how "each story is in itself complete, but the seven are gathered together quite evidently because they all bear on the supposed fact that there is some great force operating in the world around us" (231). The review goes on to claim that Glasgow "presents her own belief that this power works through the fact that ideas once definitely and strikingly resolved into action do not die but manifest themselves still living long after the individual who put his own compelling ideas into vivid action has ceased to live" (231–32). In the *New York Evening Post*, Rebecca Lowrie points to the strength of the first four stories' connections but finds the last three stories "less effective than the others" (228). Critics emphasize how Glasgow's ghost stories make visible ideas about power, or forces operating in the world around us.

Glasgow contributed to political movements—the Equal Suffrage League of Virginia, an anticensorship advisory role on the Richmond Library Board, and the founding of the Society for the Prevention of Cruelty to Animals in Richmond—but after 1916, she did not envision herself as a political activist.[38] Instead, she used her fiction to claim that injustice could be prevented through "revolt from sentimentality, less because it was false than because it was cruel" (*WW* 104). As she reflects on her contributions to the southern literary tradition, Glasgow determines that her work constitutes a rebellion against "southern sentimental fallacy" (*Certain* 14). She sympathizes with victims of tyranny and conveys this sympathy to her readers. Glasgow seeks to illuminate social injustices toward women, to eradicate cruelty, and to advocate for women's intellectual independence.

3

Preserving the Hammock in Marjorie Kinnan Rawlings's *When the Whippoorwill* (1940)

On November 17, 1945, Ellen Glasgow wrote to her friend and contemporary Marjorie Kinnan Rawlings to thank her for a gift of citrus fruit and to explain that she could not accept an invitation to visit Florida due to her rapidly deteriorating health. Glasgow ended the letter by conveying admiration for Rawlings's work and offering words of encouragement: "Do not give up. . . . You have great gifts. My love to you always" (*Perfect Companionship* 253). Their mutual friend and fellow writer James Branch Cabell sat near Glasgow as she penned the letter. It was the last letter that Glasgow wrote before her death four days later.

Rawlings and Glasgow first met in April 1941, and the meeting, according to Cabell was "a tremendous hit." Glasgow informed Cabell that the two writers had "figuratively, let down our hair and babbled out our pasts to each other without any auctorial embellishments" during the visit. Cabell laments, "If only I could have been privileged to sit by and blush in silence!"[1] The women, as Rawlings's biographer Elizabeth Silverthorne contends, "found they had much in common in their backgrounds and in their emotional sensitivity. . . . [T]hey each had sharp antennae for detecting hypocrisy and deplored social injustice" (193). In addition, Silverthorne suggests, Rawlings, like Glasgow, preferred to participate in social reform initiatives through nonpolitical means. The writers corresponded frequently and intimately for the remainder of Glasgow's life.

As the title of Ashley Andrews Lear's book indicates, Rawlings and Glasgow enjoyed a "remarkable kinship," and they were aware of the connections between their work: as Glasgow writes to Rawlings on May 30, 1940, even before they had met in person, "Superficially, our aims and our material would seem so divergent that one could not conceive of common ground. Yet, . . . it seems to me possible that our object has been more or less identical: to present human beings, as you know one type and I another, struggling against whatever is inimical within themselves or in their background" (Lear, *Remarkable* 2).

Their writings focus on the universal human struggle despite the fact that their biographies include experiences that lend themselves to more differences than similarities in perspective. Both Glasgow and Rawlings identified with their southern lineage. Glasgow was raised as a Richmond, Virginia, southern aristocrat; after residing in New York for some time, she eventually returned to her childhood home. She did not attend college. Rawlings, born almost a generation later, grew up in Washington, DC, and graduated with a degree in English from the University of Wisconsin. She benefited from a formal education, married twice, and resided in rural Florida. She met her first husband, Charles Rawlings, during college, and they worked as journalists. In November 1928, they moved to Cross Creek, Florida, hoping to support their writing careers by growing citrus (Silverthorne 12–28, 55–56).

Rural and isolated Cross Creek provided the inspiration and independence that Marjorie Kinnan Rawlings needed to write and publish successfully. As she wrote to a friend on January 6, 1931, she chose to remain at Cross Creek when Chuck traveled for work assignments. "*Scribner's* had already accepted two stories," Rawlings explains, "and I wanted to get more done while the iron was hot."[2] *Scribner's* acceptance of "Cracker Chidlings: Real Tales from the Florida Interior" and "Jacob's Ladder" marked the beginning of her recognition as a Florida writer. While her marriage to Chuck Rawlings eventually ended, Rawlings's life in the hammock, the term Cross Creek residents used to describe the region's scrubland, sustained her professionally and personally throughout most of her life (figure 3.1).

Fig. 3.1 Marjorie Kinnan Rawlings with her dog, ca. 1940, the year *When the Whippoorwill* was published. Courtesy of State Library and Archives of Florida.

Maxwell Perkins, the editor at Charles Scribner's Sons who eventually introduced Rawlings and Glasgow, first noticed Rawlings's work in *Scribner's Magazine*. Recognized as one of the most prominent editors of the first half of the twentieth century from his work with F. Scott Fitzgerald, Ernest Hemingway, Thomas Wolfe, and Eudora Welty, Perkins cultivated professional and personal relationships with his authors (see Berg). In contrast to Glasgow's tumultuous relationships with Walter Hines Page and Frank Nelson Doubleday, Perkins's approach to editing was collaborative and congenial. He was impressed with Rawlings's ability to "blend fact into fiction," and in a letter written almost a decade after their collaboration began, he assured her that "nobody's writing could interest me more deeply."[3] He encouraged her to write "about what she knew, what was intimate to her" (Rodger Tarr 24), encouragement that produced her first novel, *South Moon Under* (1933), which she developed from her early stories. Until his death in 1947, Perkins continued to recommend that she write short fiction as a starting point for her novels and, at Rawlings's request, offered detailed suggestions regarding future projects (Berg 401). It was Perkins's idea to collect her early stories in the first and only short story collection published during her lifetime, *When the Whippoorwill* (1940) (Rodger Tarr 7).

The textual history of *When the Whippoorwill* demonstrates a progressive depiction of female protagonists on the early twentieth-century Florida frontier. Rawlings uses her selection and arrangement of stories in this collection to position Quincey Dover, her most vocal protagonist and narrator, as representative of the strength and perseverance of the Florida Cracker culture. Writing to the editor of *Scribner's Magazine*, Alfred Dashiell, in March 1930, Rawlings confided, "There seems to me something so moving in these lives in the Florida interior, that I felt that fault surely would lie with me, if I could not make them alive in print" (Rawlings, *Selected Letters* 36–37). Florence Turcotte and Elizabeth Silverthorne rightly argue that Rawlings sought to connect readers to Florida's natural environment, but as C. Anita Tarr contends, her desire to preserve the Florida interior constitutes as much an ethnographic impetus as an environmental one. Rawlings sought to use her literary representations to capture the relationships between a diminishing wilderness and culture.

The concept of wilderness as both an idea and geographic place evolved between the colonization of America and the early twentieth century. As Roderick Frazier Nash examines in *Wilderness and the American Mind* (2001), colonists constructed their perception of civilization out of a wilderness, or geographic place untouched by modern civilization. Initially fearing its unknowns, they sought to conquer the early frontier, but by the end of the nineteenth century, Americans viewed the wilderness as a place in need of protection from the "self-destructive tendencies of civilization" confirmed by industrialization (xi–xiv, 108; see also Buell, *Future*; Buell, *Environmental*).[4] The first examples of wilderness preservation legislation were enacted in March 1872 for Yellowstone National Park, with further legislation protecting New York's Adirondack Mountains a decade later (see Jacoby). The first Wilderness Society was formed in 1935 (Nash 206), during the same period in which Rawlings was writing the stories that were included in *When the Whippoorwill.*

Rawlings's ideas about the Florida wilderness would have been influenced by this ideological shift. In fact, her desire to convey the Florida wilderness's beauty to readers drove her literary production. In a manuscript fragment that includes her notes for a speech on "The Relativity of Beauty," Rawlings explains that she originally had "intended to read" from *South Moon Under* because she did not think that she had "anything of value to say" but then discovered that passages in the novel "illustrated the place of beauty in the life of the Florida backwoods people." Crossing out the word "determination" and replacing it with "longing," Rawlings writes, "it is in [a writer's] fierce longing to make the intangible beauty, tangible."[5] Rawlings, as Edna Saffy concludes, wrote and revised to best articulate the beauty she recognized within "the interaction of the Florida Cracker with the natural environment" (112–13).

Like Glasgow's collection, Rawlings's short story collection followed her successful novels, such as *South Moon Under* (1933), *Golden Apples* (1935), and *The Yearling* (1938), which won the 1939 Pulitzer Prize for fiction. Also like Glasgow, Rawlings sought to place her stories in quality magazines; however, as her popularity grew, she became increasingly frustrated as the magazines "pester[ed] her about stories and articles and she hated it." She insisted that she "could not and would not write to order" (Silverthorne 154). Her literary agent, Carl Brandt, often pressed her for more stories, warning her against becoming completely dependent on Charles Scribner and Maxwell Perkins.[6] Nevertheless, she increasingly relied on her personable and collaborative relationship with Perkins.

When the Whippoorwill was published in 1940, following the end of the Great Depression, the beginning of World War II, and the publication of *The Yearling*. The collection had been delayed in press due to Rawlings's illness, and she worried that it would not be well received or that it might detract from *The Yearling*'s sales (*MM* 353–454). Both Scribner and Perkins worked to allay her concerns. On January 17, 1940, Scribner admits that the war meant that the publisher could continue its advertising expenditures on *The Yearling* but explains that the firm would "combine it with the advertising of the stories to good effect." He continues, "There is not a question in my mind but that the publication of your stories this spring will help rather than detract from the sale of *The Yearling*. . . . [I]t makes a natural peak between the earlier editions and the popular priced edition we plan for the fall."[7] Scribner was correct. *When the Whippoorwill* was a success.[8]

The short story collection contains eleven tales, all published previously in *Scribner's Magazine*, *Harper's Monthly Magazine*, or the *Saturday Evening Post*. Four of the stories—"A Crop of Beans," "Jacob's Ladder," "Gal Young Un," and "Cocks Must Crow"—demonstrate how her selection and arrangement of stories for the volume depict a progression toward female narration. "A Crop of Beans," which opens the volume, describes a sharecropping family's struggle to find independence. While protagonist Lige Gentry eventually cultivates a successful crop of beans, his prosperity is short-lived, and his wife, Drenna, must forgo her desires to keep her family from financial ruin. "Jacob's Ladder," the third story in the collection, was originally published as a short novel in *Scribner's Magazine*. It constitutes a bildungsroman about the lives of fictional characters Mart and Florry, who struggle to find work and a home on the Florida frontier. "Gal Young Un," the seventh tale from *When the Whippoorwill* and winner of a 1932 O. Henry Prize, depicts the strength and resilience of female protagonist Mattie Syles, who drives her moonshining husband off her property with a rifle during the story's conclusion. Finally, "Cocks Must Crow," the last story of the collection and the third tale narrated by protagonist Quincey Dover, portrays how a wife comes to accept her husband's need for independence.[9]

One reviewer favorably compared *When the Whippoorwill* to work by other southern luminaries, writing that Rawlings makes "these poverty-stricken, inarticulate, earthy folk as interesting as members of the Sorbonne. . . . As a regional writer she may lack Ellen Glasgow's profundity. Yet she is as lively and as funny as Erskine Caldwell, without getting as nasty; and she catches the Southern vernacular with Faulkner's fidelity, while her in-between passages make a lot more sense than his."[10] But Rawlings did not want her writing to be compared with works like Caldwell's *Tobacco Road* (1932). In the manuscript for a 1935 speech, she writes, "I'm always horrified when someone . . . speaks of the characters in [*South Moon Under*] as degenerate, and compares them with the hideous characters of such a book as *Tobacco Road*. . . . I always feel that I've failed completely as an artist when I've left anyone with a sense of ugliness."[11]

Even when she viewed comparisons to contemporary writers as complimentary, Rawlings rejected the categorization of her work as regional (Rodger Tarr 1). In a 1940 essay, Rawlings calls regional writing "not even a decent bastard" and "a betrayal of that region" (Rawlings, "Regional" 384). In this genre, "speech and customs are turned inside out for the gaze of the curious," while the people represented in these fictional portrayals "are held up naked, not as human begins, but as literary specimens" (384). Rawlings aligns regional writing with contemporary definitions of "local color."

Almost a century later, Judith Fetterley and Marjorie Pryse distinguish between local color and regional writing in *Writing out of Place: Regionalism, Women, and American Literary Culture* (2005), asserting that writers "who accept the assumptions of the regionalizing premise" should be associated with "local color," whereas writers who take exception to these assumptions should be categorized as regionalist writers (7). Rawlings demanded that her writing not be categorized as regional (in the sense that regional writing's sole purpose is to magnify the peculiarities of a place's culture), since she viewed her novels and stories as merely set in a particular region that serves as a "fitting background for the particular thoughts or emotions that cry out for articulation" of "the inner revelation of mankind" (Rawlings, "Regional" 385). Her intentional use of the Florida interior's wilderness was designed to convey her observations and insights about humanity.

Fetterley and Pryse argue that women writers use region to "create texts that can be read as autoethnographies by writing from the inside out" (117). In this light, Rawlings's work constitutes regional literature. She wrote of the Florida wilderness as both participant (a resident at Cross Creek) and observer (a writer conveying universal meaning). Moreover, she portrays geographic setting and human interaction as interdependent. Her preservation initiatives, therefore, are motivated by connections between ecology and ethnography. As she writes in "The Relativity of Beauty," Rawlings finds the people living in the Florida interior "beautiful" because "they are an integral part of their background. . . . They are not conscious of being courageous. They joke about hunger and death. But they are distinctly conscious of their harmony with their surroundings." She uses her fiction to demonstrate this beauty of survival to readers, asking, "What hope is there for any writer to pass on the particular beauty that happens to stir him? It is in his fierce longing to make intangible beauty, tangible."[12] Reminiscent of other 1930s artists' work, such as Dorothea Lange's photographs of rural workers for the Farm Security Administration and James Agee and Walker Evans's stories of three sharecropper families in *Let Us Now Praise Famous Men* (1941), Rawlings sought to record the Florida Cracker culture before that way of life disappeared.

The social history of the term *Cracker* remains contentious. Janisse Ray explains that her use of it in her first book, *The Ecology of a Cracker Childhood* (1999), "comes at a great price and part of it is the racial connotations and class connotations that are wrapped up with it" (interview 19:17–19:34). Rawlings did not intend for her use of *Florida Cracker* to be read as derogatory. Instead, in the words of anthropologists Mozell C. Hill and Bevode C. McCall, she viewed "cracker culture" as a subtype of southern regional culture distinguished by geography, social organization, and the "rationale that supports and gives meaning to the culture" (45). Primarily located in southeastern Georgia and north-central Florida, Florida Crackers were associated with living in the Florida interior, raising wild hogs and cattle, growing corn, and hunting and fishing. This culture formed the majority of Florida's white antebellum population during the nineteenth century.[13]

In an environment in which a group of people struggled to obtain daily sustenance, southern archetypal constraints for women, such as "true womanhood" and "southern lady," may have been desired by Florida Cracker men but proved impractical. As a result, Rawlings's female characters are neither mired in nineteenth-century true womanhood tropes like Caroline Compson in Faulkner's *The Sound and the Fury* (1929) nor revised as fallen archetypes like Ellie May in Caldwell's *Tobacco Road* (1932). Instead, Rawlings selects and arranges the stories in *When the Whippoorwill* to portray the inherent strength and endurance of Florida Cracker women. Rawlings's arrangement features protagonists—Drenna in "A Crop of Beans," Florry in "Jacob's Ladder," Mattie in "Gal Young Un," and Quincey Dover in "Cocks Must Crow"—who progressively deconstruct the southern female archetype to narrate their own stories. Rawlings celebrates their "bravery and fortitude, and she made fictional heroes out of them, most notably Quincey Dover, whose feminist antics and strength in adversity served as an emblem for the women at Cross

Creek" (Rawlings and Baskin 6). By envisioning herself as an ethnographer, Rawlings makes visible the previously obscured strength and determination of the Florida Cracker woman. She preserves a way of life through her literary representations of it and thus teaches readers how to appreciate its beauty.

Florida Cracker Culture

Writing from the Florida frontier on July 14, 1838, Ellen Brown, a native of Portsmouth, New Hampshire, offers a rare nondisparaging record of a nineteenth-century Florida Cracker woman's words: Brown tells her brother, Mannevillette, "I must give you an idea of the way people are . . . in this part of the world." She continues, "At a cracker wedding the other evening when it came to the bride's turn to respond instead of the usual 'I will' . . . she ejaculated 'I won't.' The justice supposing there must be some misunderstanding on her part repeated but she again astonished the company with 'I won't. I told you I would not before' and took her seat—determined not to obey!" Brown added, "I pray the example spread" (Aldrich and Anderson 87–89). Accounts of Florida Cracker culture in the 1800s primarily originated from correspondence written by aristocratic northern women or from US soldiers during the Civil War and Reconstruction.[14] Typical portrayals were critical, situating the Florida Cracker as antithetical to the plantation society of the American South. As Ellen Brown tells her brother on January 31, 1837, Crackers are "made of clay, indeed the idea of having a likeness taken is too ridiculous to mention. . . . They are the most squalid miserable creatures in the world" (Aldrich and Anderson xxiv). During the 1880s, Julia Daniels Moseley, a midwesterner who relocated to Florida with her husband for the warmer climate, compares Crackers' appearances to "dogs—lean, old, starved, sly": they "do not create a smile [and] take all the mirth out of life and leave only pity and horror" (39).

In the most comprehensive scholarship on the formation of early Florida as one of the last planter-like socioeconomic regions in the South, *Creating the Old South: Middle Florida's Plantation Fronter before the Civil War* (2002), historian Edward Baptist explains that Cracker women were not part of the plantation elite. While Baptist admits that differentiating between planter and nonplanter whites can be difficult, he argues that men who owned ten or fewer slaves had to work with their hands. Those who owned additional slaves and managed labor had "time to dream bigger dreams" about Florida's plantation frontier and possessed the power to "shape the reality . . . along the rough lines of their visions" (17).

Aristocratic southern womanhood was constructed as part of a patriarchal familial structure bolstered by slavery and consisting of qualities like submissiveness, innocence, piousness, and devotion (Scott 3–6). Florida frontier women had to be self-sufficient, cultivating the land alongside their fathers, husbands, and sons while also maintaining the home, raising children, and tending livestock. They could not enact the fictional constructs of "southern belle" and "southern lady" associated with the plantation elite.[15] Instead, their traditionally masculine work afforded opportunities to defy gender social norms for recreation. Correspondence written by northern women described Florida Cracker women as openly consuming alcohol, verbally challenging authority, and (most damning of all) using tobacco. These portrayals connected abject poverty to deviant behavior. Compared to the archetypal southern plantation woman, as historian Tracy Revels asserts, the Cracker woman was considered an "unsexed creature [without] any trace of womanly virtue or beauty" and with "ignorance stamped on [her] as plainly as though written with pen or pencil" (8, 126). Outside of the Florida frontier (and sometimes within it), Cracker women were viewed as disdained objects from a subordinate class and gender.

Nonetheless, and perhaps more than anywhere else in the antebellum South, nineteenth-century Florida offered white men and women an opportunity to transcend class. Settlement dramatically increased after the end of the Second Seminole War (1835–42), and the planter class remained disproportionate to lower class populations (Baptist 17). In 1850, only 45 people in Florida owned more than 10 slaves, whereas 428 people in other southern states owned 20–100 slaves. The Florida planter comprised "the lowest ranks of the potential planter elite," a potential that enticed nonplanter white men to adopt planter ideology (Revels 6).

Members of the nonplanter class did not work to disassemble the southern planter ideology of superiority based on race, class, and gender. Instead, they hoped to become part of the planter social structure. Since planters viewed masculinity (represented as mastery) and femininity (represented as subordination) as antithetical, nonplanters adopted and exaggerated the "need to reject and resist—by violence, if necessary—the attempts of others to force them into a position of subordination" (Baptist 102). Becoming a man accepted as equal to a planter required a refusal to take orders from another man as his tenant or employee; doing so, "suggested slavery, blackness, and femininity" (42).

In keeping with these observations, Rawlings creates Florida Cracker characters that combine her experiences from Cross Creek with her desire to convey the beauty of a diminishing culture. In an unpublished manuscript, "Notes for a Lecture on Facts vs. Fiction in Writing," she explains how she constructs fictional characters: "Sometimes the true person, the true character, in real life, stirs the writer into wanting to write about him [and] sometimes an idea or an emotion or a situation . . . cries out to be written about."[16] Her selection and arrangement of four previously published magazine stories in *When the Whippoorwill* positions female Florida Cracker characters' voices at the center of a community's interdependence and resiliency. Oppressed by southern aristocratic white male planters (who created a binary system of gender in which a southern woman either embodied a prescribed archetype or was considered unsexed) and suppressed by early Florida Cracker men (who adopted the planter ideology in the hopes of transcending poverty), Rawlings's southern female characters resist archetypal depictions.

The View from the Cockpit

The first story that Rawlings selected for *When the Whippoorwill* illustrates the planter ideology still embedded in 1920s–30s Florida Cracker culture. Rawlings wrote "A Crop of Beans" in the summer of 1931, along with her nonfiction sketch "Cracker Chidlings," which was published in *Scribner's Magazine* before "A Crop of Beans." In a June 30, 1931, letter to Perkins, she reported that "A Crop of Beans" would "probably [be] six to eight thousand words" and that the "material, basically true, is vital, and it will be my own fault if the story isn't good" (*MM* 40–42). She anticipated that the story would take two or three weeks to complete.

Rawlings's magazine publications provide a glimpse into the significant changes that had occurred in the periodical marketplace between the 1890s and the 1930s. After World War I, quality magazines took cost-saving measures, such as eliminating illustrations, and revised their editorial agendas in the hopes of procuring new readership while maintaining loyal subscribers (Mott, *History* 4:729–31). All magazines competed for advertising dollars, radio shows replaced serialized fiction, and stories often ran on nonconsecutive pages. By the end of the 1930s, many periodicals were struggling to survive.

Rawlings's magazine writings coincided with this time of transition. In its January 1932 issue, for instance, *Scribner's Magazine* opened with an editorial announcement that acknowledged the ongoing changes in American culture and the periodical marketplace and described how the magazine had been positioning itself to reach the new audience that had emerged. Three features had been added to the magazine since 1930: a short novel in each issue; a current trends section, "Straws in the Wind"; and accounts of experiences and observations from American life in "Life in the United States." *Scribner's* also confirmed that it would continue to print the "new leaders of American literature" and concluded that the magazine had "created a place distinctly its own, as a timely, brief, sharp commentary on the United States of to-day, on the lives we live, and a field for the new vigorous writers of our time" ("Editorial Announcement" 1).

From 1925 forward, *Scribner's* placed a "greater emphasis on public affairs," but the "downward curve in circulation and advertising that began in 1912 continued" (Mott, *History* 4:732–33). The new editorial policies alienated faithful subscribers, and there were not enough new subscribers to compensate for the exodus. More than fifty years old, *Scribner's Magazine* failed to make a profit in the 1930s and was sold in May 1939. The magazine could not reenvision its place among readers after the first part of the twentieth century (729).

In the early to mid-1930s, however, *Scribner's* editors, Dashiell and Harlan Logan, published emerging American modernists such as Sherwood Anderson, Erskine Caldwell, Langston Hughes, Josephine Herbst, and William Faulkner (Mott, *History* 4:729). Rawlings's "A Crop of Beans" appeared during this time on five consecutive pages in the May 1932 issue. Divided into three sections, the story did not benefit from an introductory illustration (figure 3.2) in the same way that Glasgow's "The Shadowy Third" had included an illustration of a mother embracing her child fifteen years earlier. In fact, the issue contained no illustrations.

In "A Crop of Beans," protagonist Lige Gentry begrudgingly works for Widow Sellers while dreaming of cultivating his own bean crop. He reasons that if he produces a successful crop of beans, he will obtain the independence needed to be a "rale man" (12), or a man more like the planter class

A Crop of Beans

A STORY

By Marjorie Kinnan Rawlings

A TILLIE-HAWK swooped into the top of a dead cypress. The mocking-birds and red-birds that had scurried like wind-buffeted leaves ahead of him, stirred uneasily in the live oaks and palmettos, where they had concealed themselves. The sky had emptied itself for him of living things. Against the blinding blue of the Florida afternoon hung indolent masses of white cloud. The hawk shifted from one claw to the other, hitching his shoulders like a cripple. There ran a road—a fat chicken snake—a man——

The young Cracker swung his shotgun from his waist to his shoulder in a quick semicircle. The tillie-hawk exploded into a mass of buff feathers and tumbled to the edge of the road. The Cracker girl caught her breath.

"Lige!" she reproached him. "You hadn't orter wasted a shell on a ol' tillie-hawk."

A horn sounded behind them and a truck loaded with bean hampers lurched by in the deep ruts of the sand road. Old man Tainter and his Negro driver passed without the customary "Hey!" or lift of the hand. The young woman crowded back into the dry dog-fennel. The man no more than stepped aside, unbreaching his gun. He kicked a cloud of sand after the truck.

"His beans ain't a mite better'n mine. Parts of 'em is plumb sorry-lookin'."

"They're earlier, ain't they?"

"Jest a week. He ain't no more likely to miss frost than me. Ary time, now it's a'most November, we're like to git us one o' them piddlin' leetle ol' frosts don't mean nothin'. To-night, mebbe."

They turned between chinaberries into the Widow Sellers' gate. Her sharp tongue clicked at them from the porch.

"You Lige Gentry, you, how'll I ever git my cane cut? I ain't payin' you by the week reg'lar to traipse around with your wife."

He rose to the familiar bait.

"Dog take it, ol' woman, Drenna's been a-cuttin' cane with me all evenin'. An' who'll pay fer it? Not you. I'll be hornswoggled if you ain't the meanest white woman in the county."

He stamped across the porch. Drenna dropped down on the top step, draping her gray percale skirt across her worn shoes. The widow hunched herself on the cowhide seat of her hickory rocker, drawing her shawl around her shoulders against the chill air from the northwest.

"Ain't you sick o' keepin' Drenna hangin' around where you kin look at her all the day? I ain't done laughin', the way you begun a-courtin' her, like you was huntin' a squirrel goin' acrost a oak thicket an' you tryin' to keep sight of it. How many yares ago was it? Two, three? Anyways, long enough to git you a couple o' young uns. An' you ain't sick o' lookin' at her yit!"

The young Cracker towered over her. He shook back the curly sun-bleached hair from his sweaty forehead like an infuriated bull. He plunged roaring into her trap.

"Dog take you! You ain't fitten to fish the same creek 'longside of her! Drenna, move offen the stoop away from her! You'd orter study on sayin', is she sick o' lookin' at me! A pore sorry thing like me, to git a woman——"

The Widow Sellers rocked violently in sheer delight. Her little black chinquapin eyes danced. She scratched her white head excitedly with a piece of the okra she was cutting. She shrilled above him.

"Now you said it! Now you and me agrees for onct, Mister Gentry! A pore sorry thing like you! Now you're talkin'!"

He stopped short.

"Oh, go to the devil," he said good-naturedly.

Drenna smiled uneasily. The ribald quarrelling of this pair still disturbed her. It was scandalous

Fig. 3.2 First page of Marjorie Kinnan Rawlings's "A Crop of Beans," *Scribner's Magazine* 91, no. 5 (May 1932): 283. Courtesy of Special Collections, Tampa Library, University of South Florida.

than the subservient working class.[17] Humor permeates the dialogue between Lige Gentry and Widow Sellers, satirizing the opening scene.

Caroline Gebhard argues that plantation myth fictions gained "surprising vitality" after Reconstruction, often "employ[ing] humor to deflect the threat of emasculation that arises when men take the place of women and slaves as objects of sentimental identification" (135–36). The opening of Rawlings's tale depicts this humor-masculinity paradigm by revising the traditional gender roles of characters in a plantation scene. Instead of a white male master, Widow Sellers disseminates orders to Lige from her porch. Instead of an African American slave, Lige Gentry, a young white man with a surname that ironically indicates aristocratic lineage, cultivates Widow Sellers's crops for little pay and must accept hand-me-down shoes for his children. Instead of managing the plantation as a matriarch, Lige's wife, Drenna, works alongside him in the fields. Widow Sellers's verbal mockery solidifies the satirical scene, forcing Lige to agree that he is a "pore sorry thing" with "no sense" because "no other man, black or white, would work so hard for [her] at the low wages of six dollars a week" (2–3). Her discourse augments Lige's sense of emasculation and portrays the seemingly traditional plantation scene as ironic.

Lige's inability to escape the scene that confines him derives from his insistence on employing planter ideology to solve present-day problems. He tells a stranger who asks about his occupation, "I'm a bean man!" and asserts that he will become a "rale man" if he can "make . . . crops when nobody else couldn't make 'em" (12). A "rale man," as Lige defines it, embodies independence by working for himself and supporting his family without assistance. Yet when he finally obtains this status after growing a successful crop of beans, he becomes irresponsible, neglectful of his family, and perpetually drunk. As the narrator explains, Lige previously "had been like a wild thing tamed; a 'coon or 'possum or young panther that had come to enjoy captivity. . . . [I]n his prosperity, he had broken out of the cage and was gone, dangling his ropes behind him" (14). A successful bean crop allowed Lige to momentarily escape servitude, but the remnants of his confinement in the metaphorical cage remained with him, a reminder of the planter status that he could never achieve permanently.

To eliminate the planter trope, Lige Gentry must construct a different narrative, but since he is incapable of doing so, the narrator progressively positions Drenna as adept at revising it. Initially referred to as "she" or the "Cracker girl," Drenna's anonymity and objectivity diminish as she increasingly speaks through dialogue and the narrator's descriptions of her inner thoughts. She becomes the key to the family's survival. When Lige feels discouraged, Drenna encourages him to plant another crop. When frost threatens the thriving crop, Drenna suggests that they cover and later uncover six acres of bean plants with soil. When Widow Sellers criticizes Lige for shooting at a tillie-hawk or drinking with the Brinley boys, Drenna defends his actions. Finally, when Lige insists that she deposit all the crop money in the bank, her decision to hold back fifty dollars ensures that they are not destitute after the bank's collapse. Next to the magnified voices of Widow Sellers and Lige, Drenna's relative silence makes the words she speaks especially poignant.

"A Crop of Beans" resembles a parable, and like F. Scott Fitzgerald's *The Great Gatsby* (1925), this parable warns of the inherent fallacies within the American Dream ideology. Lige Gentry achieves success, but it does not provide long-term independence or financial security. Instead, it magnifies the greed and corruption inherent in the community, a microcosm of American society that, as exemplified by the closing of the bank, has recently suffered from the stock market crash of 1929 (see Bauer). Through her depictions of Lige and Drenna, Rawlings seems to suggest that the preservation of the hammock or the Florida Cracker culture at Cross Creek is not about seeking independence but rather involves reliance on a precarious balance between individual and community.

Perhaps indicative of Rawlings's experiences in the Florida frontier, privileging interdependence over independence remains central to the narratives that follow "A Crop of Beans" in *When the Whippoorwill*. By 1931, Rawlings had lived at Cross Creek for three years, was dependent on her citrus production (not her writing) for income, and was struggling with her marriage to Chuck Rawlings; they divorced two years later (Silverthorne 96). To save money, she wrote the manuscript for the third story in the collection, "Jacob's Ladder," on the front and back of a roll of brown paper. Unrolled, the paper stretches approximately fourteen feet.[18]

"Jacob's Ladder" was published in *Scribner's* in April 1931, thirteen months before "A Crop of Beans," with an introduction by Dashiell. The editor calls the story "a real find" that "confirms the great promise shown" in "Cracker Chidlings," which had appeared in the magazine the preceding January, "and brings upon the literary scene a new writer" (Dashiell 1). This appraisal attracted Maxwell Perkins's and Charles Scribner's attention (Rawlings and

Baskin 7). The text for "Jacob's Ladder" was divided into eight sections marked by Roman numerals, corresponding to the work's eight setting changes within the Florida interior. The seven hundred dollars that Rawlings earned for the story allowed her to install an indoor bathroom at Cross Creek. She christened it with a party, complete with ice and drinks in the bathtub and a bouquet of roses in the toilet bowl (Silverthorne 64–65).

Rawlings's financial hardships resonated with most Americans in the early 1930s. Magazines sought to address readers' concerns by printing articles and editorials on the state of the US economy. In an essay that directly follows "Jacob's Ladder," for instance, social economist J. J. Spengler evaluates the results of the 1930 census in "Is America Slowing Up?" Spengler warns against communism and argues for a stationary population growth that will neither exhaust irreplaceable natural resources nor leave industries without a workforce. He concludes that the only way out of economic depression is to reorganize American economic life nationally. "Rugged individualism," Spengler argues, "must give way to national planning" (376).

Government intervention, however, constituted the antithesis of Florida Cracker culture, even though the state's "rugged" population suffered disproportionately during the Great Depression. As historian Elna Green points out in a collection of letters from Florida women in the 1920s and 1930s, the land boom of the 1920s could not be sustained, hurricanes wiped out crops, and the Mediterranean fruit fly damaged agricultural production. In addition, many Floridians remained trapped in "chronic rural poverty," since the state constitution limited the federal government's response (Green 1). As some of the 1.1 million white families who were tenants or sharecroppers in the American South, Rawlings's Cracker characters portray what historian Stuart Kidd describes as a culture that "bred poverty and oppression [but] had also preserved individualism, community, character, and self-sufficiency" (110–12). To the Florida Cracker, the encroachment of urban life would erode access to independence (Berra 3, 12).

Among Rawlings's stories, "Jacob's Ladder" most poignantly depicts the potential threats of this erosion. The tale begins with a description of a square dance attended by drunken Old Jo Leddy. When a fight ensues between Jo's current and previous love interests, his daughter, Florry, attempts to help before being dismissed by her father. She waits outside the dance, and Mart, a young Cracker man, introduces himself. Later, as Florry guides her father home, Mart follows and asks her to leave with him. Mart and Florry embark on a journey of extreme personal and economic loss, in which all of Mart's efforts to financially support them fail. The story concludes after Florry guides him back to where their journey began—her childhood home in the piney woods.

Like Lige Gentry in "A Crop of Beans," Mart practices outdated customs. When he follows Florry home after the dance, his primary concerns involve social protocol. He asks, "Reckon your daddy'll keer, me a-follerin' this way?" and after asking her to leave with him, he inquires further, "What about your daddy?" (51).[19] When Florry suggests that it would be better to leave before her father's drunkenness wears off, Mart insists, "Kin you write out a letter to leave for him?" even though Mart, Florry, and Jo cannot read or write (52). In the third part of the story, a Yankee farmer catches Mart trapping on his land. Mart offers him a portion of the profits and addresses him as an equal, but the farmer refuses to accept this proposal for a gentleman's agreement. Near the end of the story, Mart confides that he recently retrieved his traps as a way to "reassure Cap'n Tack that he was a man with property and good for his bill" (102). His preoccupation with his respectability provides Cap'n Tack with the knowledge of his traps' location, and Cap'n Tack subsequently confiscates the traps to curry favor with the local sheriff.

Each of Mart's work experiences—fishing for Cap'n Tack until Zeke burns the equipment, working as a tenant farmer for the Yankee, fishing on the Gulf of Mexico for Cap'n Harper until the storm destroys his boat, and maintaining a still for Eph Harper until he turns Mart in to the game warden—demonstrates Mart's inability to negotiate socioeconomic and political change. Eph Harper and Cap'n Tack reconstruct work and identity to survive on the new Florida frontier, but Mart cannot. After Cap'n Tack leaves with the traps, Mart tells Florry, "You belong to be skeert a'right. . . . Us been a-climbin' ol' Jacob's ladder thouten no end to it" (110). Masculinity is no longer acquired through planter-class gestures of honor; as Mart's failures demonstrate, on the early twentieth-century Florida frontier, masculinity is defined by individualism, not community—that is, by one's ability to adapt to a changing culture for one's own gain.

Originally called "High Winds," "Jacob's Ladder" developed from Rawlings's experiences at Cross Creek.[20] According to her memoir *Cross Creek* (1942), Florry and Mart are based on an incident early in her time in Florida when Rawlings's misunderstanding of social responsibility and interdependence in Cracker culture led to the departure of a tenant's and his family.

The tenant's wife "will haunt me as long as I live, and all the writing in the world will not put away the memory of her face and the sound of her voice" (76). The story's title, "Jacob's Ladder," is threaded throughout the narrative as a metaphor for the physical, economic, and social struggles that Florida Crackers faced. Taking its title from a biblical story and a nineteenth-century spiritual, Rawlings's tale seems to suggest that Florry's return is her birthright and that claiming her childhood cabin in the piney woods solves Mart and Florry's problems.[21] Florry insists, "I got me a right to Pappy's cabin. Would you jest stand up to him one time. . . . [W]e'd be safe-like right on. I got me my rights there" (111). However, the story originally ended with Mart losing his traps.

Rawlings understood that Mart and Florry's journey conveys the tensions between the old Florida Cracker culture and the new Florida frontier. Future hardships could not be avoided. Rawlings writes to Perkins on November 25, 1930, that she has a choice of three endings. In the first, Florry is not defeated, but "the last shred of security [is] swept from under her." In the second, Florry is unchanged, "living like a rabbit in the brush." In the third, "Florry's instinct would naturally draw her back in a circle, to the one sure thing she knew—the clearing in the piney-woods" (*MM* 30–31). Perkins responds on November 30, 1930, that he prefers the third option (32–33). By choosing the ending that Perkins preferred, Rawlings rewrites a realistic outcome as sentimental, more hopeful.

Despite its sentimentality, this ending locates Florry's frail figure as an embodiment of strength and resilience. Hardships in the story consistently originate at the site of her body. In part II, Mart uses all of their savings to send for the doctor when he notices that Florry has "wasted down to even more skeleton-like a figure than when Mart had taken her away" (61–62). Later in the story, when Florry becomes pregnant, Mart grudgingly agrees to work for the Yankee. Mart also kills a deer out of season because "Florry had not been well," a decision that leads to his arrest (96). Analyzing portrayals of southern women's bodies in literature, Patricia Yaeger warns that "it is crucial to examine the ways in which writing by modern southern women both adheres to and rebels against" willful miniaturization of the female body ("Beyond" 291). Miniaturization not only "ensures loss of power" but also uses "the purified, rarefied, 'transcendent' female body [as] a site for political labor" (291). Whenever Mart notices Florry's miniature body, he takes measures to protect it. Described as "thin," "emaciat[ed]," and "gaunt" (302) even in her most powerful moment on the return journey home, Florry is rendered more like a child than a woman.

Nevertheless, Florry is neither child nor dependent southern female archetype. Her physical strength is Herculean: she works alongside her father as a cypress logger and endures hunger, environmental disasters, and extreme illness with Mart. This strength, when compared to the narrator's descriptions of her miniaturized body, reconfigures perceptions of feminine weakness and creates a space for female Cracker characters' voices to emerge. Rawlings does not leave Florry miniaturized.

Indeed, Rawlings's arrangement of stories in the collection revises the seemingly fragile female protagonists in "A Crop of Beans" and "Jacob's Ladder" with the figure of Mattie Syles in "Gal Young Un." Considered by scholars to be Rawlings's most feminist narrative (see Bertolini; Morris; Rodger Tarr's editorial notes in Rawlings, *Short Stories*), "Gal Young Un" depicts Mattie Syles's confrontation with her second husband, the bootlegger and trickster figure Trax Colton. A widow left financially secure by her husband and father, Mattie possesses the economic independence that Lige Gentry and Mart struggle to obtain. Capitalizing on an opportunity, Trax preys on Mattie's self-sufficiency by marrying her to gain access to her money. Ultimately, though, Mattie harnesses her humiliation into resistance. She destroys Trax's moonshining business and drives him from her homestead with a rifle.

Dashiell considered "Gal Young Un" to be "too anti-male" and refused to print it in *Scribner's* (Rodger Tarr 3, 11). As a result, Brandt, Rawlings's literary agent, sold the story to *Harper's Monthly Magazine*, which printed it in the June and July 1932 issues of the magazine without illustration or embellishment. Rawlings wrote to a friend that it is "a bad story and I know it."[22] Her reservations about the story related to its composition more than its female-oriented perspective. Ultimately, though, "Gal Young Un" proved foundational to *South Moon Under* and won an O. Henry Prize for short fiction in 1933.

As was the case with *Scribner's Magazine*, *Harper's Monthly*'s editorial policy had changed substantially over the decade since Glasgow's stories had appeared with numerous illustrations. *Harper's* used reader questionnaires to determine how to increase circulation and sales after World War I. The magazine continued to print fiction by both established and emerging authors, but beginning in September 1925, the costly illustrations were eliminated except for a frontispiece and an orange cover (Mott, *History* 2:404). The magazine's dedication to cutting expenses and repositioning itself in the marketplace proved successful. In 1950, *Harper's Magazine* celebrated its one hundredth anniversary (Peterson 361).

Rawlings positions Mattie as antithetical to Florry's frailty. The narrator's descriptions emphasize Mattie's "muscular arms" (186), "ample breasts" (199), and "large-boned hand[s]" (205); like Widow Sellers, Mattie enjoys financial independence.[23] Since Trax cannot control Mattie physically or through financial dependence, he uses psychological manipulation to force her to submit to his patriarchal authority. When Mattie questions the propriety of Trax's moonshine operation, for example, he tells her, "Course, if you don't want to invest in my business with me, I got to be gittin back where I come from" (190). Her quick response reveals her vulnerability, "No, no! It's all right! . . . Honey, anything you want to do's all right" (190). Mattie's fear of loneliness enables Trax to master her. The narrator describes how Mattie's "adoration fed him"; his threats were "laid . . . across her like a whip" (189, 194). Simulating the role of plantation master, Trax increasingly situates Mattie as his subordinate plantation mistress.

Rawlings uses rhetoric to emphasize Mattie's newfound oppression. Each time she enacts the archetype that Trax has constructed for her, the third-person narrator replaces her dialogue with descriptions of her unspoken thoughts. Humiliated and defeated—married for her money, left for long periods of time by her husband, forced to manage a moonshine still, informed of her husband's indiscretions with other women, and eventually commanded to care for her husband's mistress, Elly, in her home—Mattie literally loses her ability to speak for herself.

To overturn her psychological subordination, Mattie must regain control over her narrative voice. She contrives a plan to destroy Trax's business and to force him to leave her home. Then she tells the Lantry boys, "I jest got word the Pro-hi's comin' lookin' fer Trax' outfit. Now I ain't quick as you-all, an' I want each one o' you should go down the road a good piece an' stay there all day" (178). When the Lantrys question her, she uses Trax's words to convince them: "Trax hisself done tole me a long ways back, if anybody had it in fer a man, that was the way they'd git at him" (178). Mattie reconfigures Trax's words to obtain their power as her own.

Rawlings extends her depiction of the Florida Crackers' socioeconomic struggles in "A Crop of Beans" and "Jacob's Ladder" to explicitly include the sense of humiliation associated with these difficulties. In "Gal Young Un," the narrator tells the reader that Mattie "understood the quality of her betrayal.

The injustice was clear. . . . Trax had taken what he had not wanted" (166). He had humiliated Mattie, "like an old mare traded in with a farm" (178). Elly embodies the humiliation most associated with this injustice.

By narratively positioning Elly and Mattie together, Rawlings magnifies their difference. The narrator explains that "beside the gray bulk of the older woman," Elly "was like a small gaudy doll" (197). According to Yaeger, alongside literary portrayals of the frail, emaciated southern female body, it is also important to notice the larger female body, since it "makes us pay attention to the miniature, the microcosmic, the quotidian" ("Beyond" 302). More childlike than womanly, Elly can only dress the part, "rock[ing] rather than walk[ing]" in the blue spike-heeled pumps that Trax bought her and the "cheap silk stockings" that are baggy "on her thin legs" (197). Elly is reminiscent of a girl playing dress-up in a pair of ill-fitting shoes, and her presence heightens the irony in Trax's attempts to possess the image of the southern female archetype to complete his plantation scene. Neither completely girl nor completely woman, she falls short of his archetypal construct because she is the reproduction of an already static representation (see Boyd).

Alison Bertolini argues that, on the one hand, Mattie does not go far enough because she "believes she has righted things simply by recognizing that she has pursued the wrong man"; on the other hand, the story "disrupts the premise of patriarchy during a time period when the patriarchal system was firmly entrenched and rarely questioned" (33–34). This disruption constitutes the foundation of Rawlings's female characters' progressive resistance in *When the Whippoorwill*. Mattie constitutes the first character to transcend silence and to revise the narrative that confines her. Furthermore, she recognizes her complicity in Elly's predicament, exclaiming, "I'd orter hided him from takin' sich a young un along his low-down way. . . . I'd orter been hided. Me an' Trax together" (215–16). With no character within earshot, her dialogue functions as both self-recognition and a warning to the reader about unwittingly perpetuating cruelty. Unlike Drenna and Florry, Mattie speaks last in the story, commanding Elly to give her "them crazy shoes," though Mattie does not throw them away (217). Instead, she puts them in her apron pockets as a reminder of subjection's power.

In *When the Whippoorwill*, Rawlings's arrangement of stories increasingly positions female protagonists as powerful voices in the Florida Cracker community while increasingly situating the reader as participatory in the construction of these narratives. This progression culminates in the collection's final story, "Cocks Must Crow." In the tale, Quincey Dover suspects that her husband, Will, is having an affair with Widow Tippett. In reality, the widow is only allowing Will to keep his prize cock with her chickens so that Quincey will not find out that he is competing in cockfights. Quincey confronts Widow Tippett and at the story's end observes the cockfight from a tree limb, realizing that Will associates cockfighting with his sense of interdependence and masculinity. Rawlings's invention of this larger-than-life Florida Cracker female narrator combines the characteristics of Drenna, Florry, and Mattie that embody strength and perseverance. "Cocks Must Crow" invites readers to evaluate perspectives that engender misplaced conclusions.

"Cocks Must Crow" comprises one of four tales from the collection published previously in the *Saturday Evening Post*.[24] Best known for its iconic Norman Rockwell illustrations, the *Post* boasts a long history. First published in the 1820s, it was purchased by Curtis Publishing Company in 1897 and was edited by George Horace Lorimer beginning in 1899. The January 29, 1898, issue was accompanied by an editorial note: "In 1729 this paper was purchased by Benjamin Franklin, and published by him as the 'Pennsylvania Gazette' until 1765" (Mott, *History* 4:682). According to Frank Luther Mott, however, the connections between the *Post* and Franklin are "tenuous": the *Post* was "first published from the shop in which the *Gazette* had perished six years before and one of its founders had been a partner of the grandson of Franklin's partner in a printing business" (684). Nonetheless, the magazine utilized this association to increase its circulation.

At the beginning of the twentieth century, the *Post* focused on business, public affairs, and romance (Mott, *History* 4:684). It grew rapidly after 1900, with "one of the largest gross incomes of any magazine" by World War I (Peterson 170). The magazine emphasized advertising and "acquired its own organizations for selling its magazines and distributing to newsstands." It utilized field workers to solicit door-to-door and had more "boy salesmen" than any other magazine before World War II (171). It targeted an average, middle-class American audience by publishing popular authors like F. Scott Fitzgerald, William Faulkner, James Branch Cabell, Stephen Crane, Edith Wharton, Ellen Glasgow, and Joel Chandler Harris (Mott, *History* 4: 704; Peterson 171).

By the time that Rawlings published her stories, the *Post*'s popularity was declining. Competition for advertising from radio programs and other weekly magazines decreased the magazine's income between 1929 and 1933. Furthermore, Lorimer, who opposed Franklin D. Roosevelt's election and the New Deal, reconfigured the magazine's focus from entertainment to political commentary, straining its readership and public support (Peterson 172–73). "Cocks Must Crow" was first printed in the November 25, 1939, issue. The *Post*'s printing of the first two pages of the story highlighted its satirical sketches to capitalize on the story's humorous scenes. The tale was divided between the beginning and the end of the issue, with its final pages sharing space with other fiction and advertisements.

Like Mattie in "Gal Young Un," Quincey Dover's physical size immediately focuses the reader on the role of appearances, exemplifying and even expanding on Mattie's contrast to Dreanna and Florry. Quincey confides to the reader that "ary piece of rations I've ever ate has just wrapped itself around my middle and stayed there. The last time I weighed myself was a ways back on the scales . . . and it balanced two hundred and twenty, and I quit weighing" (254).[25] Her personality is similarly sized, with "a tongue as sharp as a new cane knife" and a heart "as big as [her] behind" (254). By writing Quincey as a narrator capable of telling her own story, Rawlings revises nineteenth- and early twentieth-century depictions of Florida Cracker women's Otherness as a form of power that is capable of disseminating social commentary.

Quincey Dover possesses the largest body and the loudest voice among the characters and narrators in *When the Whippoorwill*. In "Cocks Must Crow," she uses her voice to unravel Will's secret while simultaneously commenting on the story's developments through narrative intrusions. These narrative intrusions are even more visible in comparisons between manuscript drafts and publications of the story. In the story's original manuscript, Rawlings directly addresses readers—"Now I got to piece this together best way I can. I ain't like them story magazine writers can make a tale come out as ever as a first prize patchwork quilt"—but the published versions add, "Life ain't slick like a story, no-ways."[26] Quincey's narration compels readers to participate in the narrative, as if they were her closest confidants.

Readers eagerly connected to Quincey Dover and speculated about her relationship to Rawlings. On June 11, 1940, Cabell wrote to Rawlings, "I confess I care about only one woman, for I care not who knows it that with Quincey Dover I am heels over head in love; and to her creator my gratitude is limitless."[27] Silverthorne speculates that Quincey Dover constitutes Rawlings's alternate persona (174); however, contemporary critic Robert McLaughlin rightly argues that "Rawlings is *not* Quincey Dover" (47). Rawlings was not a slight woman, but she was neither three hundred pounds nor born in the

Florida backwoods. She admired the Florida Cracker people but could relocate her home from Cross Creek at any time. "By creating such a unique and dominating narrator, one who cannot be simply ignored or identified with the author," McLaughlin argues, "Rawlings foregrounds the problems of experiencing, understanding, and representing reality. As a result, Quincey becomes identified, not with Rawlings, but with us as readers as Quincey's problems in knowing her world become our problems as we attempt to know ours" (47–48).

As Quincey Dover's perceptions about the meaning of events in the story change, readers—already along for the unraveling of the narrative—experience the same progression of understanding. At the beginning of the story, Quincey deems cockfighting to be cruel, but after witnessing it, she concedes that some men have adequate reasons for participating in the event. Similarly, when she discovers that her accusations about Widow Tippett's relationship with her husband are unfounded, she comprehends that her dismissive responses may have driven him to find support from another woman. She continually revises her perspectives on the story's happenings even as she conveys her tale.

In "Cocks Must Crow" Quincey Dover positions readers beside her, sharing the vantage from which she views events. The *Post*'s depiction of the scene in which Quincey spies on her husband at the cockfight places her high on the tree limb. In an illustration on the second page of the story, Quincey clings to a branch so that she can get a better look, and the caption quotes her inner dialogue: "I inched around on my limb so I got a better peephole through the branches. The men milled around, not talking much, just cutting their eyes sideways at t'other feller's chickens" (271). Quincey tells readers how to view the scene and how to revise previous assumptions about the story's happenings as she balances herself in the tree. When the limb breaks and she falls into the center of the cockfighting pit at the end of the story, readers already comprehend why, as Quincey perceives it, "cocks must crow" (273). Her subsequent explanation that winning the cockfight makes Will feel like a man is superfluous because, as readers surmise, the tale is not about cockfighting or negotiating gender differences. It is about the role of perspective when observing a scene.

Regionalist writers "create narrators who empathetically identify with the regionalist perspective" and "shift the center of perception," thereby "set[ting] up the conditions for seeing differently" (Fetterley and Pryse 121, 124). "Cocks Must Crow" guides readers to question their initial readings of a character's appearance and actions and to view the same scene from multiple perspectives. Through Quincey Dover's narration, Rawlings positions readers within the Florida Cracker culture's cockpit so that they might reconsider previous assumptions derived from unsubstantiated narratives.

Although Rawlings invites a reconsideration of popular disparaging portrayals of white Florida Crackers, she devotes little to no narrative space to the African Americans who also lived in the Cross Creek community. In fact, *When the Whippoorwill*'s few references to African Americans are primarily dismissive and pejorative. In her manuscript notes for "In This I Believe," drafted for a Voice of America radio broadcast, Rawlings refers to the struggle to sustain one's existence as "the common heritage of every man and woman on earth."[28] However, as C. Anita Tarr shows, Rawlings's stories clearly favor white perspectives.

While Rawlings's subsequent fiction and nonfiction may have increasingly demanded racial equality and her friendship with Zora Neale Hurston prompted her to question previous literary portrayals of racism (C. Anita Tarr 151; Lillios 15–17), Rawlings's hyperfocus on the Florida Cracker figure in *When the Whippoorwill* illumines social injustices related to class and gender while intentionally obscuring the presence of racial oppression. The stories do not address the violence that historians Maxine Jones and Kevin McCarthy describe as the Florida African American experience during the first half of the twentieth century. Nor does Rawlings investigate how this continued threat of violence cultivated a rhetoric and culture of racism and fear that barred African Americans from socioeconomic opportunities on the Florida frontier (241). Like Glasgow's participation in the patriarchal narratives that confine her, Rawlings cannot preserve the hammock or provide a complete ethnological reading of a region at risk without including all of its residents and community interactions.

Even if Rawlings became increasingly conscious of the racism present in Cracker culture and even if she sought to eliminate it from her subsequent publications, her revisions did not give African American figures a voice. Fifty years after Rawlings published *Cross Creek*, her housekeeper, Idella Parker, responded to her depiction in the memoir *Idella: Marjorie Rawlings' "Perfect Maid"* (1992). In the preface, Parker describes both herself and Rawlings as "imperfect human being[s]" but declares that "the truth was that most black people were afraid of whites." "I was one of those that feared," Parker confides, "I think fear caused us to be obedient and do as we were told" (ix–xiii).

The Whippoorwill's Call

The stories collected in *When the Whippoorwill* offer an account of one population—Florida Crackers—during a transitional moment between frontier and modernization. The original title, *When the Whippoorwill Calls*, originated from a "Florida backwoods saying," clarified in an inscription in the front matter of the first edition: "When the whippoorwill calls, it's time for the corn to be in the ground" (Silverthorne 180). In Rawlings's notes for a speech on "The Mechanics of Writing," she asserts that "the desire to write is the desire to say something; to say that something well; to make that something understood."[29] *When the Whippoorwill* allowed Rawlings to collect the stories that she felt said "something well" and "made that something understood"—the interdependency between nature and humanity.

Working collaboratively with Perkins, she selected and arranged the stories that best highlighted Florida Cracker culture and demonstrated the breadth of her work. All eleven tales were published in magazines between 1931 and 1939, but only three—"The Pardon," "The Enemy," and "A Mother in Mannville"—were set outside of the Florida interior (table 3.1).

Letters in *Max and Marjorie: The Correspondence between Maxwell E. Perkins and Marjorie Kinnan Rawlings* (1999) provide the textual history of Rawlings's selection and arrangement of stories for the collection. Perkins first approached Rawlings about the idea of a short-story volume in May 1938. The projected publication date was planned for early 1939, but Rawlings's poor health resulted in multiple delays. She wrote to Perkins in June 1938 that she thought she might not survive a surgical procedure (*MM* 354–55). Ultimately, she did not undergo the operation, but her health continued to hinder her ability to work throughout the summer (see *MM* 349–67). In the year before the collection's publication, she was still completing Quincey Dover stories for possible inclusion, further delaying production. As a result, the first set of proofs were rushed, and Rawlings complained that they included multiple typographical errors (*MM* 442–43). On February 15, 1940, Perkins told Rawlings that he was "worried" about the delays and "urged . . . the press to work fast when the copy came" (*MM* 443–44), perhaps contributing to the errors.

When Rawlings and Perkins began to discuss the final selection and arrangement of stories in February 1940, the previously published Quincey Dover stories loomed large. Perkins sent Rawlings "a list of the stories arranged in an order that seemed . . . pretty satisfactory" and explained,

Table 3.1: Publication History of Stories in Marjorie Kinnan Rawlings's *When the Whippoorwill* (1940)

Title (page numbers)	Original Magazine Publication
"A Crop of Beans" (1–19)	*Scribner's Magazine* 91, no. 5 (May 1932): 283–90
"Benny and the Bird Dogs" (20–40)	*Scribner's Magazine* 94, no. 4 (October 1933): 193–200
"Jacob's Ladder" (41–118)	*Scribner's Magazine* 89, no. 4 (April 1931): 351–66, 446–64
"The Pardon" (119–29)	*Scribner's Magazine* 92, no. 2 (August 1934): 95–98
"Varmints" (130–55)	*Scribner's Magazine* 100, no. 6 (December 1936): 26–32, 84–85
"The Enemy" (156–74)	*Saturday Evening Post* 212, no. 30 (January 20, 1940): 12–13, 32, 36, 39
"Gal Young Un" (175–216)	Part I: *Harper's Monthly Magazine* 165, no. 985 (June 1932): 21–33 Part II: *Harper's Monthly Magazine* 165, no. 986 (July 1932): 225–34
"Alligators" (217–32)	*Saturday Evening Post* 206, no. 13 (September 23, 1933): 16–17, 36, 38
"A Plumb Clare Conscience" (233–40)	*Scribner's Magazine* 90, no. 6 (December 1931): 622–26
"A Mother in Mannville" (241–50)	*Saturday Evening Post* 209, no. 24 (December 12, 1936): 7, 33
"Cocks Must Crow" (251–75)	*Saturday Evening Post* 212, no. 25 (November 25, 1939): 5–7, 58, 60, 62–64

Note: The stories examined in this chapter are shaded.

"I think the main problem is to separate the Quincy [*sic*] Dover stories, then to have a strong story near the end. That is the idea with which these are arranged, but if you wish to move them about, it will be easy to do" (*MM* 443–44). For many years, Perkins anticipated the possibility of a Quincey Dover short story collection, writing to Rawlings as early as December 1936 to suggest that she write more tales featuring that protagonist (*MM* 280). Five years after *When the Whippoorwill* was published, Perkins continued to promote the idea: "Of course, as you know, I have always hoped you would get Quincey Dover into a book. Won't you some time?" (*MM* 581). But Rawlings was sued for libel over depictions in *Cross Creek* in 1943, and Perkins died in 1947 (Silverthorne 154). Rawlings never returned to writing Quincey Dover stories.

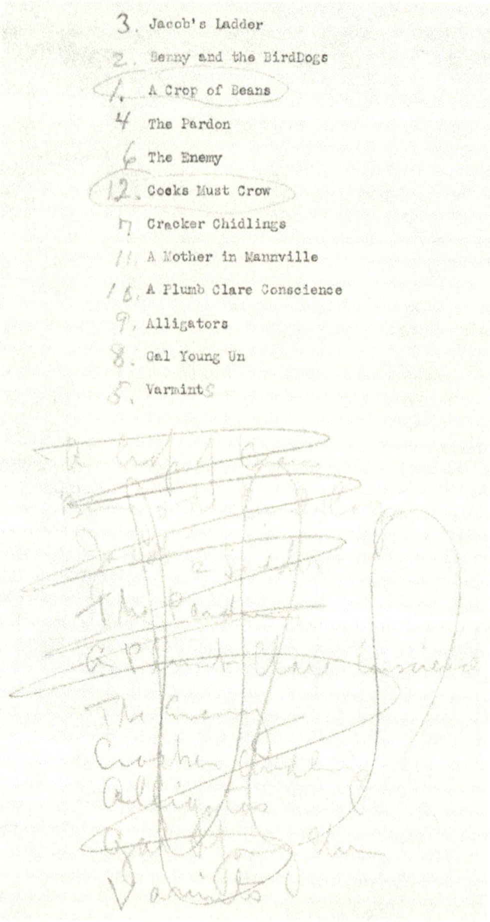
3. Jacob's Ladder
2. Benny and the BirdDogs
1. A Crop of Beans
4 The Pardon
6 The Enemy
12. Cocks Must Crow
7 Cracker Chidlings
11 A Mother in Mannville
10. A Plumb Clare Conscience
9. Alligators
8. Gal Young Un
5. Varmints

Fig. 3.3 Maxwell Perkins's typed list suggesting the order for stories in *When the Whippoorwill* with Marjorie Kinnan Rawlings's handwritten revisions, February 1940. Courtesy of Archives of Charles Scribner's Sons, Special Collections, Princeton University Library.

Rawlings followed Perkins's advice about separating the Quincey Dover stories in *When the Whippoorwill*, but she changed his proposed arrangement. Rawlings handwrote her revisions directly on Perkins's typed list, first creating her own list at the bottom of the page before scratching it out and then renumbering Perkins's list (figure 3.3).[30]

As published, *When the Whippoorwill* follows Rawlings's revisions except that "Cracker Chidlings" was eliminated later in the production process. It and another story, "Hyacinth Drift," were omitted because both Perkins and Rawlings worried that they were "almost non-fiction" and therefore did not fit (even though the similar "Alligators" was included) (*MM* 444–47). In the February 20, 1940, letter that accompanied her revisions to the list of stories,

Rawlings explains to Perkins, "I've gotten cold feet, just as you did, about opening the book of stories with too long a story. Let's begin with 'A Crop of Beans,' then 'Benny and the Bird Dogs,' then 'Jacob's Ladder.' . . . [I]f you want to end with a strong story, I say by all means use 'Cocks Must Crow'" (*MM* 444–45). Rawlings considered the strength of Quincey Dover's narration essential to the collection's conclusion. Rawlings received her first copies of the collection on April 17, 1940 (*MM* 451–52).

Contemporary critiques often dismiss Rawlings's literary contributions or primarily designate her as the children's author who wrote *The Yearling*.[31] Yet her arrangement of the stories in *When the Whippoorwill* (and arguably throughout her oeuvre) positions female characters' voices prominently as part of a larger cultural analysis. Rawlings's writing draws on a tradition of social reform narratives by nineteenth-century women writers such as Catharine Read Williams, whose *Fall River: An Authentic Narrative* (1833) reported religious leaders' cover-up of a working woman's murder, and Rebecca Harding Davis, whose publications "Life in the Iron Mills" (1861) and *A Law unto Herself* (1878) provided a public stage for labor conditions and injustices toward women. Rawlings's focus on evolving cultural perspectives about a group of marginalized people on the American frontier also resembles the work of ethnographic reform photographers like Lewis Hines, whose early 1900s photographs showed working conditions for children, and Walker Evans, whose photographs in James Agee's *Let Us Now Praise Famous Men* (1941) trace three sharecropping families during the Great Depression. Rawlings's contributions similarly magnify social inequities and interdependent relationships between environment and community.

Published individually in magazines, Rawlings's stories convey aspects of Florida Cracker culture, but when published and read together, they demonstrate her decades-long ethnographic project to preserve the Florida hammock through literary representation. Today, the impetus that drove her literary legacy remains in recreational events such as the Cracker Storytelling Festival sponsored by Polk County Parks and Recreation and a Cracker Day Celebration held annually in St. Augustine. The Florida State Fairgrounds in Tampa also maintains a permanent exhibit, "Cracker Country," a living history museum devoted to educating visitors about the early Florida Cracker way of life. Student groups visit the exhibit throughout the year, though it is open to the public only during the annual state fair. Rawlings helped to ensure Cross Creek's preservation, an accomplishment studied by geographer

Ary J. Lamme III. In "Preserving Special Places," Lamme explains that "Cross Creek, like many special places in the United States, does not have universal credentials for preservation" but rather depends on "a combination of attractive natural environments, historical associations, folk structures, discreet pastoral views, interesting social perspectives, and common recreational activities" (209). Rawlings's literary representations captured Cross Creek's culture, contributing to its survival. Her Cross Creek home, now part of Marjorie Kinnan Rawlings Historic State Park, remains a tourist destination.

In writing stories that became the foundation for her novels and that were collected in *When the Whippoorwill*, Rawlings sought to move beyond the regional depictions of the Florida Cracker that she associated with her first publication, "Cracker Chidlings" (*MM* 444–45). In her notes for a speech "On Florida and Floridians," she writes, "This is the Florida, wild and natural, that I'm calling 'the invisible Florida.' . . . I've longed to re-create, to make visible, this invisible beauty."[32] Rawlings wanted to make the "invisible beauty" of the Florida interior's culture visible to her readers through her selection and arrangement of stories.

4

Reconstructing Memory in Katherine Anne Porter's The Old Order Stories (1944, 1955, 1965)

In the 1930s, Katherine Anne Porter and Marjorie Kinnan Rawlings were writing the stories that would be published in their early 1940s collections. Unlike Kate Chopin and Ellen Glasgow's early writing career experiences, Porter and Rawlings, for the most part, benefited from collaborative relationships with editors and publishers. They were invited to lecture frequently at summer writing workshops and even mentored some of the same emerging writers (see Boggess), although biographical accounts and archived correspondence do not suggest that the two women knew each other personally.

Porter had much to contemplate in 1931. In the past two decades, she had married and divorced an abusive husband; survived tuberculosis and the 1918 flu pandemic; worked as a journalist in Mexico during the Mexican Revolution; experienced a miscarriage, a stillborn birth, and an abortion; published her first collection of stories; and, just prior to traveling from Mexico to Germany (figure 4.1), received a Guggenheim Fellowship. Now forty years old, she sailed with Eugene Dove Pressly, prepared to marry him

Fig. 4.1 Katherine Anne Porter aboard the SS *Werra* on a voyage from Veracruz, Mexico, to Bremen, Germany, September 1931. Courtesy of the Katherine Anne Porter Papers, Special Collections and University Archives, University of Maryland Libraries.

and to complete a biography on Cotton Mather that was under contract with Harcourt, Brace (Unrue 132–59).

Within a few months of their arrival, Pressly left Porter in Berlin to pursue a work opportunity in Madrid. During this time, Porter attended social events and met other expat writers, but she did not work on the Mather biography. Less than a year after her arrival, she became increasingly concerned about the rise of Nazism and left to meet Pressly in Madrid. On her way, she met friends in Paris, and captivated by the city, returned after spending only a few days in Madrid. This was the beginning of separations and reunions;

geographic relocations between Germany, France, and Switzerland; and another marriage that ended in divorce (Unrue 132–59).

In 1932, Porter began work on a project she called "Many Redeemers," drafting each day to produce the initial six stories, which eventually became known as The Old Order stories. Porter organized the project into three sections: "Legend and Memory"; "Midway of This Mortal Life"; and "The Present Day."[1] Two years later, she wrote to her father to ask for further details about the Porters because she was "trying to reconstruct the whole history of an American family (Ours, more or less) from the beginning by means of just those two things—legend, and memory."[2] In a 1935 address to the American Women's Club in Paris that was later published as "My First Speech," she defines *legend* as "those things I have been told or that I read as a child," and *memory* as a combination of "my own memory of events taking place around me" and "my present memory and explanation to myself of my personal life" (685). Even though she never completed the project as she had originally intended, it "would go on for more than thirty years, expand, change forms and titles, shed pieces of itself, and shift focus . . . becom[ing] the widest stream in her fictional canon" (Unrue 113).

She submitted "Legend and Memory" to the *Atlantic Monthly* in 1934, but the response was not what she had anticipated. The magazine's editor, Edward Aswell, recommended she combine three of the stories ("The Grandmother," part of "The Old Order," and part of "The Last Leaf") into a single tale about the characters Grandmother and Nannie.[3] She reluctantly agreed on the condition that the editing team abide by three stipulations outlined in a letter to her editor, Charles Pearce: the editors "must not change the order of episodes or the chronology" or "mutilate the sentence structure," and "they must never under any circumstances substitute one word for another." Her willingness to revise the manuscript stemmed from financial necessity: "I hope they pay fairly well. God knows how I need the money."[4]

This letter provides early evidence of the importance that Porter placed on the stories' arrangement. She felt that revisions constituted mutilation that would destroy the cohesiveness of the manuscript, which had initially been arranged according to the protagonist's chronological age. Ultimately, the *Atlantic Monthly*'s editorial team could not merge the three stories and returned the manuscript. Porter was glad, telling Pearce that she "should not like at all for it to be published in such a state. . . . [*T*]*his is not a short story and cannot be turned into one with a blue pencil*."[5]

Table 4.1: Publication History of Katherine Anne Porter's The Old Order Stories

Title	Original Magazine Publication
"The Grandmother"	"The Source," *Accent* 1, no. 3 (Spring 1941): 44–47
"Uncle Jimbilly"	Published with "The Last Leaf" as "Two Plantation Portraits: The Witness and The Last Leaf," *Virginia Quarterly Review* 2, no. 1 (January 1935): 85–92
"The Circus"	*Southern Review* 1, no. 1 (Winter 1935): 36–41
"The Old Order"	*Southern Review* 2, no. 1 (Summer 1936): 495–509
"The Grave"	*Virginia Quarterly Review* 11, no. 2 (April 1935): 177–83
"The Last Leaf"	Published with "Uncle Jimbilly" as "Two Plantation Portraits: The Witness and The Last Leaf," *Virginia Quarterly Review* 2, no. 1 (January 1935): 85–92

Notes: The stories are listed in the order in which they appear in "Legend and Memory," which I determined by combining information from Edward Aswell to Charles Pearce, May 17, 1934, Porter Papers; Alvarez 267; and "Legend and Memory" (Part 1) from *Midway of This Mortal Life* (I. "The Grandmother" ["The Source"], III. "The Circus," IV. "The Old Order" ["The Journey"]) and notes, 1934, 1937, Porter Papers. The stories examined in this chapter are shaded.

Pearce subsequently attempted to publish the "Legend and Memory" manuscript in six other magazines—*The Forum*, *Scribner's Magazine*, *Woman's Home Companion*, *Harper's Magazine*, *Ladies' Home Journal*, and the *Virginia Quarterly Review*—but none would accept the entire piece. He wrote to Porter that the editors were "interested, as they always are, in your work," but "all of them objected that the length of the manuscript made it impossible to use, or that they could not select portions to publish."[6] The *Virginia Quarterly Review* agreed to publish two selections from it, "Uncle Jimbilly" and "The Last Leaf," as a two-part story under the title "Two Plantation Portraits: The Witness and The Last Leaf," that appeared in January 1935.[7] Porter accepted the offer and eventually published the remaining stories in similar "little magazines"—that is, magazines that appealed to niche audiences and "encouraged literary experimentation"—between 1935 and 1941 (Peterson 352). The *Virginia Quarterly Review* published "The Grave" in April 1935, while "The Circus" and "The Old Order" appeared in the *Southern Review*'s winter 1935 and summer 1936 issues, respectively. Finally, Porter changed the title of "The Grandmother" to "The Source" and published it in *Accent*'s spring 1941 issue (table 4.1). Not until ten years after her original submission to the *Atlantic Monthly* did all six stories appear together, and she came to think of them (along with a seventh published later) as The Old Order stories. They

Table 4.2: Arrangement of Katherine Anne Porter's The Old Order Stories in Published Collections, 1944–1965

Collection	Arrangement of Stories (page numbers)
The Leaning Tower and Other Stories (1944)	"The Source" (3–12) "The Witness" (13–20) "The Circus" (21–32) "The Old Order" (33–58) "The Last Leaf" (59–68) "The Grave" (69–80)
The Old Order: Stories of the South (1955)	"The Source" (3–10) "The Old Order" (11–33) "The Witness" (34–38) "The Circus" (39–46) "The Last Leaf" (47–52) "The Grave" (53–62)
The Collected Stories of Katherine Anne Porter (1965)	"The Source" (321–25) "The Journey" (326–39) "The Witness" (340–42) "The Circus" (343–47) "The Last Leaf" (348–51) "The Fig Tree" (352–61) "The Grave" (362–68)

Notes: All published collections contain works in addition to The Old Order stories. In *Collected Stories*, the title of "The Old Order" is changed to "The Journey." Porter also added a seventh Old Order story in *Collected Stories*: "The Fig Tree" was originally published in *Harper's Magazine* 220, no. 1321 (June 1960): 55–77.

and Porter's short novels *Old Mortality* (1937) and *Pale Horse, Pale Rider* (1939) featured the same protagonist, Miranda Gay, tracing her memories and experiences from childhood through early adulthood.

"The Old Order" was originally the title of one of the six stories in the "Legend and Memory" submission. The story appeared again in *The Leaning Tower and Other Stories* along with the five other "Legend and Memory" stories. The table of contents does not distinguish between these stories and the other three stories in the volume until *The Old Order: Stories of the South* (1955), in which the six stories (including "The Old Order") are grouped together as "The Old Order." In *The Collected Stories of Katherine Anne Porter* (1965), the final collection to include the stories, they are again grouped as "The Old Order," but that story's title is changed to "The Journey," and a seventh story, "The Fig Tree," is added to the group. Originally written in 1928, "The Fig Tree" was not published until 1960, when it appeared in *Harper's Magazine*.

Porter did not revise The Old Order stories between their appearances in three different collections. Instead, she changed their arrangement from chronological to anachronistic (table 4.2). This persistent reordering represents a reconstructive process of memory, privileging certain episodic memories over others to demonstrate Miranda Gay's evolving perspectives on remembered childhood experiences. Individually, each story functions as one component of Miranda's construct of identity from the perspective of an adult looking backward and remembering as a child. Collectively, these stories reveal memory's process of reconstruction, transforming initial remembered experiences through arrangement and addition over time. Ultimately, these reorganizations serve as a frame for conveying social commentary.

As was the case for Rawlings and Quincey Dover, scholars and biographical evidence suggest a connection between Porter and Miranda Gay.[8] Porter calls the series "autobiographical" yet "not autobiographical": "the earlier parts are most surely very near to my own experience . . . but I take leave to use whatever experience I please and how I please."[9] Her ambiguity arises from her use of ancestral research and personal memories in the writing of the stories. Porter's rearrangements of the stories over time indicate her desire to reorganize these fictional renderings sourced from personal experience and memory.

The seven stories focus on Miranda's childhood memories and are told from a third-person limited point of view (Alvarez 266). The first story, "The Source," describes the matriarchal Grandmother, who serves as primary caretaker for her son, Harry, and his three children. Grandmother ritualistically moves the family to her farm during the summer and back to their town house during the school year, maintaining ancestral legends through repetition and order. "The Journey" portrays how Grandmother and Nannie, the Black freedwoman who remains as Grandmother's servant, reminisce about the past and reveals Grandmother's inability to accept her responsibility for Nannie's continued racial oppression. In "The Witness," Uncle Jimbilly, an elderly freedman, tells stories about slavery's violence and is both feared and revered by the grandchildren. The fourth story, "The Circus," describes a young Miranda's first circus experience, in which she becomes frightened by the man on the high wire and must be escorted home by her Black caretaker, Dicey. In "The Last Leaf," Nannie relocates and refuses to remain in servitude after Grandmother's death. The sixth story, "The Fig Tree," deals with Miranda's grief over her mother's death. Finally, "The Grave" depicts a hunting expedition on which

Miranda's brother Paul shoots and skins a rabbit, only to discover that it is pregnant. Paul warns Miranda not to tell their father about the experience. The memory unexpectedly resurfaces twenty years later.

Porter's preoccupation with memory in The Old Order stories parallels the Southern Renaissance, a period of literary production in the 1920s–30s during which writers and critics preferred a romanticized version of the South's antebellum past as emblematic of the South's modern identity. Four years before Porter submitted "Legend and Memory," the Southern Agrarians published *I'll Take My Stand: The South and the Agrarian Tradition* (1930), a collaborative, twelve-essay volume that responded to H. L. Mencken's condemnation of southern letters and argued for the return of an agrarian-based economy. However, the authors did not address the foundation of that economy—the enslavement of African Americans.[10] The Southern Agrarians sought to revise the region's identity as a tradition of elite intellectual and social culture, portraying the antebellum South as "a balanced, orderly society where the yeomanry lived in relatively cozy co-equilibrium with the planters [and] took pains to stress [the South's] almost otherworldly incompatibility with both the values and practicalities of contemporary industrialism" (Cobb 118).

Porter socialized frequently with leading Southern Agrarians, particularly Allen Tate and Caroline Gordon, throughout her literary career (Unrue 104, 166–67). She insisted that her fictional works "never confused politics with art," but as biographer Darlene Harbour Unrue contends, Porter's views, particularly during the first half of her career, aligned with those of her Southern Agrarian contemporaries (166). Prior to the Southern Renaissance, southern white women writers were considered "an 'other,'" but during this period, their work became supported and encouraged in southern letters (McHaney 132–33). Porter took advantage of this opportunity by rooting The Old Order stories in depictions of an idyllic past. Through Miranda's fictional memories, Porter sought to preserve her family's southern aristocratic legacy, as she constructed it, while simultaneously signaling to the Southern Agrarians that she upheld their vision of a return to a plantation-based society.

Unlike the other short-story collections discussed in this book, The Old Order stories do not constitute Porter's first or only published volume of collected stories. She published *Flowering Judas and Other Stories* in limited (1930) and expanded (1935) editions. The 1935 edition includes ten stories, eight of which depict Mexican culture and two of which—"The Jilting of Granny Weatherall" (now one of her most anthologized stories) and "He"—are southern stories. Porter also published a collection of "short novels" in *Pale Horse, Pale Rider: Three Short Novels* (1939), which includes Miranda Gay in *Old Mortality* and *Pale Horse, Pale Rider*, before The Old Order stories appeared in *The Leaning Tower*.

Like Chopin, Glasgow, and Rawlings, Porter demanded agency at every step of the publication process. She also used established conventions from literary genres to appeal to magazine editors, garner readership, and obtain recognition from her contemporaries. And reminiscent of Chopin's, Glasgow's, and Rawlings's story arrangements, Porter repurposed these genre conventions to magnify social injustices within a regional context, even though her progression toward this commentary may have been more protracted. The thematic focus in The Old Order stories primarily replicates the Southern Agrarians' initiative to glorify the past, while Porter's rearrangements of the tales indicate that she reconsidered the significance of their collective meaning over time, using the social commentary embedded in their narratives to question idealized portrayals of a southern antebellum past.

Memory

The resurgence of southern letters in the 1920s–30s responded to the threat of cultural change, a tradition of response in southern literature that began with the defense of slavery in the early nineteenth century and continued with the revision of northern accounts of a decimated South prior to the turn of the twentieth (see Grammer 58; McKee 11; Prince). These literary responses nearly always drew on the same geographic settings, archetypal characters, and heroic plots to narratively reconstruct the antebellum South as a romanticized, exceptional place, complete with pastoral plantation and ever-faithful slaves. Before and during the Southern Renaissance, some writers revised this tradition and repurposed the plantation as a symbol of injustice, calling for social reform through sentiment in novels and autobiographies like Harriet Beecher Stowe's *Uncle Tom's Cabin* (1852) and Harriet Ann Jacobs's *Incidents in the Life of a Slave Girl* (1861); through satire in story collections like Charles Chesnutt's *The Conjure Woman* (1892); and through the use of the grotesque in novels like William Faulkner's *Absalom! Absalom!* (1936) and Erskine Caldwell's *Tobacco Road* (1932). However, Porter's Old Order stories constitute a "fantasy narrative" that was written as realism but was rooted in Porter's desire to keep her ancestral memories and legends from disappearing permanently.[11]

In *Possessing the Past: Trauma, Imagination, and Memory in Post-Plantation Southern Literature* (2015), Lisa Hinrichsen argues that memory can serve as "a key that, when 'possessed,' can unlock a definitive identity that existed in the past" and "function as a central term in the reproduction of an ideology of southern homogeneity" (5). This "self-construction" becomes fantasy, or "the mechanism by which southerners imagine themselves as 'southern' [and become] invested in a collectively imagined public and political heritage" (3). Writing The Old Order as fiction instead of autobiography allowed Porter to construct a romanticized version of the antebellum past and to position her protagonist within a tradition of southern aristocracy. Even though her family would no longer have been considered part of the planter class after Reconstruction, Miranda's associative identity as the granddaughter of a once-aristocratic family linked her to this lineage.

Plantation literature relates place (the physical and tangible) to ideology (the psychological and intangible) through memory, positioning event and reader simultaneously in both the past and the present. While antebellum plantation culture was no longer present in the twentieth century, its continued depiction in fiction resists extinction by appropriating its tropes—both revised and stagnant—to perpetuate its mythology. In fact, between 1930 and 1939, eighty Civil War novels were published, including Margaret Mitchell's iconic *Gone with the Wind* (1936) (Hinrichsen 11). Emblematic of this "mystic fascination," the plantation "came to seem as worth preserving because of what it meant . . . what its loss would mean culturally to the South, the nation, and the world" (Wells 175–80). Aligning geographic place with sociopolitical ideology, Southern Agrarian writers repositioned the plantation as central to the South's public consciousness.

In the context of plantation fiction's popularity during the Southern Renaissance, it is not surprising that the *Atlantic Monthly*'s Aswell desired to assemble a story from the archetypal plantation characters, Grandmother and Nannie, instead of printing a series of tales about Miranda's coming of age. Aswell would have been aware of readers' interest in adaptations of plantation fiction and would have sought to capitalize on this demand. In fact, ten years after Porter's unsuccessful submission to the *Atlantic Monthly*, her publisher, Donald Brace, still hoped to attract a larger audience for Porter's stories by framing them as plantation fiction in the stories' first collected publication,

The Leaning Tower. On June 6, 1944, Brace suggests that Porter use the half title "Plantation Sketches" to designate (and highlight) a theme for the six stories.[12] Ultimately, though, the stories were published in this collection without any indication that they belonged together. While biographical accounts and correspondence do not indicate why *The Leaning Tower* did not include the half title, Porter insisted on explicitly grouping The Old Order stories in later collections as a way to remedy reviewers' confusion about the stories' relationship to other stories.[13]

In The Old Order stories, Porter uses the plantation's fixed geographic location and archetypal characters to examine Miranda's relationship with the past while only tangentially engaging the inherently problematic social issues related to race, gender, and class that permeated her memories. Miranda, as Jay Watson rightly argues, must "draw on the history of her foremothers and the lessons of her own experience in order to arrive at a viable model of womanhood upon which to found a mature identity [and] come to a fuller awareness of a woman's stake in [the traditional plantation regime] and its toll on her" (216). Grandmother, the white female matriarch, and Nannie, the Black freedwoman, represent the foundations of Miranda's earliest recollections about her ancestors. While all seven stories in *Collected Stories* reference these characters, the Grandmother and Nannie figures are most prominent in "The Source," "The Journey," and "The Last Leaf." In their entirety, Miranda's memories cannot help but to expose Nannie's continued racial oppression in a post–Civil War plantation setting.

Inherited Ideology

From the "Legend and Memory" submission to the publication of *Collected Stories*, "The Source" constitutes the first story in Miranda's memory sequence and thus the foundation of her most formative memories. For a young Miranda, whose mother had recently passed away and whose father struggled to maintain financial stability, Grandmother's presence signifies stability in a disordered and chaotic world. For the adult Miranda, recalling her childhood, Grandmother embodies one of the last connections to family legends about the antebellum South. She designates herself as the proprietor of the family's southern aristocratic lineage and therefore as an extension of its legend through her recollections of it.

Grandmother's ritualistic practices reenact the antebellum past to situate its illusion as part of present experience. As Miranda recollects it, these practices rely on three constructions of time: linear time, circular time, and Bergsonian time (see Bergson; Fetterley; McBee). Linear time, comprised of the progression of hours, days, months, and years in the narrative, schedules reoccurring happenings, such as grandchildren's recognition that "the hour came in each day when they were rounded up, captured, washed, dressed properly, made to eat what was set before them without giving battle, put to bed when the time came and no nonsense" (324).[14] Circular time connects depictions of fictional events to seasonal changes, such as Grandmother's departure from the town house at the beginning of each summer and her return to it at the end of each summer. Finally, a Bergsonian sense of time frames linear and circular occurrences by their connections to the past, present, and future, combining ritual and repetition to create a sense of endurance despite change. Leslie K. Hankins argues that Grandmother performs her departures and arrivals repetitiously and ritualistically so that there appears to be "ritual from life by detaching reality from the limits of time . . . not bound by time but transcend[ing] its control" (21). Grandmother rides her horse, Fiddler, who "would remember his youth and break into a stiff-legged gallop." Fiddler, the narrator tells us, might "drop in his tracks" at "any time," but Grandmother "would not" (325).

In a letter to Pearce, Porter explains that she uses time "as a means of showing each character as the whole sum of himself at any given moment." "The Grandmother is old," Porter explains, "but the child she was is still present in her memory, herself as child is shown beside her grand-daughter as child, and the old people live over within themselves every stage of themselves from infancy to their present."[15] Grandmother connects linear, circular, and Bergsonian time through ritualistic performances to affirm her seemingly immortal permanence.

Despite the critical acclaim for Porter's *Flowering Judas and Other Stories* and *Pale Horse, Pale Rider*, "The Source" had difficulty finding a magazine home as a consequence of its short length and sketch-like, unconventional narrative. The last of The Old Order stories to be published in a magazine, "The Source" appeared in the spring 1941 issue of *Accent*, the University of Illinois's first national literary production, known for publishing emerging writers.[16] Flannery O'Connor, Wallace Stevens, Kay Boyle, and E. E. Cummings also published selections from their early work in *Accent*. Described as "an eclectic"—a magazine "open to most of the literary currents but generally favoring straight, realistic writing and more or less conventional structural patterns"—*Accent* endeavored to "carefully balanc[e] the work of established authors with that of comparative unknowns" (Hoffman, Allen, and Ulrich 9, 350). While Porter's story was published alongside a critical essay by John Crowe Ransom, a recognized poet and contributor to *I'll Take My Stand*, most selections in that issue of *Accent* came from relatively unknown writers and reviewers.

More than any other writer examined in this book, Porter distanced herself from the process of publishing in the periodical press. When the *Atlantic Monthly* returned "Legend and Memory," Pearce and Brace negotiated the stories' publications in magazines without much direction from Porter regarding which story to place in which magazine (Unrue 155). The editors of the little magazines, unlike the men who helmed the "quality magazines," thought of their work as contributing to a particular intellectual community instead of a popular audience (Peterson 352). Known for "seeking out unrecognized artistic talent," *Accent* and similar little magazines published more than 80 percent of the post-1912 writers and critics now recognized as influencing literary movements in American literature (Hoffman, Allen, and Ulrich 2).

In the only revision between the magazine and collected versions of "The Source," Porter adds a space to separate the beginning of the story (set at the town house) and the remaining two-thirds of the story (set at Grandmother's ancestral plantation). As in Chopin's "Beyond the Bayou," geographic boundaries perpetuate the plantation's sociopolitical hierarchy. Upon arriving, Grandmother "walk[s] straight through the house, . . . pass[es] out into the yards and gardens, . . . down the narrow path past the barns, . . . and on past the canebrake to the left, the hayfields to the right, until she arrive[s] at the row of Negro huts that ran along the bois d'arc hedge" (322). Without her constant supervision, she observes, "everything was out of order" (322). She makes "instant plans for changes" and glances with "firm and purposeful censure" when she reaches the cabins previously occupied by slaves and now home to the emancipated African American laborers who remained on the plantation (322).

In the same way that the setting embodies popular images of an antebellum plantation scene, Grandmother's character assumes the role of white slave master, eagerly enacting the part of "just and efficient slave driver" (323–24). Her "wrath," which the narrator describes as the impetus for overhauling the plantation's working conditions (323), recalls previously enslaved African Americans' physical and psychological punishments in the absence of the institution of slavery. As proprietor of the family's antebellum legend, Grandmother re-creates antebellum social hierarchies, establishing herself as a master capable of sanctioning punishment. She intentionally acts the part, re-creating her memories of the past and situating the plantation myth as "another kind of reality" to preserve it (West 20–22).

By mythologizing both the setting and her role in it, Grandmother becomes the myth's caretaker and overseer, charged with its maintenance and dissemination to future generations. Before leaving the town house each summer, she admires a peach tree and tells Miranda, "I have planted five orchards in three states, and now I see only one tree bloom" (322). This "single tree, representing all her beloved trees" (322), symbolizes Miranda's future role when Grandmother can no longer maintain the myth. Miranda is charged with observing the performance so that she can disseminate the plantation myth to future generations after Grandmother's death.

Porter, like her fictional protagonist, carried her family's legends into adulthood. By the mid-1930s, she had established friendships with like-minded Southern Agrarians who praised her work. In 1935, Robert Penn Warren and Cleanth Brooks asked Porter for a story to publish in their first issue of the *Southern Review*, a literary journal that they were establishing as faculty at Louisiana State University. Porter asked Brace to send them selections from "Legend and Memory" but did not designate particular stories. Both "The Circus" and "The Old Order" appeared in the magazine's earliest issues (Unrue 155).

The *Southern Review* was "one of the most important university critical reviews in the United States" (Hoffman, Allen, and Ulrich 398). Primarily edited by New Critics and less experimental than *Accent*, the quarterly's critical essays were "devoted to the analysis of individual poets as well as to the general problem of modern poetics" and used "close structural and textual analysis" (398). Many of the Southern Agrarians considered themselves New Critics, part of a literary criticism movement that relied on close readings and eliminated sociocultural contexts to categorize texts as literature or not literature. Porter's The Old Order stories benefited from this critical approach, which focused on the psychological development of characters in lieu of situating narratives in historical, social, and political contexts. By examining solely the text, New Critics could ignore the sociopolitical contexts that perpetuated injustices in the South.

In the summer of 1936, the *Southern Review* published "The Old Order" alongside works by other well-known southern writers and critics such as Warren, Ransom, Donald Davidson, Howard Baker, Brooks, Allen Tate, and Mark Van Doren. Only one other woman writer, Harriette Simpson Arnow, perhaps best known for her novel *The Dollmaker* (1954), was published in the issue.[17] Like *Accent*, the *Southern Review* did not illustrate its fiction. Selections were printed with a simple line at the top of the page to introduce the title and author. Tate stated that the critical quarterly sought "not to give the public what it wants, or what it thinks it wants, but what—through the medium of its most intelligent members—it ought to have" (Hoffman, Allen, and Ulrich 398). Porter's invitation to contribute to the *Southern Review* thus signaled her acceptance as a Southern Renaissance artist and her inclusion in the southern literary canon.

At first glance, "The Old Order" depicts Grandmother and Nannie's friendship, but as the narrator rightly points out, their relationship was "not so much a question of affection between them as a simple matter of being unable to imagine getting along without each other" (330).[18] By placing episodic memories from Grandmother's life alongside episodic memories from Nannie's life, the narrative invites readers to piece together these fragments to fully comprehend the significance of the two women's experiences in sociocultural context.

Like her ritual performances from the antebellum South in "The Source," Grandmother's authority in "The Old Order" originates from her ancestry. From the first sentence of the story, the use of the article *the* sets Grandmother apart (Fetterley 11). She is "the Grandmother" because she was "the great-granddaughter of Kentucky's most famous pioneer" and "the daughter of a notably heroic captain in the War of 1812" (326). As a southern matriarch from a prominent family, Grandmother contends that it is "her duty to portion out activities, to urge or restrain where necessary, to teach morals, manners, and religion, and to punish and reward her own household according to a fixed code" (328). When a neighbor returns her young sons, Harry and Robert, after they attempt to run away, she first punishes them with her riding whip and then immediately forces them to kneel and pray. At the same time, however, Grandmother's role is antithetical to the antebellum southern social system in that she serves as both patriarch and matriarch after her husband's death leaves her in debt and responsible for the entire household's operations.[19]

Grandmother views her authority as ordained by God. In a particularly poignant example of her sense of omniscient power, she reassures Nannie that she will be accepted into heaven even though God, as Nannie protests, "ha[s] been so cruel to black people on earth" (337). As the narrator intrudes to elaborate further, Grandmother reassures Nannie "as if she, who had been responsible for Nannie, body and soul in this life, might also be her sponsor before the judgment seat" (337). Grandmother's use of religion to rationalize racial and gender hierarchies draws on nineteenth-century Cult of True Womanhood ideology as well as adaptations of the American Jeremiad (Puritan political sermons employed as social guidelines; see Welter; Bercovitch 179). While true womanhood positioned piety as one cornerstone of feminine behavior, the American Jeremiad accepted correction as indicative of spiritual guidance. Harnessing these principles, Grandmother affirms her social privilege by re-creating a planter society in the postbellum South. This self-conferred social positioning allows her to justify inequalities and hardships, particularly racial injustice, as part of "God's plan" (328).

Grandmother associates her silence on social injustice prior to the Civil War—a southern antebellum sociocultural expectation for women that she imposes in a postwar setting—with her (rather than Nannie's) victimization even as the narrator rightly indicts Grandmother's memories of remaining silent as complicit in the continued oppression of African Americans. When Grandmother describes how she must "keep silent and give no sign of uneasiness" regarding young men's "headstrong habits," for example, the narrator explains that she "held her breath for three days" to see whether an infant born in the slave cabins would "turn black" (337). In doing so, the narrator exposes the source of "headstrong habits" as the rape of Black female slaves instead of a less pejorative social concern that Grandmother's ambiguousness seems to suggest. Similarly, when Grandmother recalls how she inscribed "June 11, 1827, Nannie Gay (black)" into the family Bible as a young child, the narrator addresses the reader directly to explain that Nannie "did not know the [actual] year of her birth" (337, 328). This narrative intrusion makes clear that while the inscription is described in the context of childhood affection, the invented birthdate and assigned name document Nannie's identity as the property of the Gay family. Sophia Jane's behavior may appear subversive or as rebelling against "ideological codes of behavior and thinking," but in actuality, it is, "perhaps naively, perpetuating them" (Frankwitz 474). As an African American woman who was Grandmother's slave in the Old South and lifelong servant in the New South, Nannie's "place in the world . . . had been assigned to her before birth" (328). The story's third-person narrator makes clear that Grandmother's silences do not constitute her own victimization. Instead, they perpetuated and continue to perpetuate the victimization of others.

The rhetorical distance between the narrator's intrusions and descriptions of events from Grandmother's perspective expose her unwillingness to emancipate Nannie from the reenactment of the plantation myth, which Grandmother carefully preserves like the "irreplaceable treasures" that connect her to her ancestral past (326). Moreover, she engages Nannie in this preservation task through the sewing of patchworks from fine fabrics and silk floss to protect her great-grandmother's rolling pin and great-grandfather's razor and daguerreotype (326). Grandmother embellishes the tangible reminders of her ancestral past just as she venerates and romanticizes the Old South. In an examination of Black women's lives after Emancipation, social historian Thavolia Glymph argues that "white women worked to reclaim as much of the ideological terrain as possible. . . . [E]xperience [had] taught them that black women's ambitions and actions projected a sense of self, radically at odds with their own" (189, 209, 213). Grandmother positions Nannie as "faithful slave," incapable of an identity independent of her servitude, to sustain the performance of the "old order."

When analyzed in conjunction with the narrator's intrusions in the story, Porter's change of title from "The Old Order" to "The Journey" both distinguishes the grouping's title from that of the particular story and departs from the plantation myth as the cornerstone of the tales' collective vision. Perhaps chosen as indicative of two characters' memories of their life journeys, "The Journey" signals the beginnings of Miranda's critical awareness of the subjugation embedded in the plantation myth's ideology.

In "The Last Leaf," the final The Old Order story as initially proposed by Aswell in 1934, Porter complicates the perpetuation of inherited ideology by portraying Nannie after Grandmother's death. The January 1935 issue of the *Virginia Quarterly Review* published "The Last Leaf" and "The Witness" together under the title "Two Plantation Portraits." The two parts of the story were separated by Roman numerals and subtitles, without illustration.

Like the *Southern Review*, the *Virginia Quarterly Review* was edited and printed at a university—in this case, the University of Virginia. The quarterly's first issue appeared in 1925 and its mission was to engage both southern and national sociopolitical commentary (see James Southall Wilson, "*Virginia*"; James Southall Wilson, "Founding"). In a study of the magazine's publications from 1925 to 1935, Bruce Fort confirms that it upheld this mission, devoting eighty articles to literary criticism and the remaining articles to history, politics, and economics in the South, the nation, and internationally. First produced during the height of the Southern Renaissance, the quarterly established an "identity as an elite and eclectic national journal of discussion [as] a calculated, self-conscious response to the charges of cultural sterility which critics had leveled at the South. [The editors wanted to] bring the South into full partnership with the rest of the nation." Yet even as the quarterly insisted that it was a national journal, it struggled to reconcile its southern voice with national perspectives (Fort).

Most of the *Virginia Quarterly*'s contributors were "prominent white liberal Southern male journalist and academics" (Ayers). The January 1935 issue, for example, included works by H. L. Mencken and Robert Penn Warren while featuring only a few women writers (figure 4.2). As was the case for the inclusion of her work in the *Southern Review*, Porter's publication in the *Virginia Quarterly* indicated her acceptance in southern literary circles. "Two Plantation Portraits," in particular, embraces the Southern Agrarians' vision of the antebellum South, with its sketches of two former slaves that drew on African American archetypes and played into a southern (and national) audience's imagination.

Archived correspondence does not reveal why Porter called Nannie's portrait "The Last Leaf," an image that suggests the end of a season or permanent change. Nannie appears to complacently embody the "faithful slave" archetype in "The Source" and "The Old Order," but she adamantly rejects her assigned part in the staged plantation after Grandmother's death. In "The Last Leaf," Nannie refuses to continue reenacting Grandmother's inherited antebellum past. Instead, Nannie systematically and purposefully separates herself physically and psychologically from associations with her past servitude, constructing a new identity that works toward emancipating her from her continued oppression. Despite its appearance as a replication of the past through archetypal figures and setting, Nannie's narrative eliminates Grandmother's perpetuation of the plantation myth.

The portrayal of Nannie in "The Last Leaf" revises her previously prescribed narrative by changing her appearance, geographically relocating her home, and demonstrating how she gains financial independence. Nannie

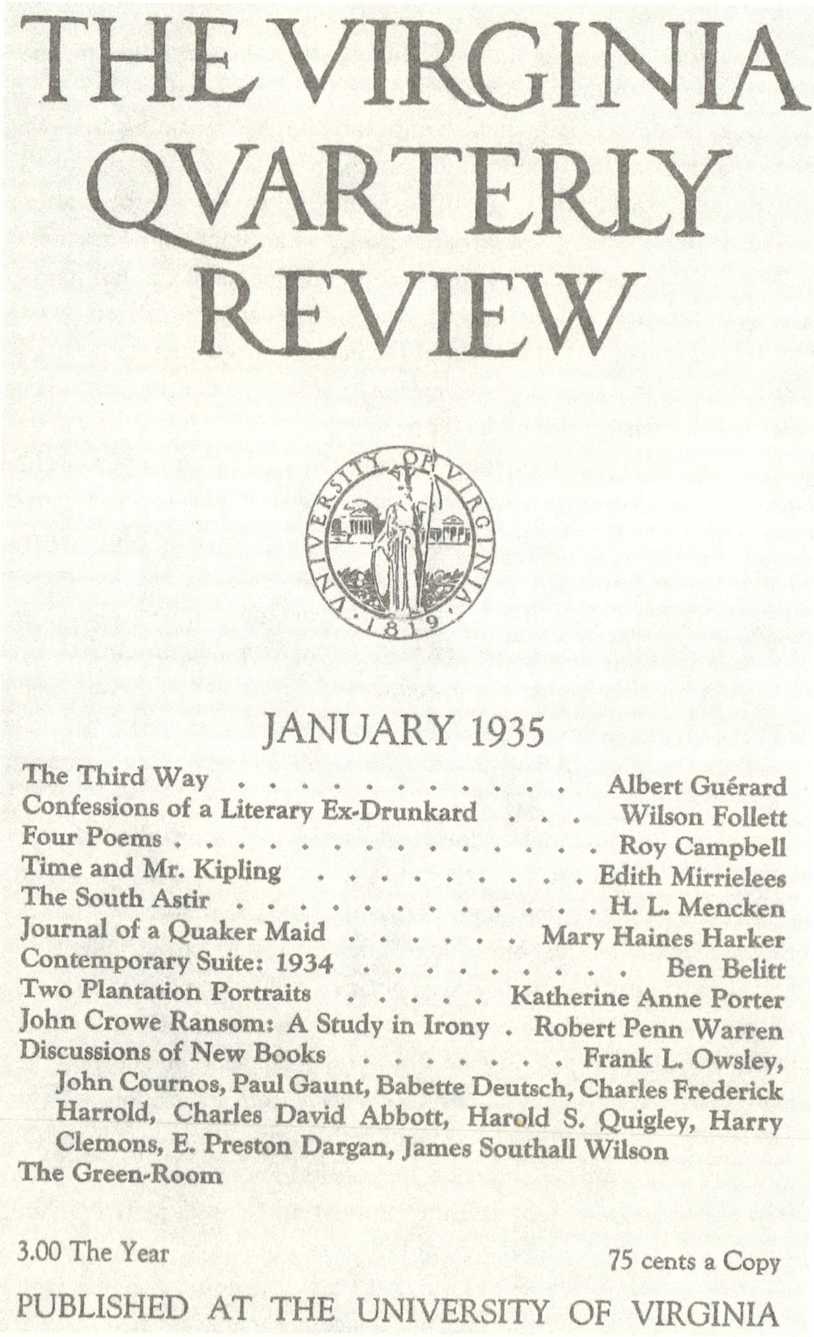

THE VIRGINIA QUARTERLY REVIEW

JANUARY 1935

The Third Way . . . . Albert Guérard
Confessions of a Literary Ex-Drunkard . . . Wilson Follett
Four Poems . . . . Roy Campbell
Time and Mr. Kipling . . . . Edith Mirrielees
The South Astir . . . . H. L. Mencken
Journal of a Quaker Maid . . . . Mary Haines Harker
Contemporary Suite: 1934 . . . . Ben Belitt
Two Plantation Portraits . . . . . Katherine Anne Porter
John Crowe Ransom: A Study in Irony . Robert Penn Warren
Discussions of New Books . . . . Frank L. Owsley, John Cournos, Paul Gaunt, Babette Deutsch, Charles Frederick Harrold, Charles David Abbott, Harold S. Quigley, Harry Clemons, E. Preston Dargan, James Southall Wilson
The Green-Room

3.00 The Year

75 cents a Copy

PUBLISHED AT THE UNIVERSITY OF VIRGINIA

Fig. 4.2 Cover of the *Virginia Quarterly Review* 2, no. 1 (January 1935). Courtesy of Special Collections, Tampa Library, University of South Florida.

"fashioned her body so as to materialize and memorialize a very different element of the African American past" (Watson 255). Changing the clothing she wore in servitude—"black wool dresses, or black and white figured calico with starchy white aprons and a white ruffled mopcap"—Nannie dons "a blue bandanna wrapped around her head" and smokes a corncob pipe (349).[20] She leaves Grandmother's ancestral plantation and insists that Mister Harry, Grandmother's son, provide her with an empty cabin so that she can have "a house of her very own" (348). For income, she weaves rugs and sells them to white visitors. She systematically replaces her lifetime's confinement to a mammy archetype with "an aged Bantu woman of independent means, sitting on the steps, breathing free air" (349).

Instead of memory as a response to societal change, Nannie embraces opportunities to emancipate herself from all remnants of past. She affirms to Grandmother's grandchildren that she is no longer responsible for their care. "Lemme go there and pass my last days in peace, chil'ren," Nannie tells them, seeming, as the narrator remarks, not to care "whether they loved her or not" (349). The narrator then conveys to the reader that Grandmother's grandchildren had "always complacently believed that Nannie was . . . perfectly happy with them" (349). They cannot reconcile her rebuke with their idealized memories of her willing servitude.

Like Grandmother's children, her husband during slavery, Uncle Jimbilly, resists Nanny's rejection of her previous caretaking role. He implies that she should allow him to live with her again, since she has independent means, but Nannie determinedly replies, "I don' aim to pas my las' days waitin on no man. . . . I've served my time, I've done my do, and dat's all" (351). In choosing to no longer submit to the plantation myth's illusions, Nannie situates her postbellum political emancipation as both physical and psychological liberation.

Kathryn B. McKee argues that there are "pockets of resistance" built "into the very progenitor of fictional plantation" (11). Nannie's refusal to maintain the narrative of her servitude despite the grandchildren's and Uncle Jimbilly's urgings, constitutes an example of this resistance. Whether or not she intended it when she composed the story for "Legend and Memory," Porter began to exploit these "pockets of resistance" to deconstruct the plantation myth even as her work was eagerly accepted by the Southern Agrarians who preferred romanticized versions of the antebellum past.

In "Portrait: Old South," an essay first published in a 1944 issue of *Mademoiselle*, Porter begins, "I am the grandchild of a lost War, and I have blood-knowledge of what life can be in a defeated country on the bare bones of privation" (Porter, *Collected* 745). She fondly recollects the stories of the experience, told to her during childhood, and describes her grandmother's memory as "the lingering perfume and the airy shimmer of grace" in "a family full of willful eccentrics and headstrong characters and unpredictable histories" (750). Drawing on these romanticized impressions, she engages tropes from plantation literature in The Old Order stories, but regardless of whether her narrative decision is a conscious one, she repurposes the genre as much as she imitates it. Porter writes Miranda into a white tradition of southern aristocratic lineage that maintained its power by oppressing Black men and women while simultaneously writing Nannie out of its "faithful slave" tradition, echoing Chopin's depiction of La Folle in "Beyond the Bayou" and Glasgow's portrayal of Mammy Rhody in "Whispering Leaves." In "The Source," Grandmother attempts to reinstate the antebellum South by mythologizing it through memory. Yet by the conclusion of "The Old Order," she is physically dead. In "The Last Leaf," Nannie rejects Grandmother's reenactments of a past that confined her to slavery and servitude. She outlives Grandmother and openly rejects the southern plantation culture that Grandmother sought to memorialize.

A Cognitive Arrangement

Unlike Glasgow, who published no further stories after *The Shadowy Third and Other Stories*, Porter viewed herself as a short-story writer. Writing in 1958 about her work on the novel *A Ship of Fools* (1962), between the second and third collected publications of The Old Order stories, she affirms, "I was and am a short story writer" (Porter, *Selected Letters* 264–67). Warren's critical review of Porter's "Miranda stories" commends her engagement with her preferred genre: "It was once fashionable to argue complacently that the popular magazine had created the short story," Warren explains, "but at the same time, and progressively, the magazine has corrupted the short story." Porter, however, does not sacrifice the "division of the artistic self of the writer" for a story's placement in a magazine (93).

Yet the short novels featuring Miranda Gay—*Old Mortality* and *Pale Horse, Pale Rider*—were initially published in magazines in 1937 and 1938, respectively and appeared together in *Pale Horse, Pale Rider: Three Short*

Novels five years before The Old Order stories' collective debut in *The Leaning Tower*. Some readers may have been familiar with Miranda's childhood stories from their magazine publications, since all except "The Source" preceded the publication of the short novels depicting her adolescence and early adulthood.

The stories were well received by readers, a trend cultivated by the periodical press but sustained by collection reprints and the Armed Services editions of her work. In particular, *The Selected Short Stories of Katherine Anne Porter* (1945) initiated extensive correspondence with readers. It included three of The Old Order stories ("The Grave," "The Witness," and "The Old Order") as well as "The Downward Path to Wisdom" from *The Leaning Tower*; "María Concepción," "That Tree," "The Cracked Looking-Glass," and "Hacienda" from *Flowering Judas and Other Stories*; and "Noon Wine" from *Pale Horse, Pale Rider*. Approximately 150,000 copies of the edition were distributed. In response, Porter received more than 600 letters from all parts of the war front and all branches of service.[21] Her readership continued to grow after the war, and *The Collected Stories of Katherine Anne Porter*, which included sections devoted to all her previously published collections, won the 1966 National Book Award and the Pulitzer Prize for Literature.

A popular writer for decades, Porter fielded multiple requests to write her biography. She responded to one such request with a rhetorical question: "How can we write a story until we know the end? In a special and almost literal way, *In my end is my beginning*; nobody will be able to see what my life meant until it is ended; how can you sum up my work until it is finished?" (Porter, *Selected Letters* 246). Like her biography, the final arrangement of The Old Order stories in *Collected Stories* comprises a beginning, or the compilation of all seven stories ordered to favor the significance of Miranda's memories beyond the chronological occurrence of the events that first engendered them.

Porter's rearrangement of Miranda's memories indicates a reconstructive process of memory, or a process of reordering, adding, eliminating, and contextualizing episodes of remembered experience over time. In 1914, psychologist Frederic Bartlett invited Cambridge students to read "The War of the Ghosts" twice and then to write out the story, word for word, after various lengths of time.[22] During the decade-long experiment, Bartlett discovered that subjects remembered some of the details from the story but that others were changed to conform to the subject's expectations or were completely omitted. Remembered text, Bartlett concluded, evolves over time (197). Porter might not have called her anachronistic rearrangements of The Old Order stories a "reconstructive process of memory" or alluded to Bartlett's experiment to contextualize her narrative decisions, but she does acknowledge the role of "craft" in her artistic renderings of legend and memory in "My First Speech," given one year after she submitted "Legend and Memory" to the *Atlantic Monthly*:

> The legend is that work of art which goes on in the human mind, adding to and arranging, harmonizing and rounding out, making larger or smaller than life, and holding the entire finished product in a good light and asking you to believe it. And it is true. No memory is really faithful. It has too far to go. . . . So the truth in art is got by change. . . . [N]othing can be accidental . . . it takes craftmanship. (693)

Porter's crafting of Miranda's memories determines a "truth" beyond the stories' original coming-of-age chronological context.

"Legend and Memory" reinforces the tales' chronological framework through textual clues that provide information about Miranda's age at the time of each event's occurrence. In "Uncle Jimbilly," Miranda is "a flighty little girl of six" (341). In "The Grave," the narrator tells us that Miranda is nine years old (362). Since Miranda's memory narrative, or an adult remembering as a child, connects her perspectives from childhood experiences to an adult's narration of those perspectives, her age is significant at the time of each memory's original experience. At the age of six, she does not question Grandmother's ritual repetitions and is frightened by Uncle Jimbilly's stories, unlike her older siblings, who question the stories' veracity. At nine years old, she buries her experience with Paul in "The Grave," only for it to emerge twenty years later in a different context. In one Old Order manuscript fragment, Porter writes that "one lives an enormous span of life between one's first memory and one's thirteenth year."[23] Miranda is younger than thirteen in all of the "Legend and Memory" sections—the first framework for ordering her memories.

"Many Redeemers," the larger project that began with "Legend and Memory," originates with a "source memory"—that is, "an experience that binds certain features of a memory episode together with certain features of another memory episode."[24] A source memory not only serves as an origin but also contributes to the future perceptual encoding for subsequent memories, connecting "separate parts of an event into a cohesive and memorable whole" (Raj and Bell 396). Porter likely developed her idea for the project from a manuscript fragment in which Miranda remembers a conversation with her father as a young child. Miranda's father demythologizes the Virgin Mary figure by asserting that "if Jesus was not the son of Joseph . . . why then he was the son of some other man." Beneath the sketch, Porter wrote "*Many Redeemers*" and outlined three sections: "1. Legend and Memory, 2. Midway this Mortal Life, 3. The Present Day."[25] The project outline beneath the sketch suggests that this narrative (which was not included in "Legend and Memory") was an impetus for The Old Order stories (figure 4.3).

As in "Legend and Memory," Porter organized the first collected publication of The Old Order stories in *The Leaning Tower* primarily chronologically.[26] When preparing for *The Leaning Tower*'s publication, Porter expressed concern about how to demonstrate that the "Legend and Memory" stories belonged together. On June 6, 1944, Brace suggested two options: (1) grouping them under a "half-title" such as "Plantation Sketches," with another half title for the remaining three; or (2) a space after the first six stories in the table of contents.[27] Despite his suggestions, the stories appear undifferentiated in the collection's table of contents. Between "Legend and Memory" and *The Leaning Tower*, Porter's most significant change was her rearrangement of the final two stories, "The Grave" and "The Last Leaf" (see table 4.2). This narrative decision initiates her revisions of the stories' chronological framework.

Porter's most significant revision of the stories' arrangement occurred in their second publication, *The Old Order: Stories of the South*. On January 25, 1955, Catharine Carver, an editor at Harcourt, Brace, proposed the collection and outlined the editorial team's story preferences.[28] However, Porter had selected and arranged the stories in all of her previous collections and was displeased with Carver's recommendations. She lamented her lack of agency in the project and firmly directed Carver to subtitle the stories "The Old Order" and to include three other southern stories: "The Jilting of Granny Weatherall," "He," and "Old Mortality." She then asked, "Does this make clear what I should like? Then no one can mistake them for random sketches, as so many reviewers did, or fragments from an unfinished novel, which they are not." And, she noted, "If this were my book, I'd never leave out these two utterly southern stories. The collection is crippled without them" (figure 4.4).[29]

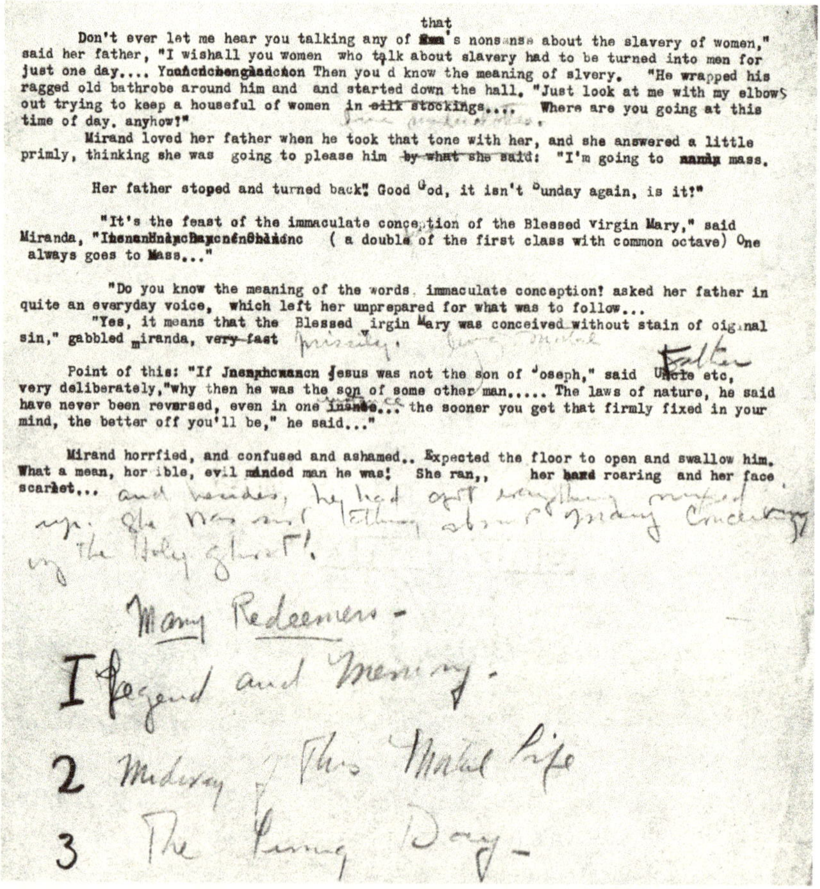

that
Don't ever let me hear you talking any of ███'s nonsense about the slavery of women," said her father, "I wishall you women who talk about slavery had to be turned into men for just one day.... Ynaǹcnchengàadchon Then you d know the meaning of slvery. "He wrapped his ragged old bathrobe around him and and started down the hall. "Just look at me with my elbows out trying to keep a houseful of women in ~~silk stockings~~.... Where are you going at this time of day, anyhow!"

Mirand loved her father when he took that tone with her, and she answered a little primly, thinking she was going to please him ~~by what she said~~: "I'm going to ~~mamix~~ mass.

Her father stoped and turned back" Good God, it isn't Sunday again, is it?"

"It's the feast of the immaculate conception of the Blessed Virgin Mary," said Miranda, "IhenanHnàpcBapcnènShàdnc (a double of the first class with common octave) One always goes to Mass..."

"Do you know the meaning of the words immaculate conception! asked her father in quite an everyday voice, which left her unprepared for what was to follow...

"Yes, it means that the Blessed Virgin Mary was conceived without stain of original sin," gabbled Miranda, ~~very fast~~ prissily.

Point of this: "If Jnenphcmancn Jesus was not the son of Joseph," said ~~Uncle~~ Father etc, very deliberately,"why then he was the son of some other man..... The laws of nature, he said have never been reversed, even in one ~~insnte~~ instance... the sooner you get that firmly fixed in your mind, the better off you'll be," he said..."

Mirand horrfied, and confused and ashamed.. Expected the floor to open and swallow him. What a mean, horrible, evil minded man he was! She ran,, her ~~hamd~~ roaring and her face scarlet... and besides, he had got everything mixed up. She was not talking about Mary Conceiving by the Holy Ghost!

Many Redeemers -
I Legend and Memory -
2 Midway of This Mortal Life
3 The [illegible] Day -

Fig. 4.3 Manuscript fragment (ca. 1930–31) that outlines Porter's "Many Redeemers" project. Courtesy of Katherine Anne Porter Papers, Special Collections and University Archives, University of Maryland Libraries.

Two days later, Porter wrote to Brace to convey similar concerns and to inform him about her letter to Carver. She agreed to "settle," even though she would prefer "*all* the southern stories," or "the six under the heading *The Old Order*, and 'Old Mortality,'" as well as "He," "Granny Weatherall," and "even 'Magic.'"[30] As the published version of *The Old Order: Stories of the South* demonstrates, her preferences eventually were accepted.

The anachronistic ordering of Miranda's childhood episodic memories in *The Old Order* eliminates the veracity of detail necessary for realistic fiction. Grandmother's mythical legend still comprises the first story, but by the end of

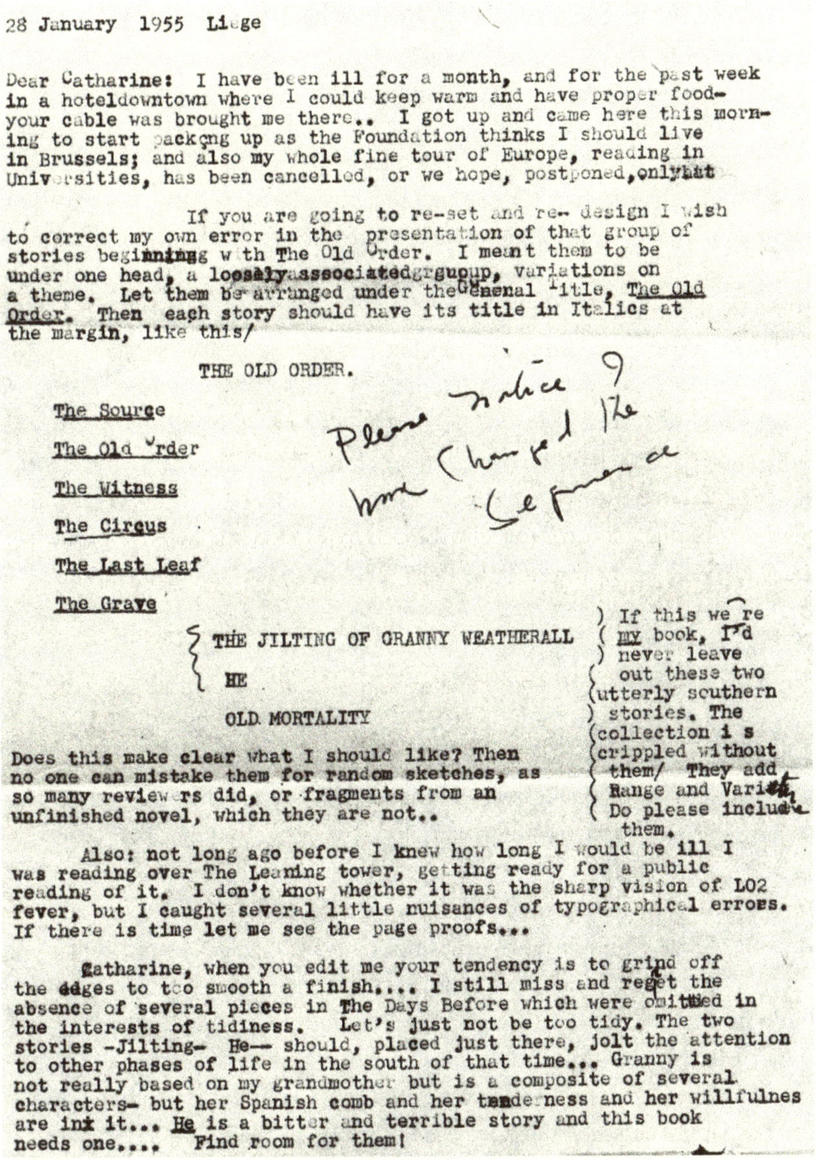

28 January 1955 Liège

Dear Catharine: I have been ill for a month, and for the past week in a hoteldowntown where I could keep warm and have proper food- your cable was brought me there.. I got up and came here this morning to start packçng up as the Foundation thinks I should live in Brussels; and also my whole fine tour of Europe, reading in Universities, has been cancelled, or we hope, postponed,onlythat

If you are going to re-set and re- design I wish to correct my own error in the presentation of that group of stories beginningg w th The Old Order. I meant them to be under one head, a loosely associatedgrgupup, variations on a theme. Let them be arranged under the General Title, The Old Order. Then each story should have its title in Italics at the margin, like this/

THE OLD ORDER.

The Source

The Old Order

The Witness

The Circus

The Last Leaf

The Grave

Please notice I have changed the sequence

THE JILTING OF GRANNY WEATHERALL

HE

OLD MORTALITY

If this were MY book, I'd never leave out these two utterly southern stories. The collection is crippled without them/ They add Range and Variety. Do please include them.

Does this make clear what I should like? Then no one can mistake them for random sketches, as so many reviewers did, or fragments from an unfinished novel, which they are not..

Also: not long ago before I knew how long I would be ill I was reading over The Leaning tower, getting ready for a public reading of it. I don't know whether it was the sharp vision of 102 fever, but I caught several little nuisances of typographical errors. If there is time let me see the page proofs...

Catharine, when you edit me your tendency is to grind off the edges to too smooth a finish.... I still miss and regret the absence of several pieces in The Days Before which were omitted in the interests of tidiness. Let's just not be too tidy. The two stories -Jilting- He-- should, placed just there, jolt the attention to other phases of life in the south of that time... Granny is not really based on my grandmother but is a composite of several characters- but her Spanish comb and her tenderness and her willfulnes are inx it... He is a bitter and terrible story and this book needs one.... Find room for them!

Fig. 4.4 First page of Katherine Anne Porter's January 28, 1955, letter to Catharine Carver outlining Porter's preferences for The Old Order collection. Courtesy of Katherine Anne Porter Papers, Special Collections and University Archives, University of Maryland Libraries.

the second story, "The Old Order," Grandmother has "dropped dead over the doorsill" (340). She miraculously resurrects herself in the third story, "The Witness," and her matriarchal voice continues to govern Miranda's experiences in "The Circus." The final two stories—"The Last Leaf" and "The Grave"—assume that Grandmother is dead (again). Grandmother's physical presences and absences, as depicted by her fictional life, burial, and narrative resurrection, allow Miranda's memories simultaneously to encompass the past, present, and future. Her memories become significant not because of their chronological framework but because of their collective remembered experience.

Porter never returned the stories to their original "Legend and Memory" arrangement. Instead, in their final publication, *Collected Stories*, she reuses *The Old Order: Stories of the South*'s arrangement and subtitle though she organizes the series under *The Leaning Tower* collection and changes the title of "The Old Order" to "The Journey." She also adds "The Fig Tree" and places it sixth, between "The Last Leaf" and "The Grave." In her preface to *Collected Stories*, Porter explains that "The Fig Tree" had been lost for more than twenty years but that she had always meant to include it in The Old Order stories. The story had "simply disappeared at the time *The Leaning Tower* was published in 1944," Porter writes, "and reappeared again from a box of otherwise unfinished manuscripts in another house, another city and a different state" many years later (v).

The history of "The Fig Tree" actually begins before the other Old Order stories. In 1928, Porter wrote to a friend, "I knocked out another wee story. . . . I called it The Fig Tree."[31] On January 12, 1930, Janet Lewis, a friend of Porter's and the publisher of a literary magazine, *Gyroscope*, apologetically returned "The Fig Tree," commenting that the story "does not quite come off, I think, or else it comes off a little too heavily with the emphasis on the lump in the throat."[32]

In "The Fig Tree," Miranda hears a weeping sound that seems to be coming from underground. She worries that a dead chick that she buried at the farm may actually have been alive but is reassured when Great-Aunt Eliza reveals that the sound is coming not from the ground but from tree frogs: "'Just think,' said Great-Aunt Eliza, in her most scientific voice, 'when tree frogs shed their skins, they pull them off over their heads like little skirts, and they eat them. Can you imagine? They have the prettiest little shapes you ever saw—I'll show you one some time under the microscope'" (362).[33] In *Collected Stories*, resurrection takes many forms: Grandmother's anachronistic death and reappearances, the resurfacing of Miranda's buried childhood memory in "The Grave," and Great-Aunt Eliza's revelation. By adding "The Fig Tree" to The Old Order, Miranda's memory narrative displaces chronological time to resurrect what lies beneath the surface of her remembered childhood experiences.

Francis Pendleton Gaines argues that the plantation literary tradition is "more reflection than determinant of public taste" (12). The Old Order stories position the plantation as relevant to the twentieth century, but the plantation was already fetishized, a staple of the nation's imagination that was continually adapted for popular consumption.[34] Porter's rearrangements of The Old Order stories over thirty years matter because by deconstructing the arrangement of her memories, she (through the fictional Miranda) begins a process of dismantling the plantation myth's underpinnings. If the initial chronological arrangement of the stories in "Legend and Memory" writes Miranda's indoctrination as future proprietor of the plantation myth, then Porter's reordering of the tales revises this indoctrination and exposes the narrative structure that maintains and perpetuates the myth's oppressiveness. Her final arrangement of The Old Order in *Collected Stories* suggests, as Solomon William argues of Porter's oeuvre, that she "was determined in her work not to smooth over the divide between troubled persons and their troubling conditions of existence" (201).

Porter's reconstructive process of memory through Miranda Gay becomes a social commentary about the perpetuation of social injustice toward white and Black women in retellings of the plantation myth—a realization developed from Porter's thirty-year reflections on the arrangement of The Old Order. In *Possessing the Past*, Lisa Hinrichsen calls for southern studies to "reexamine its own historical representation, and development, questioning its notions of self-identity, history, and community, and complicating the notion of what it means 'to remember'" (28). We must engage "critical memory," or a "form of remembrance that refuses nostalgic and unproblematic renditions of the past" (112). And we should "avoid a sense of history as something closed and complete; rather, we should always engage the past as something open and in dialogue with the present" (112). Porter's arrangements of The Old Order stories engage the past as something open and in dialogue with the present. Instead of revising the content of Miranda's memories, Porter (re)contextualizes their significance through reordering them as part of Miranda's ongoing critical engagement with the past.

Epilogue

Reading Arrangement

> To part is to die a little, it is said (in every language I can read), but my farewell to these stories is a happy one, a renewal of their life, a prolonging of their time under the sun, which is what any artist most longs for—to be read, and remembered.
>
> —KATHERINE ANNE PORTER, preface to *The Collected Stories of Katherine Anne Porter* (1965)

Arranging Stories is about how narratives are constructed and maintained to perpetuate or dismantle social injustice. The collections' textual histories demonstrate how southern white women writers used the periodical marketplace to negotiate a male-dominated publishing industry. Publishing a volume of stories indicated an author's ability to capture and preserve a loyal readership. By connecting short stories to one another within an arranged narrative space, collections guide readers through a framework of reading and interpreting meaning. Kate Chopin's *Bayou Folk* (1894), Ellen Glasgow's *The Shadowy Third and Other Stories* (1923), Marjorie Kinnan Rawlings's *When the Whippoorwill* (1940), and Katherine Anne Porter's The Old Order stories (1944, 1955, 1965) situate this frame as a conduit for social commentary about women's lives in the American South.

The final revisions for this book were completed between 2020 and 2021, during the COVID-19 pandemic. In March 2020, I watched a news brief without fully comprehending the significance of early infection outbreaks. A narrative now familiar to all of us, these numbers began multiplying quickly, universities sent students home to complete the semester online, public health officials warned of "spikes" and recommended precautionary measures, elected representatives used uncertainty to further polarize citizens, and many families lost loved ones. When I heard the situation characterized as an "unprecedented" historical moment, I recalled Porter's *Pale Horse, Pale Rider* (1936), set during the 1918 influenza pandemic. In the short novel, Miranda Gay, the (now young adult) protagonist from The Old Order stories, contracts the flu and nearly dies. Overcome by illness's delirium, her mind searches for the "feeling among her memories of words she had been taught to describe the unseen, the unknowable" (251). This feeling has the potential to comfort Miranda by shaping language to better comprehend its meaning, linking the unseen and unknowable to the visual and tangible.

Reading arrangement, whether across Porter's reordering of The Old Order stories in three collections or through Miranda's 1918 pandemic experiences as the conclusion of her three-part coming-of-age narrative, shapes our engagements with language so we can see and know. Collective arrangements not only serve as frames for reenvisioning stories in context but also are designed to invite further considerations about textual relationships. This book constitutes one case study—four authors and four short story collections—that I hope will prompt additional readings and new ways of reading, especially about the literary lives and production of historically marginalized writers.

Critical discourse about authors' narrative decisions as rhetorical strategy can be applied to other kinds of textual arrangements across genres and literary periods. Among contemporary examples, Janisse Ray alternates between ecological- and ethnographic-focused chapters in her memoirs *Ecology of a Cracker Childhood* (1999) and *Wild Card Quilt: Ecology of Home* (2007) to compel readers to view community as a responsibility to the natural environment as well as to one another. Crystal Wilkinson arranges her short story collection, *Water Street* (2002), by individual characters' voices, so that each might tell of their experiences living in an African American Appalachian community. Natasha Trethewey's *Native Guard* (2006) arranges poems in three sections, guiding readers through a spatial experience of remembering and memorializing. In the final lines from the collection's last poem, "South," the speaker maps complicated relationships between identity and place in the American South:

> where that old flag still hangs, I return
>   to Mississippi, state that made a crime
> of me—mulatto, half-breed—native
>   in my land, this place they'll bury. (lines 31–34)

The movement from infrastructure to memorialization, from symbol to legislation, and from race to geography emphasizes the entanglement of these elements. Each association with place unearths a tradition of racial oppression, or ideology bound in and disseminated through narrative.

Reading arrangement can also become an exercise for teaching narrative decisions. In an advanced composition class for future K–12 teachers offered by the Department of English at Eastern Kentucky University, students write a six-part literacy narrative that focuses on their previous experiences with writing in and out of the classroom setting. After workshopping drafts, students arrange their work to create an overarching lens that will help them develop a philosophy for teaching writing. To conceptualize this process, classes tour the current exhibit at the university's gallery or a virtual gallery with a user-guided interface. Students experience how arrangement contributes to our understanding of individual and collected texts (in the same way that Mieke Bal writes about her visits to Ken Aptekar's exhibits) and then incorporate insights from this exercise into the arrangements of their work.

How we arrange writing is part of a narrative's telling, an analysis that can be applied to other kinds of engagements with collected texts. What happens, for example, when critics compile unpublished manuscripts or rearrange previously collected stories into posthumous edited volumes?[1] A group of Chopin's stories was published nearly a century after they first appeared in magazines in *A Vocation and a Voice* (1991); an edited collection of Glasgow's stories, including stories not included in *The Shadowy Third*, was published in 1963; and all of Rawlings's short stories were published in *Short Stories by Marjorie Kinnan Rawlings* (1994), without differentiating stories from *When the Whippoorwill* from stories published outside of the collection. Edited collections like these typically arrange texts by original publication or composition dates, providing readers with a trajectory that seems to correspond with biographical information. The importance of posthumous collections should not be underestimated, since reprinting stories maintains and extends their readership beyond an author's lifetime. However, I cannot help but wonder if our editing decisions impose on authors' original intentions for their oeuvres in ways that might unintentionally revise envisioned collective meaning.

In this way, reading arrangement might also frame our understanding of authors' planned legacies. All the authors in this study insisted on control over their published work, an approach that by association often extends to their posthumous legacies. It seems fitting, then, that this book was engendered in the archives that contain the textual histories of these stories—repositories that, as much as a century later, continue to revise ideas about white southern women writers' authorial intentions. All of the writers except Chopin, whose surviving manuscripts and correspondence were meticulously transcribed and published by Per Seyersted and Emily Toth, sought to use selection and arrangement to ensure the maintenance of their narrative visions beyond their lifetimes, and for the most part, they succeeded. Glasgow, Rawlings, and Porter destroyed materials or bequeathed vetted documents to institutional repositories. Glasgow spent the latter years of her life writing her autobiography, *The Woman Within* (1954). She kept it in a locked briefcase with specific instructions for publishers to collect it directly from her home after her death. She also stipulated that her remaining personal photographs and letters were to be destroyed and that her correspondence should never be published. Even so, some letters were preserved through friends' and family members' archives (Goodman 157). Rawlings and Porter left their papers to university archives, greatly benefiting scholars, though the presences and absences within these archives sometimes complicate research. Rawlings, for instance, was careful to not include sensitive notes from her (incomplete) Ellen Glasgow biography, and Porter, in addition to typing manuscripts from the published versions of her work, asked recipients to return or to destroy some of her early correspondence (Silverthorne 335; Unrue 112).

An archived collection conveys one account of a writer's life and work from the letters and manuscripts left (either purposely or inadvertently) behind. Whether the archive is physical or digital, its selection and arrangement of documents comprises a cultural history of authors' lives and works (Steedman 81). Like a short-story collection, individual documents provide one insight; taken together, a repository depicts a collective narrative vision. For nineteenth- and early twentieth-century women writers, letters and manuscripts often remain situated in multiple geographic locations, buried in archives designated for male relatives or publishers, and marginalized for their perceived lack of value. Reading arrangement—either within an archive or between multiple archives—connects text to context and readings to relationships between readings.

When women writers construct (or deconstruct) their archives, we should read it as an extension of their narrative legacies. Writers' ability to arrange their own archives—either by bequeathing materials to a university's library or by destroying materials and writing an autobiography—provides another example of how southern white women writers sought agency in the early twentieth century.[2] It is a privileged position that reflects particular race and class statuses, but it is also a position painstakingly developed through a level of tenacity that defied a patronizing publishing culture. The writers in *Arranging Stories* wanted to secure their narrative legacies for future readers, legacies that, as Porter writes in her preface to her final short-story collection, are "what any artist most longs for—to be read, and remembered."

Notes

Introduction: Arranging Stories as a Frame for Social Commentary

1. Tom Sleigh, email to author, fall 2011. This conversation was coordinated by David Wojahn, professor of English, Virginia Commonwealth University, Richmond.

2. The term *intersectionality* was coined by legal scholar Kimberlé Crenshaw to indicate relationships between multiple sites of oppression, including (but not limited to) race, class, gender, and sexuality.

3. A few (of many) examples include Harriet Ann Jacobs's *Incidents in the Life of a Slave Girl* (1861) and Elizabeth Keckley's *Behind the Scenes, or Thirty Years a Slave and Four Years in the White House* (1868). Harper did publish a slave narrative, *Iola Leroy, or Shadows Uplifted* (1892), but this publication followed poetry collections, such as *Forest Leaves* (1845) and *Sketches of Southern Life* (1875).

4. For more on how African American women began to establish a public presence in order to confront the literary conventions of womanhood which excluded them in the mid- to late nineteenth century, see Carby.

5. For critical analysis of the stories in Dunbar-Nelson's *The Goodness of St. Rocque*, see Nagel.

6. In 2014, Nagel devoted a chapter to Dunbar-Nelson's stories in *Race and Culture in New Orleans Stories*, and in 2016, Katherine Adams, Sandra Zagarell, and Caroline Gebhard guest edited a *Legacy: A Journal of American Women Writers* special issue, "Rediscovering Alice Dunbar-Nelson for the Twenty-First Century." While Alice Walker first published "In Search of Zora Neale Hurston" in a 1975 issue of *Ms.* magazine, recovery efforts to publish Hurston's manuscripts are ongoing, including a 2018 publication of Hurston's *Barracoon: The Story of the Last "Black Cargo,"* which was completed in 1931.

Chapter One: Mapping Spatial Consciousness in Kate Chopin's *Bayou Folk* (1894)

A previous version of this chapter was published as "Mapping Spatial Consciousness in Kate Chopin's *Bayou Folk* Stories" in *South: A Scholarly Journal* 48, no. 1 (Fall 2015): 108–28.

1. The first two Chopin biographies include Rankin, *Kate Chopin and Her Creole Stories* (1932) and Seyersted, *Kate Chopin: A Critical Biography* (1969). Toth's 1999 biography, *Unveiling Kate Chopin*, was published well after the initial recovery period of Chopin's work and after years of critical attention beginning in the 1970s. In "The Shadow of the First Biographer," Toth points out that Rankin's portrayal of Chopin as a "traditional woman, devoted wife, selfless mother, and chaste widow" was influenced by his training as a Jesuit priest (288).

2. Chopin, *Kate Chopin's Private Papers*, 131. Hereafter cited as *PP*. Kate Chopin's original manuscript account books—the Bonnell Manuscript Account Book and the Wondra Manuscript Account Book—are archived digitally with the Missouri Historical Society and reprinted in *PP* 136–75.

3. This definition of true womanhood draws on Welter's seminal essay, "Cult of True Womanhood." See also Papke's examination of the influence of true womanhood ideology on the writings of Chopin and Wharton; Anne Goodwyn Jones 135–82.

4. This assertion contradicts Vanlandingham 159–60, which argues that Chopin primarily "wrote to please herself," did not concern herself with a periodical's audience or editorial policies, "misunderstood editors and mistrusted their perceptions of what the public wanted," and "naively thought she could gain the attention of the eastern literary establishment by sending review copies to newspaper and magazine editors . . . whose work she especially admired." However, my argument here aligns with Shaker, "Kate Chopin," 88, which directly counters Vanlandingham's claims and contends that Chopin was "a seasoned veteran of the periodical marketplace who honed her writing skills to take maximum advantage of the commercial opportunities available for her fiction."

5. Mott, whose five-volume *History of American Magazines* chronicles the trajectory of periodical publications in the United States from 1731 to 1930, identifies these four publications as "quality magazines," or magazines for an audience of higher socioeconomic means and intellectual interests.

6. These essays are reprinted in Rankin, *Kate Chopin and Her Creole Stories* and Chopin, *Complete Works*, 2:706–20.

7. For a historical analysis of the opportunities for white southern women to publish regionally inspired work beginning in the 1880s, see Censer, *Reconstruction*.

8. My categorizing of "Beyond the Bayou," "The Return of Alcibiade," "A Wizard from Gettysburg," and "Ma'ame Pélagie" as Civil War stories draws on Kotlarczyk's assertion that they, as well as two other stories published after *Bayou Folk*, directly engage the effects of the Civil War.

9. While Soja focuses on modern-day metropolises like Los Angeles, his conceptualizations of space can be applied to rural geographies chronologically situated in previous centuries. I borrow the term *spatial consciousness* from Soja, *Postmetropolis*, 17, which calls for "a new spatial consciousness" that aligns "spatial perspective" with "historical and sociological reasoning."

10. See "Confederate Memoirs," vols. 2 and 3, A. S. Williams III Americana Collection, University Libraries Division of Special Collections, University of Alabama. I transcribed selections from this two-volume manuscript in August 2015 as a 2015–16 Frances S. Summersell Fellow.

11. Jessie Gilley, "Confederate Memoirs," 2:209–10.

12. Joshua Morbut, "Confederate Memoirs," 2:288.

13. John West, "Confederate Memoirs," 2:218.

14. "Confederate Memoirs," 3:395–96.

15. The term was originally the *Great South*, but Lanier amended the phrase to *New South* in his article by that title. The transition to the New South following the Civil War revised the region's social structure.

16. In *Unveiling Kate Chopin*, Toth describes how Chopin organized a garden party with other mothers whose sons were serving in the Spanish-American War. These women were her "cardplaying friends," and the party "combin[ed] the United Daughters of the Confederacy and the Daughters of the American Revolution" (204). This was the sole reference to the UDC I found in Chopin's biographical material, and I could not obtain further information through correspondence with a UDC historian.

17. Koloski points out that one hundred of Chopin's stories were written for children (30).

18. "Beyond the Bayou" appears in Chopin, *Bayou Folk*, 99–110. All citations are to this version.

19. In *Production of Space*, geographer and place theorist Henri Lefebvre defines social space as "not a thing among other things, nor a product among other products: rather it subsumes things produced, and encompasses their interrelationships in their coexistence and simultaneity—their (relative) order and/or (relative) disorder. . . . Itself the outcome of past action, social space is what permits fresh actions to occur, while suggesting others and prohibiting yet others" (73). See also *In Place/Out of Place*, 11, in which geographer Tim Cresswell underscores the significance of Lefebvre's definition, asserting that social and spatial are "thoroughly imbued with each other's presence"; any attempt at "their analytical separation becomes a misleading exercise."

20. I rely on Lefebvre's definition of *nature* as constituting what creates but does not produce or labor (70–71).

21. Nixon's reading contends that since La Folle's social status has always been equivalent to slavery, her second journey can only be read as a "pathetic fallacy," confirmed by nature's "affirmation [of] the rightness of the social-racial hierarchy" (945).

22. For more on the "socialized geography of (in)justice" that informs this reading of La Folle's response in "Beyond the Bayou" and especially contemporary applications, see Soja, *Seeking*.

23. Kate Chopin, "A Free Little Mulatto," n.p., Kate O'Flaherty Chopin Papers, 1855–1975, archived digitally with the Missouri Historical Society, St. Louis.

24. Although previous scholarship dates the story's publication to December 17, 1892, the story was actually published on December 10, 1892.

25. "Return of Alcibiade" appears in Chopin, *Bayou Folk*, 113–25. All citations are to this version.

26. According to *From Ox-Teams to Eagles*, the New Orleans–Shreveport line opened on September 12, 1882.

27. The original manuscript for "White Oaks" is archived digitally in the Kate O'Flaherty Chopin Papers, 1855–1975, Missouri Historical Society, St. Louis. The poem was printed posthumously in *PP* 289.

28. For instance, Linda Wagner-Martin calls it "one of Chopin's most clichéd tales" in Edwards 142; while Nagel argues that the story "does much to unify the thematic elements of *Bayou Folk*" (135).

29. "Wizard from Gettysburg" appears in Chopin, *Bayou Folk*, 230–44. All citations are to this version.

30. J. W. Pater, "Confederate Memoirs," 2:264–65

31. "Ma'ame Pélagie" appears in Chopin, *Bayou Folk*, 245–60. Unless otherwise noted, all citations are to this version.

32. Emily Toth and Per Seyersted compiled the surviving documents and published them in *Kate Chopin's Private Papers* and *A Kate Chopin Miscellany*.

33. Chopin, *Kate Chopin Miscellany*, 110. Hereafter cited as *Miscellany*.

34. Chopin, "Ma'ame Pélagie," *New Orleans Times-Democrat*.

35. *Bayou Folk* was printed in March 1894, March 1895, February 1906, and August 1911 (Rankin 136). Rankin incorrectly dates the first publication to February instead of March 1894. Chopin also negotiated with publishers to reprint some of the stories in *Bayou Folk* outside of the collection. She did not further revise these stories after they appeared in *Bayou Folk* (*PP* 206–7).

Chapter Two: Advocating for Social Justice in Ellen Glasgow's *The Shadowy Third and Other Stories* (1923)

1. Glasgow, *Woman Within*, 139. Hereafter cited as *WW*.

2. See Coultrap-McQuin, which examines nineteenth-century women writers' negotiations within a male-dominated publishing marketplace; Showalter, whose introduction cites literary historical evidence that aligns directly with Glasgow's assertions about the exclusion of women writers in American literature (x–xii).

3. Russ identifies denial of agency, "pollution of agency," and isolation as three of eleven components that contribute to less representation in literature. I draw on Russ's analysis of pollution of agency to further contextualize characterizations of Glasgow's publishing relationships (25).

4. Glasgow to Edna Kenton, November 4, 1913, Albert and Shirley Small Special Collections Library, University of Virginia, Charlottesville.

5. Glasgow to Edna Kenton, November 4, 1913, Small Special Collections Library.

6. Anne Goodwyn Jones asserts that James Branch Cabell likely initiated the label (230).

7. Meeker discovered the twelfth story, "The Professional Instinct," as an unfinished manuscript in the University of Virginia's Special Collections. Despite Meeker's reservations, Kelly published the story. See Meeker, editor's note to "The Professional Instinct," in Glasgow, *Collected Stories*, 254.

8. Meeker argues that the stories in *The Shadowy Third* are influenced by Glasgow's failed relationship with Henry Anderson, Darwinism, Poe's narrative style, responses to World War I, and emerging psychological knowledge. Raper asserts that the short stories are difficult to categorize but constitute an "experiment in characterization" as a result of a "decade of emotional and aesthetic crisis" ("Invisible" 66, 89). Both Raper and Meeker contend that Glasgow's stories, particularly her ghost stories, are influenced by findings in psychology at the turn of the twentieth century. In addition, MacKethan argues that one of the influences on Glasgow's stories is Darwinism, and Rainwater attributes Glasgow's stories to the influences of Poe and H. G. Wells.

9. My use of *intellectual independence* derives from Kelley, *Learning to Stand and Speak*. Kelley, a historian, connects increased opportunities for women's education to women's progressive political engagement in the nineteenth century to argue that education allowed women to experience themselves as "rational being[s]" (98).

10. For more on the use of the ghost story trope, see Domínguez-Rue; Harde, which draws on Gilbert and Gubar for an analysis of Glasgow's use of this (Gothic) nineteenth-century genre.

11. For more on Glasgow's realism, see Meeker 9; Goodman 88; Mims 218; Branser 75.

12. For a reading of the role of inheritance (broadly defined) in "The Shadowy Third," see Zaugg.

13. "Shadowy Third" appears in Glasgow, *Shadowy Third and Other Stories*, 3–46. Unless otherwise noted, all citations are to this version.

14. Glasgow, "Shadowy Third," *Scribner's Magazine*, 660.

15. "Dare's Gift" appears in Glasgow, *Shadowy Third and Other Stories*, 47–106. Unless otherwise noted, all citations are to this version.

16. Glasgow, "Dare's Gift: Part I," 322.

17. Glasgow, "Dare's Gift: Part I," 322–23.

18. Nonetheless, critics have argued that women's magazines did not do enough for the suffrage movement. Burkhalter rightly notes that *Good Housekeeping* published only eight suffragist-related articles between 1918 and 1920. This finding, however, does not account for selections between 1913 and 1916. Suffragist articles were less common during the US involvement in World War I.

19. "The Past" appears in Glasgow, *Shadowy Third and Other Stories*, 107–50. Unless otherwise noted, all citations are to this version.

20. Glasgow also identifies the name of her mother's caretaker as "Mammy Rhoda" in *WW*. See also Meeker 10; MacKethan 52.

21. One explanation for this uniformity can be traced to the United Daughters of the Confederacy (UDC). Cox argues that UDC purposefully rewrote a false, romanticized version of the past and read essays about the Old South during group meetings to strategically position these writings' tropes in collective memory. In particular, their narratives reminisced about "mammies," an extension of the "faithful slave" narrative (12). See also White; McElya; Faust.

22. Julia Neely Finch, "An Old-Time Southern 'Mammy,'" Julia Neely Finch Papers, W. S. Hoole Special Collections Library, University Libraries Division of Special Collections, University of Alabama, Tuscaloosa. I transcribed this memoir in August 2016 during my time as a 2016 Frances S. Summersell Fellow.

23. Finch, "Old-Time Southern 'Mammy,'" 14–16.

24. Finch, "Old-Time Southern 'Mammy,'" 22–23.

25. For a trajectory of scholarship about Glasgow and race, see William Parker; Haytock, which argues that "literary representations of such black caretakers for white children indicate a deeper problem" (4); Griffith, which asserts that "by creating fictional figures of 'faithful slaves,' the institution of slavery becomes an abstract rather than a specific wrong [so] that despite the injustice of slavery, no one is held responsible for it" (91).

26. "Whispering Leaves," appears in Glasgow, *Shadowy Third and Other Stories*, 151–200. Unless otherwise noted, all citations are to this version.

27. This assertion applies the argument made in Anolik to "Whispering Leaves."

28. Glasgow to Cabel Tutwiler (Rebe), December 27, 1925, Marjorie Kinnan Rawlings Papers, Special and Area Studies Collections, George A. Smathers Libraries, University of Florida, Gainesville.

29. Meeker also suggests that "Between Two Shores" does not appear in *Shadowy Third and Other Stories* because it struggles to reconcile romantic love with submission and

that "Thinking Makes It So" resembles a "modern Cinderella story" that is difficult to take "seriously" (Glasgow, *Collected Stories* 39, 89).

30. See Glasgow to Maxwell Perkins, August 19, 1937, Rawlings Papers. Rawlings was writing Glasgow's biography, so copies of some of Glasgow's correspondence, Rawlings's interview notes, and other documents related to the biography's production are located in the Rawlings Papers. For more on the relationship between Glasgow and Rawlings, see Lear, *Remarkable*.

31. Maxwell Perkins to Glasgow, August 18, 1937, Rawlings Papers.

32. Glasgow to Maxwell Perkins, August 19, 1937, Rawlings Papers.

33. Writing to Perkins on August 21, 1937, Glasgow eliminates *The Descendant* because it is not set in Virginia. In another letter to Perkins dated September 23, 1937, Glasgow outlines her work into three categories: Novels of Character, Comedies of Manners, and My Social History of Virginia from the War between the States. She notes that the reprints must come from the Old Dominion Editions and that she has found twelve frontispieces. On November 18, 1937, Glasgow points out to Perkins that there "were several misprints in this page proof" and thanks him for allowing her to correct her own proofs. All letters are in the Rawlings Papers.

34. Glasgow to Maxwell Perkins, September 23, 1937, Rawlings Papers.

35. Glasgow to Maxwell Perkins, October 26, 1937, Rawlings Papers.

36. Maxwell Perkins to Glasgow, October 29, 1937, Rawlings Papers.

37. Much of Glasgow's correspondence and photographs was destroyed within days of her death (Goodman 5, 76, 157). Rouse's 1958 publication of Glasgow's letters (Glasgow, *Letters*) went against her will. Glasgow's longtime caretaker, Anne Bennett, writes to Rawlings on May 7, 1953, "I *knew* Ellen did not want her *letters* published" (Rawlings Papers). Some of Glasgow's letters were again published in Glasgow, *Perfect Companionship* (2005).

38. See Glasgow, *Five Letters*. Frazee argues that Glasgow "failed to see that the rights of women, like any serious public issue, cannot gain recognition outside the channels of politics, whether or not one is interested in political commitment" (179).

CHAPTER THREE: PRESERVING THE HAMMOCK IN MARJORIE KINNAN RAWLINGS'S *WHEN THE WHIPPOORWILL* (1940)

1. James Branch Cabell to Rawlings, April 9, 1941, Rawlings Papers.

2. Rawlings to Ethel Fairmont Snyder Beebe, January 6, 1931, Rawlings Papers.

3. Maxwell Perkins to Rawlings, October 5, 1939, in Perkins, *Max and Marjorie*, 422. Hereafter cited as *MM*.

4. While not a focus of this book's analysis of Rawlings's short story collection, the colonization and attempt to "conquer" the American frontier also contributed to the inhumane treatment and often death of Indigenous peoples.

5. Marjorie Kinnan Rawlings, "The Relativity of Beauty," Rawlings Papers.

6. See Carl Brandt to Rawlings, February 15, 1935, in Rawlings Papers.

7. Charles Scribner to Rawlings, January 17, 1940, Rawlings Papers.

8. See letters between Rawlings and Maxwell Perkins, May 16 and December 3, 1940, *MM* 455–56, 476–77.

9. "Benny and the Bird Dogs" and "Varmints" are the other two stories that feature Quincey Dover's narration.

10. Scrapbook of Book Reviews, especially *When the Whippoorwill*, 1940; transcript from Boston, May 4, 1940, "Robust Stories of Piney Woods: First Collection of Short Works of Fiction by 'The Yearling's' Author Is Rich Folklore," both in Rawlings Papers.

11. Marjorie Kinnan Rawlings, "Speech for [a] Florida College," Rawlings Papers.

12. Rawlings, "Relativity of Beauty," 3–6.

13. For descriptions of the nineteenth-century through early twentieth-century Florida frontier, including the origins of the term *Florida Cracker*, see editorial notes in Aldrich and Anderson 14, xxiv; Marjorie Kinnan Rawlings, "Florida: A Land of Contrasts," 59–66.

14. Examples of volumes of letters from the nineteenth- through early twentieth-century Florida frontier include Aldrich and Anderson; Moseley; George Gillett Keen and Williams. Keen and Williams's collection of solicited editorials, written in the early twentieth century as a response to late-nineteenth-century recollections of living on the Florida frontier, constitutes a rare example of Florida Cracker culture experiences written by Florida Crackers during this period.

15. As Scott notes, an elite plantation woman who enacted the ideals of the southern lady would be "loved and respected and supported," but a woman who "defi[ed] the pattern and behave[d] in ways considered unladylike" would "be unsexed, rejected, unloved," and she would "probably starve" (20–21).

16. Marjorie Kinnan Rawlings, "Notes for a Lecture on Facts vs. Fiction in Writing," Rawlings Papers.

17. "Crop of Beans" appears in Rawlings, *When the Whippoorwill*, 1–19. Unless otherwise noted, all citations are to this version.

18. Marjorie Kinnan Rawlings, "Jacob's Ladder," Rawlings Papers.

19. "Jacob's Ladder" appears in Rawlings, *When the Whippoorwill*, 41–118. Unless otherwise noted, all citations are to this version.

20. Perkins suggested that title be changed from "High Winds," which had recently been used by another author (Silverthorne 63).

21. In the biblical story, Jacob falls asleep and dreams of a stairway between heaven and earth with ascending and descending angels. In the dream, God's voice tells him that he will have many children and that everyone on earth will be blessed through him and his offspring. Jacob's dream follows his escape from the wrath of Esau, his older brother. In conspiracy with his mother, Jacob had deceived his blind father into giving him the blessing and birthright that would traditionally have been given to the first son (Genesis 28:10–22). The last verse of the nineteenth-century African American spiritual, developed into a hymn, repeats "we are climbing higher / soldiers of the cross" ("Jacob's Ladder #418"). For a reading that focuses on Jacob's dream and other biblical allusions in Rawlings's story, see Weiser.

22. Rawlings to Bernice Baumgarten Hawthorne, received October 19, 1933, Rawlings Papers.

23. "Gal Young Un" appears in Rawlings, *When the Whippoorwill*, 175–216. Unless otherwise noted, all citations are to this version.

24. The other three stories were "The Enemy" (January 1940), "Alligators" (September 1933), and "A Mother in Mannville" (December 1936).

25. "Cocks Must Crow" appears in Rawlings, *When the Whippoorwill*, 251–75. Unless otherwise noted, all citations are to this version.

26. Marjorie Kinnan Rawlings, "Cocks Must Crow," 6, Rawlings Papers. For the added sentence, see Rawlings, "Cocks Must Crow," in *When the Whippoorwill*, 256.

27. James Branch Cabell to Rawlings, June 11, 1940, Rawlings Papers.

28. Marjorie Kinnan Rawlings, "In This I Believe," in "Short Writings," 3, Rawlings Papers.

29. Marjorie Kinnan Rawlings, "The Mechanics of Writing," 6, Rawlings Papers.

30. Perkins's list is referenced in an editor's note in *Max and Marjorie* (*MM* 445) but is not included in the volume. The list is housed in the Archives of Charles Scribner's Sons, Special Collections, Princeton University Library.

31. See Lowe; Morris, which argues that Rawlings is excluded from essay collections such as *The Feminine Tradition in Southern Literature*, edited by Carol S. Manning (1993) because her "work does not tell a woman's story" and that she could not write "with a focus on women's concerns" because her writing would not have been taken seriously (31).

32. Marjorie Kinnan Rawlings, "On Florida and Floridians," Rawlings Papers.

Chapter Four: Reconstructing Memory in Katherine Anne Porter's The Old Order Stories (1944, 1955, 1965)

Portions of this chapter expand on "Representations of Truth: The Significance of Order in Katherine Anne Porter's The Old Order Stories" in *Janus Head: Journal of Interdisciplinary Studies in Literature, Continental Philosophy, Phenomenological Psychology, and the Arts* 14, no. 2 (October 2015): 201–25; and "(Re)Positioning through Remembering and Forgetting in Katherine Anne Porter's 'The Source,' 'The Journey,' and 'The Last Leaf'" in *Southern Studies: An Interdisciplinary Journal of the South* 21, no. 2 (Fall/Winter 2014): 75–97.

1. For Katherine Anne Porter's work on "Legend and Memory," see Porter to Caroline Gordon, June 16, 1932, Porter to Harrison Porter, May 31, 1934, Katherine Anne Porter Papers, Special Collections and University Archives, University of Maryland Libraries, College Park; Porter to Josephine Herbst, August 3, 1934, Porter to Caroline Gordon, June 9, 1935, in Porter, *Letters*, 109–10, 125–28. See also Unrue 144.

2. Porter to Harrison Porter, May 31, 1934, Porter Papers.

3. Edward Aswell to Charles Pearce, May 17, 1934, Porter Papers.

4. Porter to Charles Pearce, May 31, 1934, Porter Papers.

5. Porter to Charles Pearce, June 8, 1934, Porter Papers.

6. Pearce to Katherine Anne Porter, December 3, 1934, Porter Papers.

7. Pearce to Katherine Anne Porter, December 3, 1934, Porter Papers.

8. Several literary scholars contend that Miranda is either the fictional rendering of Porter as a child or her alternate persona. See, for example, Schwartz; Wimsatt 85; Titus 182.

9. Porter to Charles Pearce, May 31, 1934, Porter Papers.

10. *I'll Take My Stand* contains essays by twelve southern writers and critics from Vanderbilt University, three of whom self-identified as members of the Fugitive Poets: Donald Davidson, John Gould Fletcher, Henry Blue Kline, Lyle Lanier, Andrew Nelson Lytle, Herman Clarence Nixon, Frank Lawrence Owsley, John Crowe Ransom, Allen Tate, John Donald Wade, Robert Penn Warren, and Stark Young. In "Sahara of the Bozart," originally published in the *New York Evening Mail* (1917), Mencken argued that southern culture had diminished so dramatically since the Civil War that the South was incapable of intellectual production.

11. The term *fantasy narrative* is borrowed from Hinrichsen.

12. Brace to Katherine Anne Porter, June 6, 1944, Porter Papers.

13. Porter to Catharine Carver, January 28, 1955, Porter Papers.

14. "The Source" appears in Porter, *Collected Stories*, 321–25. Unless otherwise noted, all citations are to this version.

15. Porter to Charles Pearce, May 31, 1934, Porter Papers.

16. For *Accent*'s publication history, see Lynn. See also Hoffman, Allen, and Ulrich 350.

17. *The Dollmaker* depicts an Appalachian family's struggle to survive in the industrialized North. In some of her previous publications, Arnow used the pseudonym H. L. Simpson to deter publishers from rejecting her work based on her gender.

18. "The Old Order" appears as "The Journey" in Porter, *Collected Stories*, 326–39. Unless otherwise noted, all citations are to this version.

19. Fox-Genovese argues that this social system defined gender conventions that "simultaneously formed and influenced social relations and operated like a language or discourse that helped individuals make sense of their place in the world" (194).

20. "The Last Leaf" appears in Porter, *Collected Stories*, 348–51. Unless otherwise noted, all citations are to this version.

21. See S. Scott Spencer to Katherine Anne Porter, May 16, 1945, Porter Papers.

22. For contemporary analysis of Bartlett's experiment and its applications, see Winter 210–18.

23. Porter, "Old Order Fragments," Porter Papers.

24. My use of the term *source memory* comes from Raj and Bell, which argues that the contextual detail of an episodic memory attributes a memory episode to its source, which, in turn, provides an experience that binds together certain features of a memory episode and certain features of another memory episode (384).

25. Porter, "Many Redeemers, c. 1930–31," Porter Papers.

26. Donald Brace Anne Porter, June 2, 1944, June 6, 1944, Porter Papers.

27. Donald Brace to Katherine Anne Porter, June 6, 1944, Porter Papers.

28. Catharine Carver to Porter, January 25, 1955, Porter Papers.

29. Porter to Catharine Carver, January 28, 1955, Porter Papers.

30. Porter to Donald Brace, January 30, 1955, in Porter, *Letters*, 474.

31. Porter to Josephine Herbst, 1928, Porter Papers.

32. Janet Lewis to Porter, January 12, 1930, Porter Papers.

33. For an analysis of "The Fig Tree," see Fox, "Resurrecting."

34. This assertion draws on two sources. First, in "From *Uncle Remus* to *Song of the South*," Daniel Stein examines Walt Disney's adaptation of Joel Chandler Harris's *Uncle Remus* tales and calls for the study of "individual adaptations within a broader cultural framework" to trace how a "whole cultural mythology" and its "images of race and spaces can migrate from one century to another through the chain of remediation from folktales to literature to film" (22). According to Stein, "adaptation and remediation are indeed ubiquitous practices of national making and remaking that urge us to view *America* as a fiction that has, for better or worse, returned again and again to the southern plantation" (22). Second, my reference to the popular consumption of southern ideology through literary production comes from Romine, which argues that the South sells its ideology.

Epilogue: Reading Arrangement

1. See Hutchisson, whose examinations of "restored" or re-edited texts invites questions applicable to a collection of stories: "If a re-edited version of a novel is supposed to replace the 'classic' version of the book, then what are the rights and responsibilities for the publishers and editors who are ushering them into print? What arguments can these editors make for claiming one version to be superior (in whatever context) over the other?

For 'lost' or unpublished manuscripts, is there a tacit fiduciary responsibility that the editor must assume toward Rawlings or Hemingway to act in the best interests of the posthumous reputation of the author? And finally, what, in general, is to be gained or lost from altering, retouching, or restoring a literary masterpiece?" (346).

2. This assertion about women's archives borrows from Fox and Stuckey.

Bibliography

Adams, Katherine, Sandra A. Zagarell, and Caroline Gebhard. "Rediscovering Alice Dunbar-Nelson for the Twenty-First Century: An Introduction." *Legacy: A Journal of American Women Writers* 33, no. 2 (2016): 213–53.

Agee, James, and Walker Evans. *Let Us Now Praise Famous Men.* New York: Houghton Mifflin, 1941.

Aldrich, Corinna Brown, and Ellen Brown Anderson. *Echoes from a Distant Frontier: The Brown Sisters' Correspondence from Antebellum Florida.* Edited by James M. Denham and Keith L. Huneycutt. Columbia: University of South Carolina Press, 2004.

Alvarez, Ruth M. "Katherine Anne Porter." In *A Companion to the American Short Story,* edited by Alfred Bendixen and James Nagel. Oxford: Blackwell, 2010.

Anolik, Ruth Bienstock. "Introduction: The Dark Unknown." In *The Gothic Other: Racial and Social Constructions in the Literary Imagination,* edited by Ruth Bienstock Anolik and Douglas L. Howard, Jefferson, NC: McFarland, 2004.

Aptekar, Ken. "I'm Six Years Old and Hiding." 1996. http://kenaptekar.net/1997-2/.

Arnow, Harriette Simpson. *The Dollmaker.* New York: Macmillan, 1954.

Ayers, Edward L. "*The Virginia Quarterly Review* and the American South, 1925–2000." *Virginia Quarterly Review* 76, no. 2 (Spring 2000). https://www.vqronline.org/essay/southern-chronicle-virginia-quarterly-review-and-american-south-1925%E2%80%932000.

Bal, Mieke. "Memories in the Museum: Preposterous Histories for Today." In *Acts of Memory: Cultural Recall in the Present,* edited by Mieke Bal, Jonathan Crewe, and Leo Spitzer. Lebanon, NH: University Press of New England, 1999.

Bal, Mieke. *Narratology: Introduction to the Theory of Narrative.* 2nd ed. Toronto: University of Toronto Press, 1997.

Baptist, Edward E. *Creating an Old South: Middle Florida's Plantation Frontier before the Civil War.* Chapel Hill: University of North Carolina Press, 2002.

Bartlett, Frederic C. *Remembering: A Study in Experimental and Social Psychology.* Cambridge: Cambridge University Press, 1964.

Bauer, Gerri. "Pollution in Paradise: Betrayal and the Nature of Salvation in Marjorie Kinnan Rawlings's 'A Crop of Beans' and *Golden Apples.*" *Marjorie Kinnan Rawlings Journal of Florida Literature* 23 (2015): 34–57.

Bellamy, Francis. "National School Celebration of Columbus Day." *Youth's Companion* 45, no. 36 (September 8, 1892): 446.

Bercovitch, Sacvan. *The American Jeremiad.* Madison: University of Wisconsin Press, 1978.

Berg, A. Scott. *Max Perkins: Editor of Genius.* Boston: Dutton, 1978.

Bergson, Henri. *Time and Free Will: An Essay on the Immediate Data of Consciousness.* Crows Nest, Australia: Allen and Unwin, 1921.

Berra, Monica. "Conservative Rebels: Marjorie Kinnan Rawlings and Cracker Country." *Journal of Florida Studies* 1, no. 3 (Spring 2014): 1–24.

Bertolini, Alison. "The Decentering of the Male in Rawlings's 'Gal Young Un': A Derridean Analysis." *Marjorie Kinnan Rawlings Journal of Florida Literature* 14 (January 2005): 27–34.

Best, Stephen, and Sharon Marcus. "Surface Reading: An Introduction." *Representations* 108, no. 1 (Fall 2009): 1–21.

Boggess, Carol. "Letters of Understanding: James Still's Correspondence with Marjorie Rawlings and Katherine Anne Porter, 1936–1945." *Appalachian Heritage* 38, no. 4 (Fall 2010): 53–62.

Bonner, Thomas, Jr. "Kate Chopin: Tradition and the Moment." In *Southern Literature in Transition: Heritage and Promise*, edited by Philip Castille and William Osborne. Memphis, TN: Memphis State University Press, 1983.

Boyd, Janet L. "Cinderella in the Swamp: Marjorie Kinnan Rawlings's Fractured Fairy Tale." *Marjorie Kinnan Rawlings Journal of Florida Literature* 2 (January 1988): 1–22.

Branser, Stephanie. "'Experience Illuminated': Veristic Representation in Glasgow's Short Stories." In *Ellen Glasgow: New Perspectives*, edited by Dorothy Scura. Knoxville: University of Tennessee Press, 1995.

Buell, Lawrence. *The Environmental Imagination: Thoreau, Nature Writing and the Formation of American Culture.* Cambridge: Belknap Press of Harvard University Press, 1995.

Buell, Lawrence. *The Future of Environmental Criticism: Environmental Criticism and Literary Imagination.* Oxford: Blackwell, 2005.

Burkhalter, Nancy. "Women's Magazines and the Suffrage Movement: Did They Help or Hinder the Cause?" *Journal of American Culture* 19, no. 2 (Summer 1996): 13–24.

Burns, Ken, dir. *The Civil War.* Public Broadcasting Service, 1990.

Caldwell, Erskine. *Tobacco Road.* New York: Grosset and Dunlap, 1932.

Carby, Hazel V. *Reconstructing Womanhood: The Emergence of the Afro-American Woman Novelist.* Oxford: Oxford University Press, 1987.

Castillo, Susan. "'Race' and Ethnicity in Kate Chopin's Fiction." In *The Cambridge Companion to Kate Chopin*, edited by Janet Beer. Cambridge: Cambridge University Press, 2008.

Caws, Mary Ann. *Reading Frames in Modern Fiction.* Princeton: Princeton University Press, 1985.

Censer, Jane Turner. *The Reconstruction of White Southern Womanhood, 1865–1895.* Baton Rouge: Louisiana State University Press, 2003.

Censer, Jane Turner. "The Southern Lady and the Northern Publishers: A Tumultuous Relationship." *Journal of Southern History* 85, no. 1 (February 2019): 7–32.

Chesnutt, Charles. *The Conjure Woman.* New York: Houghton Mifflin, 1899.

Chopin, Kate. "As You Like It." In *The Complete Works of Kate Chopin*, edited by Per Seyersted. Baton Rouge: Louisiana State University Press, 1969.

Chopin, Kate. *At Fault.* 1890. New York: Penguin Classics, 2002.

Chopin, Kate. "At the 'Cadian Ball." *Two Tales* 3, no. 33 (October 22, 1892): 145–52.

Chopin, Kate. *The Awakening*. Chicago: Stone, 1899.

Chopin, Kate. *Bayou Folk*. New York: Houghton Mifflin, 1894.

Chopin, Kate. "The Bênitous' Slave." *Harper's Young People* 8, no. 642 (February 16, 1892): 280.

Chopin, Kate. "Beyond the Bayou." *Youth's Companion* 66, no. 24 (June 15, 1893): 302–3. New York: Houghton Mifflin, 1894.

Chopin, Kate. "Boulôt and Boulotte." *Harper's Young People* 13, no. 632 (December 8, 1891): 112.

Chopin, Kate. *The Complete Works of Kate Chopin*. Edited by Per Seyersted. Baton Rouge: Louisiana State University Press, 1969.

Chopin, Kate. "The Father of Désirée's Baby." *Vogue* 1 (January 14, 1893): 70–71, 74.

Chopin, Kate. "For Marse Chouchoute." *Youth's Companion* 64, no. 34 (August 20, 1891): 450–51.

Chopin, Kate. "A Gentleman of Bayou Têche." In *Bayou Folk*. New York: Houghton Mifflin, 1894.

Chopin, Kate. "In and out of Old Natchitoches." *Two Tales* 5, no. 57 (April 8, 1893): 103–14.

Chopin, Kate. "In Sabine." In *Bayou Folk*. New York: Houghton Mifflin, 1894.

Chopin, Kate. *A Kate Chopin Miscellany*. Edited by Per Seyersted and Emily Toth. Oslo, Norway: Universitetsforlaget; Natchitoches, LA: Northwestern State University Press, 1979.

Chopin, Kate. *Kate Chopin's Private Papers*. Edited by Emily Toth, Per Seyersted, and Cheyenne Bonnell. Bloomington: Indiana University Press, 1998.

Chopin, Kate. "La Belle Zoraïde." *Vogue* 3 (January 4, 1894): 2, 4, 8–10.

Chopin, Kate. "A Lady of Bayou St. John." *Vogue* 2 (September 21, 1893): 154, 156–58.

Chopin, Kate. "Loka." *Youth's Companion* 65, no. 51 (December 22, 1892): 670–71.

Chopin, Kate. "Love on the Bon-Dieu." *Two Tales* 2, no. 20 (July 23, 1892): 148–56.

Chopin, Kate. "The Lover of Mentine." *Vogue* 1 (January 14, 1893): 74–75.

Chopin, Kate. "Ma'ame Pélagie." *New Orleans Times-Democrat*, December 24, 1893.

Chopin, Kate. "Madame Célestin's Divorce." In *Bayou Folk*. New York: Houghton Mifflin, 1894.

Chopin, Kate. *A Night in Acadie*. Chicago: Way and Williams, 1897.

Chopin, Kate. "A No-Account Creole." *The Century* 47, no. 3 (January 1894): 382–93.

Chopin, Kate. "Old Aunt Peggy." In *Bayou Folk*. New York: Houghton Mifflin, 1894.

Chopin, Kate. "On Certain Brisk, Bright Days." *St. Louis Post-Dispatch*, November 26, 1899.

Chopin, Kate. "A Point at Issue." *St. Louis Post Dispatch*, October 27, 1889.

Chopin, Kate. "The Return of Alcibiade." *St. Louis Life* 7, no. 131 (December 10, 1892): 6–8.

Chopin, Kate. "A Rude Awakening." *Youth's Companion* 66, no. 7 (February 2, 1893): 54–55.

Chopin, Kate. "A Turkey Hunt." *Harper's Young People* 8, no. 642 (February 16, 1892): 287.

Chopin, Kate. "A Very Fine Fiddle." *Harper's Young People* 13, no. 630 (November 24, 1891): 79.

Chopin, Kate. *A Vocation and a Voice*. New York: Penguin, 1991.

Chopin, Kate. "White Oaks." In *Kate Chopin's Private Papers*, edited by Emily Toth, Per Seyersted, and Cheyenne Bonnell. Bloomington: Indiana University Press, 1998.

Chopin, Kate. "Wiser Than a God." *Philadelphia Musical Journal*, December 1889.

Chopin, Kate. "A Wizard from Gettysburg." *Youth's Companion* 65, no. 27 (July 7, 1892): 346–47.

Cobb, James C. *Away Down South: A History of Southern Identity*. Oxford: Oxford University Press, 2005.

Collins, Patricia Hill. *Black Feminist Thought: Knowledge, Consciousness, and the Politics of Empowerment*. London: Routledge, 2000.

Colvert, James B. "Agent and Author: Ellen Glasgow's Letters to Paul Revere Reynolds." *Studies in Bibliography* 14 (1961): 177–96.

Cooper, Anna Julia. *A Voice from the South*. 1892. New York: Schomburg, 1999.

Coultrap-McQuin. Susan. *Doing Literary Business: American Women Writers in the Nineteenth Century*. Chapel Hill: University of North Carolina Press, 1990.

Cox, Karen L. *Dixie's Daughters: The United Daughters of the Confederacy and the Preservation of Confederate Culture*. Gainesville: University Press of Florida, 2003.

Cram, Mildred. "The Victory." *Scribner's Magazine* 67–68 (1916): 702–9.

Crenshaw, Kimberlé. *On Intersectionality: Essential Writings*. New York: New Press, forthcoming.

Cresswell, Tim. *In Place/Out of Place: Geography, Ideology, and Transgression*. Minneapolis: University of Minnesota Press, 1996.

Cresswell, Tim. *Place: An Introduction*. 2nd ed. Hoboken, NJ: Wiley Blackwell, 2015.

Dashiell, Alfred. "Editor's Introduction." *Scribner's Magazine* 89, no. 4 (April 1931): 1.

Davidson, Donald, et al. *I'll Take My Stand: The South and the Agrarian Tradition*. 1930. Baton Rouge: Louisiana State University Press, 2006.

Davis, Rebecca Harding. *A Law unto Herself*. Philadelphia: Lippincott, 1878.

Davis, Rebecca Harding. "Life in the Iron Mills." *Atlantic Monthly* 7, no. 42 (April 1861): 430–51.

Denham, James M., and Keith L. Huneycutt. Introduction to *Echoes from a Distant Frontier: The Brown Sisters' Correspondence from Antebellum Florida*. Columbia: University of South Carolina Press, 2004.

Dillard, R. H. W. "The Writer's Best Solace: Textual Revisions in Ellen Glasgow's 'The Past.'" *Studies in Bibliography* 19 (1996): 245–50.

Domínguez-Rue, Emma. "Madwoman in the Drawing-Room: Female Invalidism in Ellen Glasgow's Gothic Stories." *Journal of American Studies* 38, no. 3 (December 2004): 425–38.

Donaldson, Susan V., and Anne Goodwyn Jones. Introduction to *Haunted Bodies: Gender and Southern Texts*, edited by Susan V. Donaldson and Anne Goodwyn Jones. Charlottesville: University Press of Virginia, 1997.

Doubleday, Frank Nelson. *The Memoirs of a Publisher*. New York: Doubleday, 1972.

Douglass, Frederick. *Narrative of the Life of Frederick Douglass, an American Slave*. Dublin, Ireland: Webb and Chapman, 1845.

Dunbar-Nelson, Alice. *The Goodness of St. Rocque and Other Stories*. New York: Dodd, Mead, 1899.

Dunbar-Nelson, Alice. *Violets and Other Tales*. Boston: Monthly Review, 1895.

"An Editorial Announcement." *Scribner's Magazine* 91, no. 1 (January 1932): 1.

Edwards, Bradley. "Allusion and the Evolution of Artistry in Kate Chopin's 'A Wizard from Gettysburg' and 'After the Winter.'" *American Literary Realism* 39, no. 2 (2007): 138–49.

Ewell, Barbara C. "Kate Chopin." In *The History of Southern Women's Literature*, edited by Carolyn Perry and Mary Louise Weaks. Baton Rouge: Louisiana State University Press, 2002.

Ewell, Barbara C. "Kate Chopin and the Dream of Female Selfhood." In *Kate Chopin Reconsidered: Beyond the Bayou*, edited by Lynda S. Boren and Sara deSaussure Davis. Baton Rouge: Louisiana State University Press, 1992.

Faulkner, William. *Absalom! Absalom!* New York: Penguin Random House, 1936.
Faulkner, William. *The Sound and the Fury*. New York: Cape and Smith, 1929.
Faust, Drew Gilpin. *Mothers of Invention: Women of the Slaveholding South in the American Civil War*. Chapel Hill: University of North Carolina Press, 1996.
Feinsodane, Aleta, and Susan Alves, eds. *"The Only Efficient Instrument": American Women Writers and the Periodical, 1837–1916*. Iowa City: University of Iowa Press, 2001.
Fetterley, Judith. "The Struggle for Authenticity: Growing Up Female in *The Old Order*." *Kate Chopin Newsletter* 2, no. 2 (1976): 11–19.
Fetterley, Judith, and Marjorie Pryse. *Writing out of Place: Regionalism, Women, and American Literary Culture*. Champaign: University of Illinois Press, 2005.
Fitzgerald, F. Scott. *The Great Gatsby*. New York: Scribner's, 1925.
Fort, Bruce. "*The Virginia Quarterly Review*, 1925–1935: A 'National Journal' in the New South." *Virginia Quarterly Review* (June 11, 2009). https://www.vqronline.org/web-exclusive/virginia-quarterly-review-1925%E2%80%931935-%E2%80%9Cnational-journal%E2%80%9D-new-south.
Foucault, Michel. *The Order of Things: An Archaeology of the Human Sciences*. 1966. New York: Vintage, 1994.
Fox, Heather. "Mapping Spatial Consciousness in Kate Chopin's *Bayou Folk* Stories." *South: A Scholarly Journal* 48, no. 1 (Fall 2015): 108–28.
Fox, Heather. "(Re)Positioning through Remembering and Forgetting in Katherine Anne Porter's 'The Source,' 'The Journey,' and 'The Last Leaf.'" *Southern Studies: An Interdisciplinary Journal of the South* 21, no. 2 (Fall/Winter 2014): 75–97.
Fox, Heather. "Representations of Truth: The Significance of Order in Katherine Anne Porter's The Old Order Stories." *Janus Head: Journal of Interdisciplinary Studies in Literature, Continental Philosophy, Phenomenological Psychology, and the Arts* 14, no. 2 (October 2015): 201–25.
Fox, Heather. "Resurrecting Truth in Katherine Anne Porter's 'The Fig Tree.'" *The Explicator* 72, no. 3 (September 2014): 219–23.
Fox, Heather, and Amanda Stuckey. "Archive Stories: Narrating Boundary Conditions in the Archives of Women Writers and Readers, 1830s–1930s." Special Session Proposal, Modern Language Association Convention, 2017.
Fox-Genovese, Elizabeth. *Within the Plantation Household: Black and White Women of the Old South*. Chapel Hill: University of North Carolina Press, 1998.
Frankwitz, Andrea K. "Katherine Anne Porter's Miranda Stories: A Commentary on the Cultural Ideologies of Gender Identity." *Mississippi Quarterly* 57, no. 3 (Summer 2004): 473–89.
Frazee, Monique Parent. "Ellen Glasgow as Feminist." In *Ellen Glasgow Centennial Essays*, edited by M. Thomas Inge. Charlottesville: University Press of Virginia, 1976.
From Ox-Teams to Eagles: A History of the Texas and Pacific Railway. Dallas: Texas and Pacific Railway, 1946. Available at the Texas Transportation Archive, www.ttarchive.com.
Fuller, Margaret. "American Literature: Its Position in the Present." 1852. In *Essays on American Life and Letters*, edited by Joel Myerson. Washington, DC: Rowman and Littlefield, 1978.
Gaines, Francis Pendleton. *The Southern Plantation: A Study in the Development and the Accuracy of a Tradition*. New York: Columbia University Press, 1924.
Gardner, Sarah E. *Blood and Irony: Southern White Women's Narratives of the Civil War, 1861–1937*. Chapel Hill: University of North Carolina Press, 2004.

Garvey, Ellen Gruber. *The Adman in the Parlor: Magazines and the Gendering of Consumer Culture, 1880s–1910s.* Oxford: Oxford University Press, 1996.

Gebhard, Caroline. "Reconstructing Southern Manhood: Race, Sentimentality, and Camp in the Plantation Myth." In *Haunted Bodies: Gender and Southern Texts*, edited by Anne Goodwyn Jones and Susan V. Donaldson. Charlottesville: University Press of Virginia, 1997.

Genette, Gérard. *Narrative Discourse: An Essay in Method.* Translated by Jane E. Lewin. Ithaca: Cornell University Press, 1980.

Genette, Gérard. *Palimpsests: Literature in the Second Degree.* Translated by Channa Newman and Claude Doubinsky. Lincoln: University of Nebraska Press, 1997.

Genette, Gérard. *Paratexts: Thresholds of Interpretation.* Translated by Jane E. Lewin. Cambridge: Cambridge University Press, 1997.

Gilbert, Sandra M., and Susan Gubar. *The Madwoman in the Attic: The Woman Writer and the Nineteenth-Century Literary Imagination.* New Haven: Yale University Press, 1979.

Gilman, Charlotte Perkins. "The Yellow Wallpaper." *New England Magazine* 5 (January 1892): 647–56.

Glasgow, Ellen Anderson Gholson. "The Artless Age." *Saturday Evening Post* 196, no. 8 (August 25, 1923): 10–11, 89, 91, 93.

Glasgow, Ellen Anderson Gholson. *Barren Ground.* 1925. New York: Harcourt Brace Jovanovich, 1985.

Glasgow, Ellen Anderson Gholson. "Between Two Shores." *McClure's Magazine* 12, no. 4 (February 1899): 345–52.

Glasgow, Ellen Anderson Gholson. *A Certain Measure: An Interpretation of Prose Fiction.* New York: Harcourt, Brace, 1938.

Glasgow, Ellen Anderson Gholson. *The Collected Stories of Ellen Glasgow.* Edited by Richard Meeker. Baton Rouge: Louisiana State University Press, 1963.

Glasgow, Ellen Anderson Gholson. "Dare's Gift: Part I." *Harper's Monthly Magazine* 134, no. 801 (February 1917): 322–30.

Glasgow, Ellen Anderson Gholson. "Dare's Gift: Part II." *Harper's Monthly Magazine* 134, no. 802 (March 1917): 515–24.

Glasgow, Ellen Anderson Gholson. "The Difference." *Harper's Monthly Magazine* 147, no. 877 (June 1923): 28–42.

Glasgow, Ellen Anderson Gholson. "Feminism." *New York Times*, November 30, 1913.

Glasgow, Ellen Anderson Gholson. *Five Letters from Ellen Glasgow Concerning Censorship and Other Matters of Interest to a Library Board Member.* Richmond, VA: Friends of the Richmond Public Library, 1962.

Glasgow, Ellen Anderson Gholson. *The Freeman and Other Poems.* New York: Doubleday, Page, 1902.

Glasgow, Ellen Anderson Gholson. "Jordan's End." In *The Shadowy Third and Other Stories.* New York: Doubleday, Page, 1923.

Glasgow, Ellen Anderson Gholson. *Letters of Ellen Glasgow.* Edited by Blair Rouse. New York: Harcourt, Brace, 1958.

Glasgow, Ellen Anderson Gholson. "No Valid Reason against Giving Votes to Women." *New York Times*, March 23, 1913.

Glasgow, Ellen Anderson Gholson. "The Novel in the South." *Harper's Monthly Magazine* (December 1, 1928): 93–100.

Glasgow, Ellen Anderson Gholson. *The Old Dominion Edition of the Works of Ellen Glasgow.* New York: Doubleday, Duran, 1929–33.

Glasgow, Ellen Anderson Gholson. "The Past." *Good Housekeeping* 71 (October 1920): 64–66, 155, 157–64.

Glasgow, Ellen Anderson Gholson. *Perfect Companionship: Ellen Glasgow's Selected Correspondence with Women*. Edited by Pamela R. Matthews. Charlottesville: University of Virginia Press, 2005.

Glasgow, Ellen Anderson Gholson. "A Point in Morals." *Harper's New Monthly Magazine* 98, no. 588 (May 1899): 976–82.

Glasgow, Ellen Anderson Gholson. "The Shadowy Third." *Scribner's Magazine* 60, no. 6 (December 1916): 659–71.

Glasgow, Ellen Anderson Gholson. *The Shadowy Third and Other Stories*. New York: Doubleday, Page, 1923.

Glasgow, Ellen Anderson Gholson. "Thinking Makes It So." *Good Housekeeping* 64, no. 2 (February 1917): 18–21.

Glasgow, Ellen Anderson Gholson. *The Virginia Edition of the Works of Ellen Glasgow*. New York: Scribner's, 1938.

Glasgow, Ellen Anderson Gholson. "Whispering Leaves: Part I." *Harper's Monthly Magazine* 146, no. 872 (January 1923): 145–57.

Glasgow, Ellen Anderson Gholson. "Whispering Leaves: Part II." *Harper's Monthly Magazine* 146, no. 873 (February 1923): 334–43.

Glasgow, Ellen Anderson Gholson. *The Woman Within: An Autobiography*. 1954. Edited by Pamela R. Matthews. Charlottesville: University Press of Virginia, 1994.

Glaspell, Susan. "The Hearing Ear." *Harper's Monthly Magazine* 134, no. 800 (January 1917): 234–41.

Glaspell, Susan. *Trifles*. 1916. In *The Norton Introduction to Literature*, edited by Kelly J. Mays, 11th ed. New York: Norton, 2014.

Glymph, Thavolia. *Out of the House of Bondage: The Transformation of the Plantation Household*. Cambridge: Cambridge University Press, 2008.

Goodman, Susan. *Ellen Glasgow: A Biography*. Baltimore: Johns Hopkins University Press, 1998.

Grammer, John M. "Plantation Fiction." In *A Companion to the Literature and Culture of the American South*, edited by Richard Gray and Owen Robinson. Hoboken, NJ: Blackwell, 2004.

Grant, Robert. "Feminism in Fiction and Real Life." *Scribner's Magazine* 60, nos. 67–68 (1916): 749–50.

Greeson, Jennifer Rae. *Our South: Geographic Fantasy and the Rise of National Literature*. Cambridge: Harvard University Press, 2010.

Green, Elna C. *Looking for the New Deal: Florida Women's Letters during the Great Depression*. Columbia: University of South Carolina Press, 2007.

Griffith, Jean Carol. *The Color of Democracy in Women's Regional Writing*. Tuscaloosa: University of Alabama Press, 2009.

Hall, Joan Wylie. "Louisiana Writers of the Postbellum South." In *The History of Southern Women's Literature*, edited by Carolyn Perry and Mary Louise Weaks. Baton Rouge: Louisiana State University Press, 2002.

Hankins, Leslie K. "Ritual: Representation and Reversal in Katherine Anne Porter's 'The Old Order.'" In *Ritual in the United States: Acts and Representations*, edited by Don Harkness. Bloomington: Indiana University Press, 1985.

Harde, Roxanne. "'At Rest Now': Child Ghosts and Social Justice in Nineteenth-Century Women's Writing." In *Transnational Gothic: Literary and Social Exchanges in the Long*

Nineteenth Century, edited by Monika Elbert and Bridget M. Marshall. Farnham, UK: Ashgate, 2013.

Hardwig, Bill. *Upon Provincialism: Southern Literature and National Periodical Culture, 1870–1900*. Charlottesville: University of Virginia Press, 2013.

Harper, Frances Ellen Watkins. *Forest Leaves*. Ca. 1846. *Common-Place: The Journal of Early American Life*. http://jtoaa.common-place.org/wp-content/uploads/sites/3/2016/12/ForestLeaves.pdf.

Harper, Frances Ellen Watkins. *Iola Leroy, or Shadows Uplifted*. Philadelphia: Garrigues, 1892.

Harper, Frances Ellen Watkins. *Sketches of Southern Life*. 1872. Philadelphia: Ferguson, 1891.

Harwell, Richard B. "The Stream of Self-Consciousness." In *The Idea of the South: Pursuit of a Central Theme*, edited by Frank E. Vandiver. Chicago: University of Chicago Press, 1964.

Haytock, Jennifer. "Gender, Class, and Ghosts: Ellen Glasgow and the Single Woman." *Ellen Glasgow Newsletter* 49 (Fall 2002): 3–5.

Hill, Mozell C., and Bevode C. McCall. "'Cracker Culture': A Preliminary Definition." *Transforming Anthropology* 17, no. 1 (2009): 45–50.

Hinrichsen, Lisa. *Possessing the Past: Trauma, Imagination, and Memory in Post-Plantation Southern Literature*. Baton Rouge: Louisiana State University Press, 2015.

Hoffman, Frederick J., Charles Allen, and Carolyn F. Ulrich. *The Little Magazine: A History and a Bibliography*. Princeton: Princeton University Press, 1947.

The Holy Bible. New International Version. Nashville, TN: Holman, 1986.

hooks, bell. *Feminist Theory from Margin to Center*. Brooklyn, NY: South End, 1984.

Howells, William Dean. *Criticism and Fiction*. New York: Harper, 1891.

Howells, William Dean. "Editor's Easy Chair." *Harper's Monthly Magazine* 134 (February 1917): 442–45.

Howells, William Dean. "Editor's Easy Chair." *Harper's Monthly Magazine* 134 (March 1917): 594–97.

Hurston, Zora Neale. *Barracoon: The Story of the Last "Black Cargo."* New York: Harper Collins, 2018.

Hutchinson, Coleman. *Apples and Ashes: Literature, Nationalism, and the Confederate States of America*. Athens: University of Georgia Press, 2012.

Hutchisson, James M. "On the Restoration of Texts: The Scholar as 'Better Editor.'" *Text* 16 (2006): 344–55.

Jacobs, Harriet Ann. *Incidents in the Life of a Slave Girl*. Boston: Thayer and Eldridge, 1861.

"Jacob's Ladder #418." *United Methodist Hymnal*. Hymnary.org. http://www.hymnary.org/hymn/UMH/418.

Jacoby, Karl. *Crimes against Nature: Squatters, Poachers, Thieves, and the Hidden History of American Conservation*. Chapel Hill: University of North Carolina Press, 2001.

James, Henry. *Daisy Miller*. New York: Harper, 1878

James, Henry. *The Turn of the Screw*. New York: Macmillan, 1898

Janney, Caroline. *Burying the Dead but Not the Past: Ladies' Memorial Associations and the Lost Cause*. Chapel Hill: University of North Carolina Press, 2012.

Jones, Anne Goodwyn. *Tomorrow Is Another Day: The Woman Writer in the South, 1859–1936*. Baton Rouge: Louisiana State University Press, 1981.

Jones, Maxine, and Kevin M. McCarthy. *African Americans in Florida*. Sarasota, FL: Pineapple Press, 1993.

Keckley, Elizabeth. *Behind the Scenes, or Thirty Years a Slave, and Four Years in the White House.* New York: Penguin, 2005.

Keen, George Gillett, and Sarah Pamela Williams. *Cracker Times and Pioneer Lives.* Edited by James M. Denton and Canta Brown Jr. Columbia: University of South Carolina Press, 2000.

Keen, Suzanne. *Narrative Form.* 2nd ed. New York: Palgrave Macmillan, 2015.

Kelley, Mary. *Learning to Stand and Speak: Women, Education, and Public Life in America's Republic.* Chapel Hill: University of North Carolina Press, 2006.

Kelly, William. "The Professional Instinct: An Unpublished Short Story." *Western Humanities Review* 15, no. 4 (Autumn 1962): 301–17.

Kenton, Edna. "The Militant Women—and Women." *Century Magazine* 86 (November 1913): 13–19.

Kidd, Stuart. "Visualizing the Poor White." In *A Companion to the Literature and Culture of the American South*, edited by Richard Gray and Owen Robinson. Hoboken, NJ: Blackwell, 2004.

Koloski, Bernard. "*Bayou Folk*." In *Kate Chopin: A Study of the Short Fiction.* Woodbridge, CT: Twayne, 1996.

Kornasky, Linda. "Ellen Glasgow's Disability." *Mississippi Quarterly* 49, no. 2 (Spring 1996): 281–93.

Kotlarczyk, Adam. "Before PTSD: Combat Trauma in the Civil War Short Stories of Kate Chopin." *Notes on American Literature* 23 (2014): 23–30.

Kreyling, Michael. *Figures of the Hero in Southern Narrative.* Baton Rouge: Louisiana State University Press, 1987.

Kreyling, Michael. *Inventing Southern Literature.* Jackson: University Press of Mississippi, 1998.

Kreyling, Michael. *The South That Wasn't There: Postsouthern Memory and History.* Baton Rouge: Louisiana State University Press, 2010.

Lamme, Ary J., III. "Preserving Special Places." *Geographical Review* 79, no. 2 (April 1989): 195–209.

Lanier, Sidney. "The New South." *Scribner's Magazine* 20, no. 6 (October 1880): 840–51.

Lanser, Susan S. "Toward a Feminist Narratology." *Style* 20, no. 3 (Fall 1986): 341–63.

Lanser, Susan S. "Toward (a Queerer and) More (Feminist) Narratology." In *Narrative Theory Unbound: Queer and Feminist Interventions.* Columbus: Ohio State University Press, 2015.

Lear, Ashley Andrews. "Ellen Glasgow: The 'Feminine' Façade and the 'Masculine' Mind." *Ellen Glasgow Journal of Southern Women Writers* 2 (2009): 16–37.

Lear, Ashley Andrews. *The Remarkable Kinship of Marjorie Kinnan Rawlings and Ellen Glasgow.* Gainesville: University of Florida Press, 2018.

Lefebvre, Henri. *The Production of Space.* Translated by Donald Nicholson-Smith. Hoboken, NJ: Blackwell, 1991.

Levine, Caroline. *Forms: Whole, Rhythm, Hierarchy, Network.* Princeton: Princeton University Press, 2015.

Lewis, Nghana Tamu. *Entitled to the Pedestal: Place, Region, and Progress in White Southern Women's Writing, 1920–1945.* Iowa City: University of Iowa Press, 2007.

Lillios, Anna. *Crossing the Creek: The Literary Friendship of Zora Neale Hurston and Marjorie Kinnan Rawlings.* Gainesville: University Press of Florida, 2010.

Llewellyn, Dara. "Reader Activation of Boundaries in Kate Chopin's 'Beyond the Bayou.'" *Studies in Short Fiction* 33, no. 2 (1996): 255–62.

Lloyd, Henry Demarest. "The Story of a Great Monopoly." *Atlantic Monthly* 47, no. 281 (March 1881): 317–34.

Lowe, John. "The Construction and Deconstruction of Masculinity in *The Yearling*." *Mississippi Quarterly* 57, no. 2 (Spring 2004): 231–46.

Lowrie, Rebecca. "Good Short Stories." *New York Evening Post*, November 17, 1923.

Lynn, Andrea. "Writing Program at Illinois Publishes Inaugural Issue of Literary Magazine." *Illinois News Bureau*. https://news.illinois.edu/view/6367/207628.

MacKethan, Lucinda H. *Daughters of Time: Creating Woman's Voice in Southern Story*. Athens: University of Georgia Press, 1990.

Manning, Carol S., ed. *The Female Tradition in Southern Literature*. Urbana: University of Illinois Press, 1993.

McBee, Melinda W. "'A Soft, Enjoyable Melancholy': Memory, Silence, and Rhetoric as a Way of Knowing in Katherine Anne Porter's 'The Source.'" *CCTE Studies* 69 (2004): 36–44.

McElya, Micki. *Clinging to Mammy: The Faithful Slave in Twentieth-Century America*. Cambridge: Harvard University Press, 2007.

McHaney, Pearl Amelia. "Southern Women Writers and Their Influence." In *The Cambridge Companion to the Literature of the American South*, edited by Sharon Monteith. Cambridge: Cambridge University Press, 2013.

McKee, Kathryn B. "Region, Genre, and the Nineteenth-Century South." In *The Cambridge Companion to the Literature of the American South*, edited by Sharon Monteith. Cambridge: Cambridge University Press, 2013.

McLaughlin, Robert. "The 'On-Natural' Narratives of Quincey Dover." *Marjorie Kinnan Rawlings Journal of Florida Literature* 4 (1992): 41–48.

McPherson, Tara. *Reconstructing Dixie: Race, Gender, and Nostalgia in the Imagined South*. Durham: Duke University Press, 2003.

Meeker, Richard. Introduction to *The Collected Stories of Ellen Glasgow*. Edited by Richard Meeker. Baton Rouge: Louisiana State University Press, 1963.

Mencken, H. L. "The Sahara of the Bozart." *New York Evening Mail*, November 13, 1917.

Mercy Street. Public Broadcasting Service, 2016.

Mims, Edwin. *The Advancing South: Stories of Progress and Reaction*. New York: Doubleday, Page, 1926.

Mitchell, Margaret. *Gone with the Wind*. New York: Macmillan, 1936.

Moore, Marianne. "Poetry." In *Complete Poems: Marianne Moore*. New York: Macmillan, 1994.

Morgan, Thomas L. "Criticizing Local Color: Innovative Conformity in Kate Chopin's Short Fiction." *Arizona Quarterly* 70, no. 1 (Spring 2014): 135–71.

Morris, Rhonda. "Engendering Fictions: Rawlings and a Female Tradition of Southern Writing." *Marjorie Kinnan Rawlings Journal of Florida Literature* 7 (January 1996): 27–39.

Moseley, Julia Daniels. *"Come to My Sunland": Letters of Julia Daniels Moseley from the Florida Frontier, 1882–1886*. Edited by Julia Winifred Moseley and Betty Powers Crislip. Gainesville: University Press of Florida, 1998.

Mott, Frank Luther. *American Journalism: A History of Newspapers in the United States through 260 Years: 1690 to 1950*. New York: Macmillan, 1950.

Mott, Frank Luther. *A History of American Magazines*. Vols. 2–5, Cambridge: Harvard University Press, 1957–68.

Nagel, James. *Race and Culture in New Orleans Stories: Kate Chopin, Grace King, Alice Dunbar-Nelson, and George Washington Cable*. Tuscaloosa: University of Alabama Press, 2014.
Nash, Roderick Frazier. *Wilderness and the American Mind*. New Haven: Yale University Press, 2001.
Neary, Gwen M. "Glasgow's Ghost Stories and 'The Pattern of Society.'" *Ellen Glasgow Newsletter* 36, no. 1 (Spring 1996): 6–8.
Nixon, Timothy K. "Same Path, Different Purpose: Chopin's La Folle and Welty's Phoenix Jackson." *Women's Studies* 32, no. 8 (2003): 937–56.
O'Brien, Michael. *The Idea of the American South, 1920–1941*. Baltimore: Johns Hopkins University Press, 1979.
O'Brien, Michael. *Placing the South*. Jackson: University Press of Mississippi, 2007.
Okker, Patricia. *Social Studies: The Magazine Novel in Nineteenth-Century America*. Charlottesville: University of Virginia Press, 2003.
Outka, Paul. *Race and Nature: From Transcendentalism to the Harlem Renaissance*. New York: Palgrave Macmillan, 2008.
Page, Ruth. "Feminist Narratology in Context." In *Literary and Linguistic Approaches to Feminist Narratology*. New York: Palgrave Macmillan, 2006.
Page, Thomas Nelson. *In Ole Virginia, or Marse Chan and Other Stories*. New York: Scribner's, 1895.
Page, Walter Hines. *A Publisher's Confession*. New York: Doubleday, Page, 1905.
Papke, Mary E. *Verging on the Abyss: The Social Fiction of Kate Chopin and Edith Wharton*. Santa Barbara, CA: Greenwood, 1990.
Parker, Idella. *Idella: Marjorie Kinnan Rawlings's "Perfect Maid."* Gainesville: University Press of Florida, 1992.
Parker, Nate, dir. *The Birth of a Nation*. Fox Searchlight, 2016.
Parker, William. "Ellen Glasgow: A Gentle Rebel." *English Journal* 10, no. 3 (March 1931): 187–94.
Perkins, Maxwell E. *Max and Marjorie: The Correspondence between Maxwell E. Perkins and Marjorie Kinnan Rawlings*. Edited by Rodger L. Tarr. Gainesville: University Press of Florida, 1999.
Peterson, Theodore. *Magazines in the Twentieth Century*. Urbana: University of Illinois Press, 1956.
Porter, Katherine Anne. "The Circus." *Southern Review* 1, no. 1 (Winter 1935): 36–41.
Porter, Katherine Anne. *The Collected Stories of Katherine Anne Porter*. New York: Harcourt, Brace, and World, 1965.
Porter, Katherine Anne. *The Cracked Looking-Glass*. New York: Scribner's, 1932.
Porter, Katherine Anne. "The Fig Tree." *Harper's Magazine* 220, no. 1321 (June 1960): 55–77.
Porter, Katherine Anne. *Flowering Judas and Other Stories*. New York: Harcourt, Brace, 1935.
Porter, Katherine Anne. "Go Little Book." In *The Collected Stories of Katherine Anne Porter*. New York: Harcourt, Brace, and World, 1965.
Porter, Katherine Anne. "The Grave." *Virginia Quarterly Review* 11, no. 2 (April 1935): 177–83.
Porter, Katherine Anne. "He." In *Flowering Judas and Other Stories*. New York: Harcourt, Brace, 1935.
Porter, Katherine Anne. "The Jilting of Granny Weatherall." In *Flowering Judas and Other Stories*. New York: Harcourt, Brace, 1935.

Porter, Katherine Anne. "The Journey." In *The Collected Stories of Katherine Anne Porter*. New York: Harcourt, Brace, and World, 1965.

Porter, Katherine Anne. "The Last Leaf." 1935. In *The Collected Stories of Katherine Anne Porter*. New York: Harcourt, Brace, and World, 1965.

Porter, Katherine Anne. *The Leaning Tower, and Other Stories*. New York: Harcourt, Brace, 1944.

Porter, Katherine Anne. *Letters of Katherine Anne Porter*. Edited by Isabel Bayley. New York: Atlantic Monthly Press, 1990.

Porter, Katherine Anne. "My First Speech." In *Katherine Anne Porter: Collected Stories and Other Writings*, edited by Darlene Harbour Unrue. New York: Library of America, 2008.

Porter, Katherine Anne. "The Old Order." *Southern Review* 2, no. 1 (Summer 1936): 495–509.

Porter, Katherine Anne. *The Old Order: Stories of the South from The Leaning Tower, Pale Horse, Pale Rider, and Flowering Judas*. New York: Harcourt, Brace, 1955.

Porter, Katherine Anne. *Pale Horse, Pale Rider: Three Short Novels*. New York: Harcourt, Brace, 1939.

Porter, Katherine Anne. "Portrait: Old South." *Mademoiselle* 18 (February 1944): 89, 151–54.

Porter, Katherine Anne. "Recent Southern Fiction: A Panel Discussion," October 28, 1960. In *Katherine Anne Porter: Conversations*, edited by Joan Givner. Jackson: University Press of Mississippi, 1987.

Porter, Katherine Anne. *Selected Letters of Katherine Anne Porter: Chronicles of a Modern Woman*. Edited by Darlene Harbour Unrue. Jackson: University Press of Mississippi, 2012.

Porter, Katherine Anne. *Selected Short Stories of Katherine Anne Porter*. New York: Editions for the Armed Services, 1945.

Porter, Katherine Anne. *Ship of Fools*. New York: Little, Brown, 1960.

Porter, Katherine Anne. "The Source." *Accent* 1, no. 3 (Spring 1941): 44–47.

Porter, Katherine Anne. "Two Plantation Portraits: The Witness and The Last Leaf." *Virginia Quarterly Review* 2, no 1 (January 1935): 85–92.

Porter, Katherine Anne. "The Witness." In *The Collected Stories of Katherine Anne Porter*. New York: Harcourt, Brace, and World, 1965.

Price, Kenneth M., and Susan Belasco Smith. *Periodical Literature in Nineteenth-Century America*. Charlottesville: University Press of Virginia, 1995.

Prince, K. Stephen. *Stories of the South: Race and Reconstruction of Southern Identity, 1865–1915*. Chapel Hill: University of North Carolina Press, 2014.

Punday, Daniel. *Narrative Bodies: Toward a Corporeal Narratology*. New York: Palgrave Macmillan, 2003.

Rainwater, Catherine. "Ellen Glasgow's Outline of History in *The Shadowy Third and Other Stories*." In *The Critical Response to H. G. Wells*, edited by William J. Scheick. Santa Barbara, CA: Greenwood, 1995.

Raj, Vinaya, and Martha Ann Bell. "Cognitive Processes Supporting Episodic Memory Formation in Childhood: The Role of Source Memory, Binding, and Executive Functioning." *Developmental Review* 30 (2010): 384–402.

Rankin, Daniel S. *Kate Chopin and Her Creole Stories*. Philadelphia: University of Pennsylvania Press, 1932.

Raper, Julius Rowan. "Invisible Things: The Short Stories of Ellen Glasgow." *Southern Literary Journal* 9, no. 2 (1977): 66–90.

Raper, Julius Rowan. *Without Shelter: The Early Career of Ellen Glasgow*. Baton Rouge: Louisiana State University Press, 1971.

Rawlings, Marjorie Kinnan. "Alligators." *Saturday Evening Post* 206, no. 13 (September 23, 1933): 16–17, 36, 38.
Rawlings, Marjorie Kinnan. "Benny and the Bird Dogs." *Scribner's Magazine* 94, no. 4 (October 1933): 193–200.
Rawlings, Marjorie Kinnan. "Cocks Must Crow." *Saturday Evening Post* 212, no. 25 (November 25, 1939): 5–7, 58, 60, 62–64.
Rawlings, Marjorie Kinnan. "A Crop of Beans." *Scribner's Magazine* 91, no. 5 (May 1932): 283–90.
Rawlings, Marjorie Kinnan. *Cross Creek*. 1942. New York: Simon and Schuster, 1996.
Rawlings, Marjorie Kinnan. "The Enemy." *Saturday Evening Post* 212, no. 30 (January 20, 1940): 12–13, 32, 36, 39.
Rawlings, Marjorie Kinnan. "Florida: A Land of Contrasts." In *A Marjorie Kinnan Rawlings Reader*, edited by Dorothy Abbott. St. Petersburg: Florida Endowment for the Humanities, 1989.
Rawlings, Marjorie Kinnan. "Gal Young Un: Part I." *Harper's Monthly Magazine* 165, no. 985 (June 1932): 21–33.
Rawlings, Marjorie Kinnan. "Gal Young Un: Part II." *Harper's Monthly Magazine* 165, no. 986 (July 1932): 225–34.
Rawlings, Marjorie Kinnan. *Golden Apples*. New York: Macmillan, 1935.
Rawlings, Marjorie Kinnan. "Jacob's Ladder." *Scribner's Magazine* 89, no. 4 (April 1931): 351–66, 446–64.
Rawlings, Marjorie Kinnan. "A Mother in Mannville." *Saturday Evening Post* 209, no. 24 (December 12, 1936): 7, 33.
Rawlings, Marjorie Kinnan. "The Pardon." *Scribner's Magazine* 92, no. 2 (August 1934): 95–98.
Rawlings, Marjorie Kinnan. "A Plumb Clare Conscience." *Scribner's Magazine* 90, no. 6 (December 1931): 622–26.
Rawlings, Marjorie Kinnan. "Regional Literature of the South." *College English* 1, no. 5 (February 1940): 381–89.
Rawlings, Marjorie Kinnan. *Selected Letters of Marjorie Kinnan Rawlings*. Edited by Gordon E. Bigelow and Laura V. Monti. Gainesville: University Press of Florida, 1983.
Rawlings, Marjorie Kinnan. *Short Stories by Marjorie Kinnan Rawlings*. Gainesville: University Press of Florida, 1994.
Rawlings, Marjorie Kinnan. *South Moon Under*. New York: Scribner's, 1933.
Rawlings, Marjorie Kinnan. "Varmints." *Scribner's Magazine* 100, no. 6 (December 1936): 26–32, 84–85.
Rawlings, Marjorie Kinnan. *When the Whippoorwill*. New York: Scribner's, 1940.
Rawlings, Marjorie Kinnan. *The Yearling*. New York: Scribner's, 1938.
Rawlings, Marjorie Kinnan, and Norton S. Baskin. *The Private Marjorie: The Love Letters of Marjorie Kinnan Rawlings to Norton S. Baskin*. Edited by Rodger Tarr. Gainesville: University Press of Florida, 2004.
Ray, Janisse. *Ecology of a Cracker Childhood*. Minneapolis: Milkweed, 1999.
Ray, Janisse. Interview by Hugh Huppersburg for Georgia Writers Hall of Fame, June 9, 2016. https://www.youtube.com/watch?v=38ztIKCrloo.
Ray, Janisse. *Wild Card Quilt: Ecology of Home*. Minneapolis: Milkweed, 2007.
Revels, Tracy J. *Grander in Her Daughters: Florida's Women during the Civil War*. Columbia: University of South Carolina Press, 2004.

Romine, Scott. *The Real South: Southern Narrative in the Age of Cultural Reproduction.* Baton Rouge: Louisiana State University Press, 2008.

Rose, Gillian. *Feminism and Geography: The Limits of Geographical Knowledge.* Minneapolis: University of Minnesota Press, 1993.

Russ, Joanna. *How to Suppress Women's Writing.* Austin: University of Texas Press, 1983.

Saffy, Edna. "Marjorie Kinnan Rawlings's Theory of Composition." *Journal of Florida Literature* 2 (1998): 109–29.

Schwartz, Edward G. "The Fictions of Memory." In *Katherine Anne Porter: A Critical Symposium.* Athens: University of Georgia Press, 1969.

Scott, Anne Firor. *The Southern Lady: From Pedestal to Politics, 1830–1930.* 1970. Charlottesville: University Press of Virginia, 1995.

Scura, Dorothy M. *Ellen Glasgow: The Contemporary Reviews.* Cambridge: Cambridge University Press, 1992.

Seyersted, Per. *Kate Chopin: A Critical Biography.* Oslo, Norway: Universitetsforlaget, 1969.

Shackelford, Lynne P. "Houghton Mifflin and Company." In *American Literary Publishing Houses, 1638–1899*, edited by Peter Dzwonkoski. Farmington Hills, MI: Gale, 1986.

"The Shadowy Third." *New York Times*, October 28, 1923.

Shaker, Bonnie James. *Coloring Locals: Racial Formation in Kate Chopin's Youth's Companion Stories.* Iowa City: University of Iowa Press, 2003.

Shaker, Bonnie James. "Kate Chopin and the Periodical: Revisiting the Re-Vision." In *"The Only Efficient Instrument": American Women Writers and the Periodical, 1837–1916*, edited by Aleta Feinsodane and Susan Alves. Iowa City: University of Iowa Press, 2001.

Shaker, Bonnie James, and Angela Gianoglio Pettitt. "'Her First Part' as Her Last Story: Recovering Kate Chopin's Fiction." *Legacy: A Journal of American Women Writers* 30, no. 2 (2013): 384–96.

Showalter, Elaine. *A Jury of Her Peers: Celebrating American Women Writers from Anne Bradstreet to Annie Proulx.* New York: Vintage, 2009.

Silverthorne, Elizabeth. *Marjorie Kinnan Rawlings: Sojourner at Cross Creek.* New York: Overlook, 1998.

Sleigh, Tom. *Army Cats: Poems.* Minneapolis: Graywolf, 2011.

Smythe, Ted Curtis. *The Gilded Age Press, 1865–1900.* Santa Barbara, CA: Praeger, 2003.

Soja, Edward W. *Postmetropolis: Critical Studies of Cities and Regions.* Hoboken, NJ: Blackwell, 2000.

Soja, Edward W. *Seeking Spatial Justice.* Minneapolis: University of Minnesota Press, 2010.

Spengler, J. J. "Is America Slowing Up?" *Scribner's Magazine* 89, no. 4 (April 1931): 367–76.

Spielberg, Steven, dir. *Lincoln.* Amblin and Kennedy/Marshall, 2012.

Steedman, Carolyn. *Dust: The Archive and Cultural History.* New Brunswick, NJ: Rutgers University Press, 2001.

Stein, Daniel. "From *Uncle Remus* to *Song of the South*: Adapting American Plantation Fiction." *Southern Literary Journal* 47, no. 2 (Spring 2015): 20–35.

Stowe, Harriet Beecher. *Uncle Tom's Cabin.* Boston: Jewett, 1852.

Tarbell, Ida M. *The History of the Standard Oil Company.* New York: McClure, Phillips, 1904.

Tarr, C. Anita. "The Evolution of a 'Southern Liberal': Marjorie Kinnan Rawlings and Race." *Journal of Florida Literature* 15 (2007): 141–62.

Tarr, Rodger L. Introduction to *Short Stories by Marjorie Kinnan Rawlings.* Gainesville: University Press of Florida, 1994.

Titus, Mary. *The Ambivalent Art of Katherine Anne Porter*. Athens: University of Georgia Press, 2005.

Tompkins, Jane. *Sensational Designs: The Cultural Work of American Fiction, 1790–1860*. Oxford: Oxford University Press, 1986.

Toth, Emily. "The Shadow of the First Biographer: The Case of Kate Chopin." *Southern Review* 26 (Spring 1990): 285–92.

Toth, Emily. *Unveiling Kate Chopin*. Jackson: University Press of Mississippi, 1999.

Trethewey, Natasha. *Native Guard*. New York: Houghton Mifflin, 2007.

Tuan, Yi-Fu. *Space and Place: The Perspective of Experience*. Minneapolis: University of Minnesota Press, 1977.

Turcotte, Florence M. "For This Is an Enchanted Land: Marjorie Kinnan Rawlings and the Florida Environment." *Florida Historical Quarterly* 90, no. 4 (Spring 2012): 488–504.

Unrue, Darlene Harbour. *Katherine Anne Porter: The Life of an Artist*. Jackson: University Press of Mississippi, 2005.

Van Dyke, Henry. "War-Music." *Scribner's Magazine* 60, nos. 67–68 (1916): 647–48.

Vanlandingham, Phyllis. "Kate Chopin and Editors, 'A Singular Class of Men.'" In *Perspectives on Kate Chopin: Proceedings from the Kate Chopin International Conference, April 6–8, 1989*. Natchitoches, LA: Northwestern State University Press, 1992.

Walker, Alice. *In Search of Our Mothers' Gardens*. San Diego: Harcourt Brace Jovanovich, 1983.

Walker, Alice. "In Search of Zora Neale Hurston." *Ms. Magazine*, March 1975, 74–79, 89.

Walker, Nancy A. *Kate Chopin: A Literary Life*. New York: Palgrave, 2001.

Wallace, Emma Gary. "The Business of Housekeeping: Good Food and Its Relation to Success." *Good Housekeeping* 71 (October 1920): 63.

Wagner, Linda W. *Ellen Glasgow: Beyond Convention*. Austin: University of Texas Press, 1982.

Warhol, Robyn, and Susan S. Lanser. Introduction to *Narrative Theory Unbound: Queer and Feminist Interventions*. Columbus: Ohio State University Press, 2015.

Warner, Susan. *The Wide, Wide World*. 1850. New York: Feminist Press, 1987.

Warren, Robert Penn. "Irony with a Center." In *Katherine Anne Porter: A Collection of Critical Essays*, edited by Robert Penn Warren. Englewood Cliffs, NJ: Prentice Hall, 1979.

Watson, Jay. *Reading for the Body: The Recalcitrant Materiality of Southern Fiction, 1893–1985*. Athens: University of Georgia Press, 2012.

Weiser, David K. "Jacob and Esau in *The Yearling*." *Marjorie Kinnan Rawlings Journal of Florida Literature* 24 (2016): 33–47.

Wells, Jeremy. *Romances of the White Man's Burden: Race, Empire, and the Plantation in American Literature, 1880–1936*. Nashville: Vanderbilt University Press, 2011.

Welter, Barbara. "The Cult of True Womanhood: 1820–1860." *American Quarterly* 18, no. 2 (Summer 1966): 151–74.

West, Ray B., Jr. "Katherine Anne Porter and 'Historic Memory.'" *Hopkins Review* 6, (1952): 16–27.

White, Deborah Gray. *Ar'n't I a Woman? Female Slaves in the Plantation South*. New York: Norton, 1999.

Whitman, Walt. *Democratic Vistas*. 1871. *American Studies at the University of Virginia*, 2009. http://xroads.virginia.edu/~Hyper/Whitman/vistas/vistas.html.

Wilkinson, Crystal. *Water Street*. New Milford, CT: Toby, 2002.

William, Solomon. "Politics, Rhetoric, and Death in Katherine Anne Porter." In *Modernist Women Writers and American Social Engagement*, edited by Jody Cardinal, Deirdre E. Egan-Ryan, and Julia Lisella. Lanham, MD: Lexington Books, 2019.

Williams, Catharine Read. *Fall River: An Authentic Narrative*. Boston: Lilly, Wait, 1833.

Williamson, Joel. *The Crucible of Race: Black-White Relations in the American South since Emancipation*. Oxford: Oxford University Press, 1984.

Wilson, Augusta Jane Evans. *Macaria, or Altars of Sacrifice*. Richmond, VA: West and Johnson, 1863.

Wilson, James Southall. "The Founding of *The Virginia Quarterly Review*." *Virginia Quarterly Review* 16, no. 2 (Spring 1940). https://www.vqronline.org/web-exclusive/founding-virginia-quarterly-review.

Wilson, James Southall. "*The Virginia Quarterly Review* and Its Contributors." *Virginia Quarterly Review* 1, no. 1 (Spring 1925). https://www.vqronline.org/green-room/virginia-quarterly-review-and-its-contributors.

Wimsatt, Mary Ann. "The Old Order Undermined: Daughters, Mothers, and Grandmothers in Katherine Anne Porter's Miranda Tales." In *Southern Mothers: Fact and Fictions in Southern Women's Writing*, edited by Nagueyalti Warren, Sally Wolff, and Elizabeth Fox-Genovese. Baton Rouge: Louisiana State University Press, 1999.

Winter, Alison. *Memory: Fragments of a Modern History*. Chicago: University of Chicago Press, 2012.

Wolff, Cynthia Griffin. "Kate Chopin and the Fiction of Limits: 'Désirée's Baby.'" *Southern Literary Journal* 10, no. 2 (1978): 123–33.

Yaeger, Patricia. "Beyond the Hummingbird: Southern Women Writers and the Southern Gargantua." In *Haunted Bodies: Gender and Southern Texts*, edited by Anne Goodwyn Jones and Susan V. Donaldson. Charlottesville: University Press of Virginia, 1997.

Yaeger, Patricia. *Dirt and Desire: Reconstructing Southern Women's Writing, 1930–1990*. Chicago: University of Chicago Press, 2000.

Young, Rose. "What Is Feminism?" *Good Housekeeping* 58 (May 1914): 679–84.

Zaugg, Brigitte. "Inheritance in Ellen Glasgow's 'The Shadowy Third.'" In *Thy Truth Then Be Thy Dowry: Questions of Inheritance in American Women's Literature*, edited by Stephanie Durrans. Newcastle, UK: Cambridge Scholars, 2001.

Index

References to illustrations and tables appear in **bold**.

About the Author

Photo Credit: Violet Fox

Heather A. Fox is an assistant professor of English at Eastern Kentucky University in Richmond. Her work has appeared in *South*, *Southern Studies*, *Janus Head*, *The Explicator*, and the *Faulkner Journal*. She also publishes on the integration of archival research in the classroom.

CPSIA information can be obtained
at www.ICGtesting.com
Printed in the USA
BVHW090120200622
640161BV00001B/4

9 781496 840516